# The First Female Stars

# THE FIRST FEMALE STARS

## *Women of the Silent Era*

David W. Menefee

Westport, Connecticut
London

**Library of Congress Cataloging-in-Publication Data**

Menefee, David W., 1954–
   The first female stars : women of the silent era / David W. Menefee.
       p.   cm.
   Includes bibliographical references and index.
   ISBN 0–275–98259–9
   1. Motion picture actors and actresses—United States—Biography. 2. Actresses—United States—Biography. 3. Silent films—United States—History and criticism. I. Title.
PN1998.2.M454 2004
791.4302'8'0922—dc22          2003025652

British Library Cataloguing in Publication Data is available.

Library of Congress Catalog Card Number: 2003025652
ISBN: 0–275–98259–9

First published in 2004

Praeger Publishers, 88 Post Road West, Westport, CT 06881
An imprint of Greenwood Publishing Group, Inc.
www.praeger.com

Printed in the United States of America

The paper used in this book complies with the
Permanent Paper Standard issued by the National
Information Standards Organization (Z39.48–1984).

10   9   8   7   6   5   4   3   2   1

All Photographs used in this book are from the author's personal collection.

# CONTENTS

# PREFACE

*The First Female Stars: Women of the Silent Era* is the result of several years of research in the archives of Southern Methodist University, The Academy of Motion Picture Arts and Sciences, The British Film Institute, The Library of Congress, The American Film Institute, and the pages of silent-era publications such as *Moving Picture World, Photoplay, Motion Picture Classic, Motion Picture Stories,* and *Screenplay.*

Another incredible source of material proved to be rare Gosset & Dunlap Photoplay Editions of popular novels made into films, each book a treasure trove of stills from films, often the only surviving images from titles deemed lost.

My fascination with women and the early achievements of the gallant, daring actresses who dared to venture into the new art of silent motion pictures has been a 35-year obsession. There is a strong theme of daredevil exploration motivating each of the women profiled in this book.

Their stories are rich with faith in the medium of silent motion pictures. They radiated a positive assurance that audiences would understand their messages, discern their thoughts, and share their emotions. As role models, they are inspiring today. Though too often forgotten, their testaments to the willpower of youth and the temerity of talent deserve to resurface and be remembered.

# ACKNOWLEDGMENTS

First and foremost, to my faith in Jesus Christ, without whom nothing would be possible.

And to my mother and father, Eunice and Doyle Menefee, who told me there was a purpose to my life.

Kate Stanworth from the British Film Institute earns my applause for helping to research many rare photos.

Michael Derfler who kindly inspired me to focus on the best format and theme, a tremendous encouragement.

Kristine Krueger from the Margaret Herrick Library of The Academy of Motion Picture Arts and Sciences Center for Motion Picture Study and National Film Information Service boosted this manuscript with many rare articles she researched from their vast files.

I am in debt to Randy Jones who enabled me to create all the digital files of the manuscript and photos by volunteering to spend an entire weekend setting up a computer system.

Ronald Raburn was the greatest of help with the photo restorations, training me in the subtle nuances of digital enhancement techniques and sharing with me the mysterious secret of the Gaussian blur.

My sincere gratitude goes to Eric Levy from Greenwood Publishing, for encouraging me to go forward with this project.

Special thanks must go to the staff of the Dallas Public Library for their help in researching biographical information.

Kevin Brownlow painstakingly offered insights from his renowned knowledge of film history. Without his guidance, this book would not have been possible.

# INTRODUCTION

The world cannot allow to be forgotten the paintings of a Rembrandt or the music of a Mozart, so how is it that more than a thousand motion pictures and the women who made them became lost or forgotten?

Women and youth have been the two integral ingredients in motion pictures since their inception. When Mary Pickford first amassed a vast fortune from her work in films, the floodgates of the infant industry opened and brought many talented, young women who believed in themselves and what they had to offer.

Every film studio was owned and operated by tough business men, in most cases immigrants who rose from obscurity on the tidal wave of nickels rolling in from the storefront movie shows around the world. Women found themselves not only competing for opportunities within the industry, but against each other as well. In the battle for the attention of audiences, certain women succeeded because of their tenacity, determination, and sheer hard work. These women deserve to be remembered because they were the original molds from which every motion picture success story has been cast since.

Hollywood has been its own worst enemy. Motion pictures have been with us for a little over a century, developing from primitive, one-reel films to dynamically edited, mind-bending epics. The men and women who pioneered this development rarely imagined the long-term appeal of their work, often thinking of their productions as temporary amusements, like daily newspapers, to be circulated and then thrown away. The American Film Institute has estimated that more than 80 percent of films made before 1930 were lost by the very studios producing them. This deliberate destruction of titles has played a major role in the extinction of the first female stars from pop culture. Sixty years from now, if virtually every film made by Meryl Streep or Barbra Streisand is wiped off the face of the earth, how many people will remember them? This is the fate that befell Dorothy Gish, Gene Gauntier, and Beverly Bayne. Even Helen Keller, early champion of the handicapped, once starred in a motion picture. She paved the way for physically challenged actors such as Marlee Matlin, Harold Russell, and Lionel Barrymore to appear in films, yet her one starring role in *Deliverance* has been forgotten.

I believe the transition from silent films projecting at about 18 frames per second to sound films projecting at 24 frames per second also caused many titles to slip into obscurity as they simply could not be correctly shown on existing equipment. Watching a silent film shown sped-up by a third is the same as listening to a music recording pressed on a 33 rpm vinyl disc spun at 45 rpm. In addition, modern audiences have often shunned silent films because they have difficulty accepting their silence, accustomed as they are to the added appeal of dialogue and music.

The worst enemy of certain stars has proven to be time. Actors simply grow strangely dim in the light of the glory and presence of each decade's new stars. Few people today remember Pauline Frederick or Laurette Taylor, and this is as unfortunate as having missed the work of Meryl Streep or Barbra Streisand.

I hope this book rejuvenates the dim memory some have of these daring women and enlightens others to the wonderful fun and delightful imagination evidenced by their struggle to succeed in motion pictures.

# THEDA BARA

Theda Bara was born Theodosia Goodman to a tailor and his wife in Cincinnati, Ohio, on July 29, 1885. Theda was a pretty, blonde school girl with an interest in theatrical arts. When she finished high school, she dyed her hair black and went to New York in search of roles to fulfill her dream to be a great actress.

In 1908 she earned an opportunity to perform in a stage play titled *The Devil.* In 1911 she joined a touring company and gained much-needed experience traveling on the road for several years. When she returned to New York in 1914, movies were a source of anonymous income for many struggling actors, offering quick employment and daily cash to tide them over as they made the rounds of casting offices. She obtained several bit parts and, while observing the activities inside the Fox Studios, caught the eye of a producer, Frank J. Powell. He was beginning preparations on a film adaptation of a 1914 stage hit, *A Fool There Was,* and needed a girl to play the vamp in the lurid story.

According to Richard Griffith in *The Movie Stars,* Frank J. Powell remembered seeing Theda loitering around the studio one day: "She was angling for bigger parts, but half-heartedly, in fact, everything she did was halfhearted. She had a sort of negative personality, but she had a body. And she had big dark eyes that I thought we could make even bigger with the heavy kohl eye make-up we used then."

Two exciting films were released in 1915: D.W. Griffith opened his epoch film, *The Birth of a Nation,* and Fox unveiled *A Fool There Was,*

Theodosia Goodman, the actress known as Theda Bara,
ca. 1915.

making Theda Bara an overnight star and coining the abbreviated word
"vamp."

*A Fool There Was* had a powerful theme that tried to courageously show
a man's downfall at the hands of a truly evil woman. Bara's performance
was fantastic and seemingly leaped from the screen with its voracity. Her
characterization was shocking.

The film persona of Theda Bara was created with an elaborate promo-
tion, built around the fictional legend claiming her name was an anagram,
the letters of which, when rearranged, spelled "Arab Death." She was
reported to be a new star, known worldwide, but unheard of in America.
Her personality was fabricated by the studio's publicity machinery; she
was described not only as an actress, but also as a witch that hypnotized
unwary men to commit shameful sins. Her past was reputed to include
monstrous crimes against domesticity. She was alleged to have been born
in Egypt in the shadow of the Sphinx, half-Arab and half-French, an exotic
woman of the world who devoured men and wasted them. On screen she

Theda Bara, ca. 1918 in her image as a vampire, shockingly
portrayed dangerous and destructive women.

was obnoxious, arrogant, and rude to servants, a delightfully detestable
requirement of any woman in the early 20th century who conveyed unbridled eroticism. Theda Bara was a mass-produced, manufactured phenomenon, an instant celebrity known to millions of people.

The precensorship public of 1914 loved it and flocked to the steady
series of dramas picturing the vampire's dangerous lifestyle. The studio
made a fortune, and Theodosia Goodman earned $4,000 a week at a time
when the average wage-earner pulled in $1,500 a year or less.

She was rushed through a brief flash of a career, portraying a gallery
of destructive, historical and fictional characters: Cleopatra, Camille,
DuBarry, and Cigarette. She also played softer legends such as Carmen,

Kathleen Mavourneen, one of *The Two Orphans,* the heroine of *Easy Lynne,* and Esmeralda in Victor Hugo's *The Hunchback of Notre Dame.* Theda Bara was wildly popular, had a good sense of humor about fame, and soon became a pop icon whose image is still prominent today.

Frances Marion noted in *Off With Their Heads* the burgeoning trend of producing extravagantly longer films. Once made, the decision to propel resident stars into elaborate spectacles meant bigger and better stories, productions, and publicity. "What followed this decision was exactly what we had expected: Mr. Fox, realizing that the public was tiring of Theda Bara in vampire roles, announced that he would star her in a production of *Romeo and Juliet,*" she illustrated. "The imagination took wild flight at this news, especially among devotees of Shakespeare. Juliet was a slender flower of a fourteen-year-old girl, and it was difficult to associate large, bosomy, and rather heavily thighed Theda with Romeo's poetic outpourings of his love, which would be flashed on the screen in subtitles.

In 1918 Sarah Bernhardt was seen in *Mothers of France.* The public was flooded with propaganda films in the wake of America's entry into World War I. Among those getting attention as *Salome* was prepared for release were *To Hell With the Kaiser, The Heart of Humanity, The Beast of Berlin,* and *Hearts of the World.*

Other films without war themes were attracting huge crowds that same year, including Alla Nazimova in *Eye for Eye,* Pauline Frederick in *La Tosca,* John Barrymore in *Here Comes the Bride* and *On the Quiet,* Beverly Bayne in *Social Quicksands,* Norma Talmadge in *The Forbidden City,* Constance Talmadge in *A Pair of Silk Stockings,* Pearl White in *The House of Hate,* and Mae Marsh in *The Beloved Traitor.*

In the year 1918, Mary Pickford signed a contract with First National for $1,050,000, a new record in the industry. As an added inducement for her to leave her previous studio and join First National, a bonus of $50,000 was offered plus a contract for her brother, Jack Pickford, for a series of motion pictures at $50,000 each. Their mother, Charlotte Pickford, did a good job that year as their agent.

*Salome* (1918) was a lush example of Theda Bara in her prime, a typical Fox film of the period, projecting a highly cinematic and lurid conception of the Bible's wicked heroine. J. Gordon Edwards directed the story with tasteless splendor, taking advantage of the shock value of Miss Bara simulating near nakedness in daring costumes.

The Kansas Board of Censors strongly objected to the film's content, claimed George C. Pratt in *Spellbound in the Darkness,* and the censors refused to allow the film exhibition without specific excisions of footage deemed unacceptable by their community standards. Records of their

One-sheet poster for the William Fox film, *Salome* (1918), starring Theda Bara.

demands include: "Eliminate close-up of Salome in opening bathing scene. Shorten scenes and titles of Salome with John in his cell so as to eliminate her sensual advances to him. Shorten to a flash Salome stretched on floor with head on platter." These demands were accomplished by the Fox Film Corporation, and according to Imri Zumwalt, State Printer for the Topeka, Kansas State Printing Plant, 1919, the revised film was approved with eliminations.

Loosely based on the Biblical account of the real-life Salome, the scenario follows the action of Herodias, who divorces her husband and marries his brother Herod Antipas, governor of Judea. The prophet, John the Baptist, is imprisoned for protesting their marriage. Salome, daughter of

Theda Bara and cast in *Salome* (1918).

Herodias and both niece and stepdaughter to Herod, dances seductively and wins the prize of anything she asks of Herod. The prize she asks for is the head of John the Baptist.

In *The New York Times,* July 1918, a reviewer wrote,

> William Fox last night presented Theda Bara in *Salome* on the screen of the Forty-Fourth Street Theatre, in a photoplay which for richness and extent of pageantry, sumptuousness of setting, and color of detail has few equals among motion picture productions. And Theda Bara in the title role was all that those who have seen her in other films might expect—every minute the vampire. While there is much on the screen that could not be included in either the opera or in the play, it must be admitted that the story itself loses nothing in dramatic power when limited to pictures.
>
> Assurances from Mr. Fox were to the effect that J. Gordon Edwards, who directed the picture, followed the best historical guides in staging it and, accepting this evidence of authenticity, one was inclined to feel indebted to the producer for a vivid presentation of ancient Jerusalem and the life of its people. A freshly barbered John the Baptist struck perhaps a discordant note, however. It seemed something of an anachronism to represent the prophet of the wilderness carrying a cross in these scenes.

The Fox Corporation announced the big production was the greatest of Miss Bara's feature films. "Its success was instant and of such proportions as to cause the Fox office to feel that it will be even a bigger gold mine for the local exhibitor than *Cleopatra*," stated William Fox in an article in the trade publication, *Moving Picture World.*

After seven more films in 1919, concluding with *The Lure of Ambition,* Theda's contract was dropped by Fox. Her career as the archetypical vamp had reached the stage where each role was a caricature of the style. Her career would never be the same again.

She briefly tried the stage in a serious play, *The Blue Flame,* opening at the Shubert Theater in New York on March 15, 1920, but audiences laughed when she entered and blurted out her first line, "Did you remember to bring the cocaine?" The play ran for 48 performances and closed. She never attempted the stage again.

In 1921 she married director Charles Brabin and enjoyed the life of one of Hollywood's leading socialites. She tried a film comeback role in *The Unchastened Woman* in 1925, and in 1926 she made her final film, *Madame Mystery,* a lampoon of her previous characterizations, and happily retired from films at the age of 41.

Until a print of *Salome* is unearthed from some forgotten resting place, it is regrettably considered a lost film, as are all but two of Theda Bara's other films. Her incredible career is a prime example of the tragic, gross neglect of the major studios with their own products. She starred in nearly 40 films in four years. Most of the prints and negatives were either worn to shreds, tossed aside, or melted down for their silver content.

Theda Bara struck against the grain of convention and created breakthrough characterizations of women as aggressors in love. In an adventurous example of the dozens of films she made in her prime, Theda Bara in *Salome* was the greatest vamp of them all, an icon of the silent cinema, the dark lady of early films who wrecked marriages and drove men to destruction. The unconventional Theda Bara image shocked and amused audiences until the vogue waned, and Theodosia Goodman retired securely with a happy marriage, money, and fame, content to have made her mark in the world of theater and films, her youthful dream fulfilled.

## SILENT FILMOGRAPHY OF THEDA BARA

A Fool There Was (1915) ★ The Kreutzer Sonata (1915) ★ The Clemenceau Case (1915) ★ The Devil's Daughter (1915) ★ The Two Orphans (1915) ★ Lady Audley's Secret (1915) ★ Sin (1915) ★ Carmen (1915) ★ The Galley Slave (1915) ★ Destruction (1915) ★ Siren of Hell (1915) ★ The Serpent (1916) ★ Gold and the Woman (1916) ★ The Eternal Sappho (1916) ★ Under Two Flags (1916) ★ Her Double Life (1916) ★ Romeo and Juliet (1916) ★ The Vixen (1916) ★

East Lynne (1916) ★ The Tiger Woman (1917) ★ Her Greatest Love (1917) ★ Heart and Soul (1917) ★ Camille (1917) ★ Cleopatra (1917) ★ Madame DuBarry (1917) ★ The Rose of Blood (1917) ★ The Darling of Paris (1917) ★ The Forbidden Path (1918) ★ Salome (1918) ★ When a Woman Sins (1918) ★ Under the Yoke (1918) ★ The Soul of Buddha (1918) ★ The She Devil (1918) ★ The Light (1919) ★ A Woman There Was (1919) ★ Kathleen Mavoureen (1919) ★ La Belle Russe (1919) ★ When Men Desire (1919) ★ The Siren's Song (1919) ★ The Lure of Ambition (1919) ★ The Prince of Silence (1921) ★ The Unchastened Woman (1925) ★ Madame Mystery (1926)

# BEVERLY BAYNE

Beverly Pearl Bain was born on November 22, 1893, in Minneapolis. Her parents divorced, and her childhood years were located in Philadelphia and Chicago. School plays were her first love, and the Essanay Film Company was an early distraction to Beverly. She and her teenage friends regularly attended the local movie theaters, and the Chicago-based film company entranced the aspiring actress. Her family made the acquaintance of Henry McRae Webster, a director at Essanay, and he invited 16-year-old Beverly to a tour of the inner workings of the studio. She brought along her photographs and a pair of white gloves, and the director put her into a scene in a short film he was directing that week. Beverly was invited to come back the following day and told to report regularly from 9 A.M. until 5 P.M. each weekday, and 9 A.M. until 1 P.M. on Saturday. Within three years she was crowned Queen of the Movies at the Panama-Pacific International Exposition in San Diego.

According to Richard J. Maturi in his book, *Beverly Bayne, Queen of the Movies,* her first lead role was in *The Loan Shark,* released on March 12, 1912. "It must have been awful, and I, too! But they were all awful in those days," Beverly later recalled. "Most of the time there wasn't even a script to work on. The director and a sort of 'idea man' just worked it out as we went along.... I had nothing to resort to but some powder, lipstick and an eyebrow pencil—and Henry McRae Webster's kindly direction.... In the silent movies we didn't learn lines. We learned a story's continuity and how to put ideas across with expressions and gestures."

Essanay featured a roster of imposing stars, including Charlie Chaplin and Ben Turpin, popular western star, "Bronco Billy" Anderson, the matinee idol Francis X. Bushman, and Wallace Beery. She appeared in several comedies with Beery, and soon earned a role with Francis X. Bushman. *A Good Catch* first paired the two in a comic short. Bushman liked working with Beverly and he asked for her to play the principal role in another film, *The Legacy of Happiness* (1912). Their work was praised in film reviews at the time, and both young stars emerged as major players in a long series of films made during 1912 and 1913.

Location filming in Ithaca, New York, including the Cornell University campus area, soon brought the two together in a number of films during the summer of 1913. She was always willing to participate fully in dangerous scenes, including clinging to a sinking raft under breaking waves in *The Stigma.*

Beverly was a charming player, and her photographic possibilities won her immediate favor with audiences. Her increasing fame earned full-page coverage in motion picture magazines and newspapers like *The Chicago News*. She made great strides, considering her humble beginnings and complete lack of experience. If she feared her lack of stage experience was a hindrance, Beverly soon learned naivety was an advantage. The motion picture camera recorded those with youthful innocence, while the old posturing of stage actors was glaringly amplified in the performances of many actors who failed to adapt their technique to the intimacy of the cinema. The reality of genuine emotional feeling for a scene photographed more tellingly than stagy acting, and Beverly radiated a quiet sincerity appreciated by audiences.

*One Wonderful Night* (1914) was a lavish production featuring the most outstanding work from the young actress up to that time. The breathless action of the adventure story stirred audience's pulses and cemented her image together with Francis X. Bushman. The film was heavily promoted with photo cards, sheet music, and advertisements.

*Photoplay* conducted polls of their readers asking them to name their favorite actress, and in 1914 Beverly Bayne tallied 231,400 votes, just behind Mary Fuller (239,500), Mary Pickford (260,150), Mabel Normand (272,450), Kathlyn Williams (274,350) and Margarita Fischer (318,100). Beverly appeared in at least 22 films in 1914.

By the following year, Bayne and Bushman represented Essanay's most valuable asset. The romantic team's popularity was crystallized in a variety of movie collectable items, including portraits and postcards, silver spoons, china plates, and pocket mirrors.

Francis X. Bushman left the Essanay company over a dispute concerning salary and billing, and he signed a lucrative, long-term contract with the fledgling Metro Company. Beverly continued to work at Essanay until wires from Bushman pleaded with her to join him at Metro. Beverly signed a flattering, two-year contract and soon headed to Hollywood with her mother. Metro's new acquisition was notably heralded in the trade publications. Their first film was a five-reel comedy-drama, *Pennington's Choice.* After making one other picture, Beverly moved their production back to the East, setting up Rolfe Photoplays Inc. in production facilities in New York.

Their next film, *Man and His Soul,* was unveiled in January 1916, and received many good reviews. Beverly was noted for her versatile and life-like playing. *The Red Mouse, The Wall Between,* and *Boots and Saddles* followed.

In September 1916, Metro announced grand plans for a large-scale production of William Shakespeare's *Romeo and Juliet,* teaming Francis X. Bushman with Beverly Bayne in a silent movie adaptation of the tale of the star-crossed lovers of Verona.

Frances Marion, who by 1916 was an avowed screen writer for Adolph Zukor, marveled at the audacity of William Fox when he announced that a competing version would be filmed, starring Theda Bara. In her book, *Off With Their Heads,* she illustrated the competitive situation looming within the film industry with the pending release of two versions of *Romeo and Juliet:* "We had no sooner recovered from this shock when it was announced that Francis X. Bushman and Beverly Bayne were to appear in another screen version of Shakespeare's immortal play," she remembered. "We wondered if sophisticated viewers might laugh, and nothing was more dreaded than laughter when drama was being enacted (not acted) on a broad scale."

In the short history of the motion picture and even through the centuries of theater since Shakespeare's day, no stars were ever gilded in costumes more elaborate than those worn by the Metro stars. No sets for a Shakespearean drama boasted such baronial halls, or buried actors under more profuse arrangements of flowers than in this impressive production. Both the Fox and Metro pictures were successful, and industry observers realized how impossible it was to prophesy whether a film would succeed or fail.

Beverly Bayne never played Shakespeare prior to this first attempt, and she triumphed in competition against the powerful presence of Francis X. Bushman. Metro's sumptuous presentation was a gallant attempt to translate the spoken word into silent, moving images.

*Romeo and Juliet* has been filmed more often than any other play, Shakespearean or otherwise. In the summer of 1915, after Metro announced the production of William Shakespeare's *Romeo and Juliet* starring the cinema's great love-team, Francis X. Bushman and Beverly Bayne, principal photography on the film was completed. This early feature-length film was mounted on eight reels, running about 90 minutes. Their artistic challenge was to present the all-dialogue play in silence. Metro advertised the spectacle as having a cast of 600 and a cost of $250,000, the first full-length version of the timeless romance of the two star-crossed lovers. They succeeded in translating the classic words into floating images and earned tremendous plaudits for their effort.

The outlay of new titles in 1916 was impressive, and *Romeo and Juliet* rolled into theaters at the same time D. W. Griffith made film history with his unforgettable masterpiece, *Intolerance.* His film took 20 months to make and ran for three and a half hours on the screen. It was also the year the price of two dollars a seat was inaugurated for films shown in legitimate theaters around the country.

As Metro was preparing the release of *Romeo and Juliet* starring Francis X. Bushman and Beverly Bayne, other stupendous productions were already in circulation. Annette Kellerman was drawing crowds and critical praise in *A Daughter of the Gods.* Geraldine Farrar and Wallace Reid were appearing in *Maria Rosa,* directed by Cecil B. DeMille. Marie Doro had a banner year and was seen in a film adaptation of her stage triumph, *Oliver Twist,* followed by *The Wood Nymph.* Lou-Tellegen was making his first series of Lasky features, including *The Unknown* and *The Victoria Cross.* Mae Murray appeared with Wallace Reid in *To Have and To Hold,* Mary Pickford starred in *Less Than the Dust* and *Poor Little Peppina,* Pauline Frederick emoted in *Lydia Gilmore, Ashes of Embers, The Woman in the Case,* and *The Moment Before.* John Barrymore won praise in *The Lost Bridegroom.* Theda Bara was tearing up homes in Fox features such as *Destruction.* Alla Nazimova made her film debut in the sensational *War Brides,* while Pearl White starred in *Hazel Kirke* and the serial *Pearl of the Army.*

*Romeo and Juliet* joined this imposing array of outstanding titles, demanding its share of the audiences around the country. Metro released the film with great fanfare, and the film was lauded by George Blaisdell in the November 1916 *Moving Picture World* as "a great production, one that easily will rank with the best cinematographic efforts that have gone before."

"Francis X. Bushman and Beverly Bayne head the cast. It is an ideal combination. Mr. Bushman, above all else, possesses the physique of a 'well-governed youth,' of a man to encounter Tybalt, he appears to unusual advantage in the scanty garb of the period—in the language of Juliet's

Beverly Bayne played her first Shakespearean role in
*Romeo and Juliet* (1916).

Nurse, 'his leg excels all men's.' He fits the part, and he plays it. Miss
Bayne is a rare Juliet. Kindly endowed by nature in figure and feature, she
has entered into the interpretation of the role of the heroine with marked
sympathy and feeling."

Supporting these two stars was a splendid cast—and also perhaps the
longest in the history of motion pictures at that time excepting the multiple-
storied *Intolerance*. There were exactly one hundred names in the cast list
furnished by the Metro company, including a Booth, a Sothern, a Mantell,
a Kemble, and a Davenport, all famous names in the annals of American
theatricals.

It was hoped *Romeo and Juliet* would appeal to picture lovers as an all-
around experience, entrancing viewers with a distinct double appeal—to
the eye and to the mind. The eye would be fascinated by the action and

the text, consisting of subtitles lifted from the Shakespearean play, which would stimulate the audience's mind, forcing recall of the immortal play. The Metro organization proved its Shakespearean devotion by the use of many literal transcriptions of the original play as titles.

At the Broadway theater on the initial presentation, October 19, nearly two and one-quarter hours were devoted to the running of the eight thousand feet of film. Each scene was tightened to keep the presentation taut. Approximately a full reel was devoted to the single scene of the balcony in which Romeo climbs the Capulet wall following the feast of the Capulets. The conversation from Romeo on the ground to Juliet on the balcony was a romantic highlight of the production. Great care was given to insure the portrayal of this famous play would reach the same dramatic heights on the screen as viewers experienced in the stage play would expect. The balcony scene was considered remarkable on its own merit, and when taken with the film's entirety, a crowd-pleasing standout. The balcony scene was framed in an exquisite bower of foliage and some of the love scenes took place in a beautiful garden. The few glimpses of the Capulet castle added to the atmosphere. The background never intruded; it was subtly appropriate framing for the story's events. The natural settings seemed to be those with the best effect. Studio art in 1915 had not reached rivalry with reality, but the artificial settings were painstaking and sufficient.

The January 1917 *Photoplay* reviewed the film, calling Bushman's performance the best of his career.

> We have the Metro organization to thank for a sun-painting of the great Veronese love-tragedy. From time to time the little fluttering hearts whose musky notes grace the whittled pine desk of our blind, deaf, ninety-year old answer-man make much wailing to-do and what-not over this department's abuse of Mr. Bushman. Abate, gentle cardiac earthquakes, for as Romeo this department found Mr. Bushman not only in the best role of his career, but doing the best acting he has ever shot into the transparencies. Medically, we might term Mr. Bushman the acting hypochondriac. He has always been thinking of himself and his pretty clothes and his sweet biceps and grand smile, and forgetting his character. He may have been "scairt" into doing a superb Romeo by the overwhelming splendor and tradition of the soulful Italian lad; nevertheless, the fact remains that he is a super Romeo, performing with discretion, dignity, an unusual amount of reserve and astounding sincerity.

Bushman was far from "scairt." As a student of Shakespeare, he made extensive research of the role and the values of the drama in order to achieve the highest standard of excellence of his career.

Francis X. Bushman and Beverly Bayne in the balcony scene
from *Romeo and Juliet* (1916).

*Photoplay* went on to say, "Miss Bayne is the sweetest of Juliets, but
one could ask a little more fervor, at moments. This Juliet would scarcely
have risked immurement in the grisly tomb of the Capulets. I think she
would have married her cousin, heckled him into an affinity's arms, then
the divorce of outraged chastity, and Romeo; provided Romeo had waited.
In the tender, childish moments of Juliet's love she may be characterized
only by the word exquisite."

The *Photoplay* reviewer was also quick to give notice to the honorable
performance of Robert Cummings in the role of Friar Laurence. Other
actors in supporting roles gave admirable performances.

One of the highlights of the film, in addition to the famous balcony
scene, was the authentic replication of the period in direction, location,
and costuming. Metro had never approached a film with such an attention
to detail. Audiences loved the ghostly procession past the bier of Juliet
after she made her untimely sacrifice of life on the altar of unrequited love.
The marriage scene was also beautifully rendered.

Jerome Hart wrote in the March 1923 *Motion Picture Classic* that the film suffered in the translation to silent movies.

> The solitary screen production known of *Romeo and Juliet* to the writer is that made a few years ago with Francis X. Bushman and Beverley Bayne. The story lost a great deal for those who knew it and loved Shakespeare's matchless lines, although it had its picturesque and vital moments. Miss Bayne was a very pretty, but rather colorless Juliet, while Mr. Bushman was a handsome but mature Romeo. So much is inevitably lost in transferring Shakespeare to the screen that one feels about such an attempt much the same sort of annoyance that many of us experience at witnessing the "expressionistic" Shakespearean productions of Mr. Arthur Hopkins.

*Variety,* October 27, 1916, said the following of Metro's eight-part version of *Romeo and Juliet:*

> [The play was an] earnest, intelligent effort to put the Shakespearean classic on the screen understandably for the cinema public; to make it interesting and (this is a particularly worthy aim) to do as little violence as possible to the stage traditions of the greatest love tragedy in the language.
>
> The men concerned in the production have approached their task with reverence. They have given the photoplay followers as nearly an adequate presentation of the actual story as the limitations of the new art permit. This was to be expected. But they have gone beyond that and managed in some degree to impart a little of its poetic flavor. This leads to an interesting point. The film has an unusual footage of titles. At most of the more familiar passages quotations are used freely. When Romeo, for example, leans over Juliet in the tomb the printed lines beginning 'Death hath sucked the beauty from thy breath'—flash upon the screen. Of course, the words are not necessary to an understanding of the action, but the beauty of the old familiar words enhances the poetry of the scene. It is as though a painting of a biblical subject received emphasis and illumination from a particularly noble and well remembered quotation from holy writ. This is a detail and its effectiveness may perhaps be open to debate. Certainly the excessive use of printed titles when they have no poetic beauty in themselves and are made necessary only because of the badly handled story, are not to be defended. That is not the case here. The titles add to the artistic value of the work. To the same end the directors have selected their backgrounds with utmost care.

The directors were fortunate in their selection of actors and with the availability of the two stars, already famous as a love-team. Francis X. Bushman made a manly Romeo, playing simply, and if anything could be cited as an error, it was in his unusual employment of restraint, a positive virtue before the camera. He avoided all temptation to play a Romeo that grimaced and strutted. Beverly Bayne's appealing brunette beauty was made to order for Juliet. In repose she realized the character perfectly. But some critics and admirers would have been satisfied to see in her acting a little more fire and spirit. The death scene was especially well done, both by the actors concerned and by the directors who arranged it. Pictorially, the rose-banked bier centered in the bare stone tomb and crowned with the lovely Juliet was stunning, and the falling petals about the dead duo were a fine bit of artistic theatrical trickery.

The scenario was submitted by John Arthur; Rudolph De Cordova modified and augmented it, and John W. Nobel made the final changes. Nobel was general director and Cordova was the Shakespearean advisor. The data furnished to an invited audience that filled the Broadway theatre at the premier said the production cost $250,000.

*Wid's,* Thursday, October 26, 1916, thought less of the film than other reviewers:

Considered as a whole, the offering will impress most people as a big production because of the subject and the apparent painstaking effort in the picturization. Surely, Director Nobel has given us an impressive atmosphere, with beautiful, well-chosen exteriors and fitting interiors. Unfortunately this is too long as it stands and becomes tiresome.

The fatal error made in this offering was that the characters were not brought sufficiently close to the camera in most of the scenes, nor were they lighted in such a manner as to make it easily possible to catch their emotions. There was a very noticeable lack of close-ups. The result of this technique was that the production impressed rather as a visualization of something which should be accepted as good because it was a classic rather than enjoyed because it was a human story of conflicting emotions.

In other words, the characters in this film, instead of being red-blooded humans, seemed to be actors upon the stage. In seeing Shakespeare done in the theater we are accustomed to theatrics, but, to my way of thinking, if Shakespeare is to be done for presentation on the screen his characters should be made to appear as human beings, since that is the chief advantage of screen presentation over the theatrical presentation.

As we see *Romeo and Juliet* here, I would say that there is entirely too much Romeo. Time after time, when it is entirely unnecessary, we have scenes of Mr. Bushman walking into a scene, pausing for a moment so that the camera might notice him, and then walking off.

Miss Bayne as Juliet was sweet, but not nearly so beautiful as she has been in other films, because most of the lighting failed to show her to the best advantage.

The supporting cast was generally very good, but they were kept entirely in the background, no personality being allowed to become sufficiently prominent as to compete with Francis Romeo.

After trying through a number of scenes to determine who was playing Paris, I finally referred to my program and found that it was that very capable young actor, John Davidson. I was rather surprised, and continued to try to verify my information, but can truthfully say that without a program I would have been unable to have recognized him throughout the offering, so carefully was he kept from an opportunity to register his features any place near the foreground. I mention this just as an instance of the predominating star situation.

The reviewer from *Wid's* went on to lament the use of extras in the outdoor scenes, particularly a site of a street scene with a well-constructed exterior set filled with people, but populated with natives who didn't walk about very much. The manipulation of the throngs of extras utilized in the outdoor duel scenes was thought to have been badly composed, with no one within 20 feet of them on the side where the camera stood. In another scene there was said to be a noticeable lack of locals when Romeo and a couple of his friends met for a friendly chat on the main thoroughfare, as if no one seemed to have any business downtown that day.

The *Wid's* reviewer concluded by lamenting the use of spoken titles with a label telling who made the speech.

I have always fought against this because it kills the illusion. Certainly the use of this technique injured the effectiveness of this production and helped to keep it from being anything but a puppet show.

The lack of intimate close-ups seemed to detract some viewers from the big films, creating an offering more theatric than filmic. This was obviously a planned technique, as close-ups were profusely used in many films of 1916, including those made by Metro. The producers were seemingly holding true to the tradition of Shakespeare's tragic romance as a stage presentation, a style deemed unfortunate by some critics.

Not to be outdone by Metro's prestigious effort, William Fox's company simultaneously threw together an elaborate and decidedly more lurid version starring Theda Bara as Juliet. Both films were very successful. The Fox Company rushed into distribution their version of *Romeo and Juliet,* opening it on the same day as the Metro production, the two films pitted against each other in the marketplace.

*The New York Times,* in October of 1916, compared this Metro production with Francis X. Bushman and the other production from the Fox Company, starring Theda Bara, cast against her archetypical vamp image:

It is a pity William Shakespeare did not live to see the movies, for he might have learned about play writing from them. If he had witnessed the first showing of a motion picture called *Romeo and Juliet* at the Academy of music yesterday, for instance, he might have like the ending better than the one he wrote for the play.

It will be recalled that Mr. Shakespeare's Romeo came to the tomb, and when he saw his Juliet on her bier, dead as he thought, he drank the deadly poison the apothecary had given him and died instantly. Then a moment afterward Juliet awoke and, seeing her husband dead, took her own life with a dagger. Look on this picture from the studio of William Shakespeare Fox. Upon awaking from her coma, Juliet discovers Romeo and is overjoyed when he tells her he has come to take her away to Mantua. But her joy is short lived, for she learns in a moment that he has taken the poison and death is upon him, so she kills herself. The result is the same, of course, but the brief colloquy between the lovers shrouds the play in still deeper gloom when the happy ending that seemed imminent fades away.

This little variation was the only important change in the immortal drama to be detected in either of two movie versions shown publicly for the first time yesterday. The other picture was from the Metro studios and was exhibited at the Broadway. It had for its stars Francis X. Bushman and Beverly Bayne, While Theda Bara and Harry Hilliard acted the title roles for the Fox film. Both proved creditable attempts to translate to the screen the greatest romance of all ages.

Both films have been regrettably lost, so it would be difficult to say if either excelled over the other, for the two were said to have some points of excellence in common with each other. The Metro picture boasted a more elaborate and longer presentation more closely following the traditional stage drama, while the Fox version, because it was more condensed, took certain liberties with the text and utilized a more filmic approach.

Generally speaking, the interior or studio scenes of the Fox film were said to have been better than those of the Metro, while the outdoor scenes of the Metro picture were reportedly much finer than those of the Fox picture.

The choice of Francis X. Bushman for the role of Romeo was a wise one, as his popularity with female audiences began years earlier during the earliest of motion pictures with appearances in lantern slides that were shown in the early nickelodeons.

Bushman soon joined the Essanay Film Manufacturing company as a strong leading man, the same studio that boasted Broncho Billy and Charlie Chaplin. He was an eminent star of scores of short films for the studio, and helped pioneer the acting technique of showing thought through the eyes rather than speaking or gesturing.

Francis X. Bushman and Beverly Bayne in the death scene from *Romeo and Juliet* (1916).

Chaplin had difficulties with the management of Essanay. In his autobiography he said,

> Francis X. Bushman, then a great star with Essanay, sensed my dislike of the place. "Whatever you think about the studio," he said, "it is just the antithesis." But it wasn't; I didn't like the studio and I didn't like the word "antithesis." Circumstances went from bad to worse. When I wanted to see my rushes, they ran the original negative to save the expense of a positive print. This horrified me. And when I demanded that they should make a positive print, they reacted as though I wanted to bankrupt them.

Bushman was loyal to the studio and performed in 134 films for the company. He served as one of the assistant directors on *Romeo and Juliet.*

Gloria Swanson was another of Essanay's big stars, and she remembered Bushman as the "great god of Essanay" in her autobiography, *Swanson on Swanson.* "Mr. Bushman wore a large violet amethyst ring on his finger and he had a spotlight inside his lavender car that illuminated his famous profile when he drove after dark. Everybody at Essanay knew he was married and had five children, but to the public that was a deep dark secret.

Studios felt that if word got out that stars were married and had children like ordinary people, it might destroy their image as romantic lovers." She recalled the Essanay rule that male performers were not supposed to come anywhere near the women's dressing rooms, but Francis seemed to easily find his way into Beverly Bayne's room often enough. "Whenever we heard whispering in Miss Bayne's dressing room, we always knew Mr. Bushman was breaking the rules. We would climb on our dressing tables and try to hear what was going on."

Beverly Bayne and Francis X. Bushman were in love, no doubt mesmerized by their image as lovers on the screen. Their love took a lethal turn when Bushman divorced his wife and married Beverly Bayne. The public scandal tore through the media with a vengeance, shocking wartime audiences and ultimately wrecking both their careers.

The makers of this version of *Romeo and Juliet* were brave in their attempt to translate the written play by Shakespeare into the visual imagery of a silent film. The prestige the studio gained from this sterling production was so powerful, MGM reached for it again when Irving Thalberg presented his wife, Norma Shearer, in the first sound version made in the 1930s. He did not care if the film made money. It was the desire to do something fine and lasting that propelled the effort. The same desire drove the makers of this silent version, and by all accounts, they succeeded admirably.

*Romeo and Juliet,* produced by Metro in 1916, is considered to be another lost film, a victim of nitrate film decomposition and careless neglect by the Hollywood studios infamous for their systematic destruction of their own creations. One can only hope that somewhere on the Earth a lone print is hoarded by a selfish collector or hidden in a European archive in a mislabeled can, possibly destined to re-emerge into the light of projectors one day. By all accounts, Beverly Bayne, never having played Shakespeare prior to this first attempt, triumphed against the powerful presence of Francis X. Bushman, with producers who were gallant in their effort to translate Shakespeare's words into silver shadows.

Louis B. Mayer forced Beverly Bayne to play in a 14-chapter serial, *The Great Secret,* immediately after completion of *Romeo and Juliet,* an appearance both Bayne and Bushman rightfully felt was wrong for their image and audience. The series played from January to May of 1917, and the quality of each episode mysteriously declined with each passing week. Beverly claimed they were forced to create the story as they went along, even resorting to throwing an automobile in front of an onrushing train in one episode in an attempt to stimulate interest in the story. *The Great Secret* was mercifully ended and the team returned to work on a series of four films more suited to their style.

Some critics thought Mayer was trying to destroy both of their careers. Bushman played directly into Mayer's plans when he announced he was leaving his wife and five children to marry Beverly Bayne. They were married on July 31, 1918, and a few months later, the Mall and Alhambra theaters in Cleveland, Ohio announced they would not screen any pictures in which Bushman and Bayne appeared. Moral delinquency was the crime the public, press, and other theaters charged against them in a backlash. Metro responded by declining to renew either star's contract. They rigged their final film, *God's Outlaw,* with comedy titles, turning the unreleased drama into a lampoon of their tainted romance. It proved to be the death nail in their film careers.

Vitagraph, the studio so often an employer of desperate actors, paid the two to appear in *Daring Hearts* in 1919, a film that earned generally dismal reviews and was quickly dismissed by theaters.

The ironically titled *Smiling All the Way* offered them again to the public in 1920, but there were few smiles as Bushman's possessions were being sold to raise funds to pay off the hounding creditors of his extravagant lifestyle. Bushman had maintained an apartment with Beverly while listing a permanent address with his wife near Baltimore for some time, and as the expense of financing two separate lives mounted, he was forced to sell as many personal possessions as he could.

They fell back on a stage tour of a play called *The Master Thief* in late 1919, trekking the country well into the following year and packing theaters with those curious to see the two famous stars in person. *Poor Rich Man* proved to be another successful play in which the two stars toured throughout 1921 and 1922 on the Orpheum Vaudeville circuit, meeting with great enthusiasm wherever they appeared. The aptly titled film *Modern Marriage* was produced by Bushman's own company in 1923, and boasted the unique feature of the two stars in person interrupting the middle of the screening to cajole audiences with their live narration of the remaining half of the picture.

Francis X. Bushman determined to perform with Beverly Bayne or not at all, and managed an existence on this level for some time. Their dramatic pairings ceased when he accepted the coveted role of Messala—the heavy—in MGM's massive production of *Ben-Hur.*

Beverly signed a 1924 contract with Warner Bros. and teamed with Monte Blue in *Her Marriage Vow,* followed by *The Tenth Woman* and *The Age of Innocence.* The pressure of living and working without Bushman, who was sequestered in Italy during the elongated production of *Ben-Hur,* along with other marital differences, caused the two to separate and finally divorce on April 17, 1925.

For the next three years Beverly appeared on the vaudeville circuit, acting in a series of skits. In 1929 she toured in a stock company production of *This Thing Called Love,* later retitled and revamped under the name *Gala Night.* She joined the Westchester Theater in Mount Vernon, New York, appearing in a series of productions, and participated in various promotional stunts on the road touring in a variety of other plays. The 1935 film, *Seven Keys to Baldpate,* brought Beverly into sound films for an insignificant role.

Another marriage to Charles T. Hvass ended in divorce in 1944. Bayne continued supporting the World War II effort by joining a United Theatrical War Activities presentation of *You Can't Take it With You,* performing for troops in 1945.

Broadway beckoned, and she returned to the New York stage in 1946 in *I Like It Here,* followed by a road tour of a revival of *Claudia.* She recreated the same part in a 1950 production at the Lakeside Theater in Landing, New Jersey.

Summer stock productions and television appearances rounded out her career, and she appeared in her final role in a 1958 production of *Claudia,* co-starring with Carl Betz, soon to gain great fame as the husband in television's *The Donna Reed Show.*

Both Francis X. Bushman and her son Richard died in the 1960s; Beverly drifted into a comfortable retirement, virtually forgotten until a revival of interest in silent movies mushroomed in the 1970s and again brought her into the spotlight. She was honored at several film society screenings, even performing the balcony scene from *Romeo and Juliet* for The Cinephiles Society ceremony at the Cinecon 8 film festival in September 1972.

In her last years, she gave the robe she wore in *Romeo and Juliet* to the Hollywood Museum. Her passing on August 28, 1982 ended an era. There is a Hollywood star immortalizing her in the sidewalk at 1770 Vine Street.

## SILENT FILMOGRAPHY OF BEVERLY BAYNE

A Good Catch (1912) ★ White Roses (1912) ★ The Butterfly Net (1912) ★ The Understudy (1912) ★ The New Church Organ (1912) ★ The Old Wedding Dress (1912) ★ The Magic Wand (1912) ★ House of Pride (1912) ★ The Penitent (1912) ★ The Iron Heel (1912) ★ Billy McGrath's Love Letters (1912) ★ When Soul Meets Soul (1913) ★ What George Did (1913) ★ The Farmer's Daughter (1913) ★ Hypnotism in Hicksville (1913) ★ Love and Lavallieres (1913) ★ Teaching Hickville to Sing (1913) ★ The Gum Man (1913) ★ The

Tale of a Clock (1913) ★ The Trail of the Itching Palm (1913) ★ The White Rose (1913) ★ The Will-Be Weds (1913) ★ A Brother's Loyalty (1913) ★ The Right of Way (1913) ★ The Way Perilous (1913) ★ The Toll of the Marshes (1913) ★ The Little Substitute (1913) ★ The Stigma (1913) ★ Sunlight (1913) ★ The Snare (1913) ★ Love Lute of Romany (1913) ★ The Hermit of Lonely Gulch (1913) ★ Through the Storm (1914) ★ The Girl at the Curtain (1914) ★ Oh, Doctor (1914) ★ The Fable of the Brash Drummer and the Nectarine (1914) ★ The Countess (1914) ★ His Stolen Fortune (1914) ★ One Wonderful Night (1914) ★ The Masked Wrestler (1914) ★ Under Royal Patronage (1914) ★ The Plum Tree (1914) ★ In the Glare of the Lights (1914) ★ The Private Officer (1914) ★ Scars of Possession (1914) ★ The Fable of the Bush League Lover Who Failed to Qualify (1914) ★ Every Inch a King (1914) ★ Any Woman's Choice (1914) ★ Three Little Powders (1914) ★ The Prince Party (1914) ★ One-Two-Three (1914) ★ A Foot of Romance (1914) ★ The Epidemic (1914) ★ Curing a Husband (1914) ★ Dear Old Girl (1915) ★ The Ambition of the Baron (1915) ★ Thirteen Down (1915) ★ The Accounting (1915) ★ The Great Silence (1915) ★ Graustark (1915) ★ Providence and Mrs. Urmy (1915) ★ The Crimson Wing (1915) ★ Pennington's Choice (1915) ★ Thirty (1915) ★ Man and His Soul (1916) ★ The Red Mouse (1916) ★ The Wall Between (1916) ★ A Million a Minute (1916) ★ In the Diplomatic Service (1916) ★ Romeo and Juliet (1916) ★ A Virginia Romance (1916) ★ The Great Secret (1917) ★ Their Compact (1917) ★ The Adopted Son (1917) ★ The Voice of Conscience (1917) ★ Red, White and Blue Blood (1917) ★ Under Suspicion (1918) ★ The Brass Check (1918) ★ With Neatness and Dispatch (1918) ★ Cyclone Higgins, D.D. (1918) ★ Social Quicksands (1918) ★ A Pair of Cupids (1918) ★ The Poor Rich Man (1918) ★ God's Outlaw (1919) ★ Daring Hearts (1919) ★ Smiling All the Way (1920) ★ Modern Marriage (1923) ★ Her Marriage Vow (1924) ★ The Age of Innocence (1924) ★ Who Cares (1925) ★ Passionate Youth (1925) ★ The Tenth Woman (1925)

# SARAH BERNHARDT

The existence of Sarah Bernhardt remains the supreme marvel
of the nineteenth century. The astounding range she exhibited
as an actress baffled the imagination of the public. Her words
boomed and crashed with a superhuman resonance which shook
the spirit of the listener like a leaf in the wind. The unique sound
of her voice has often been raved over; but in Sarah Bernhardt's
voice there was more than gold: there was thunder and lightning; there was Heaven and Hell.

Edmond Rostand, *Le Cinema,* 1923

Sarah Bernhardt was the greatest stage actress of the nineteenth century, if
greatness can be measured by worldwide fame. The secret of Bernhardt's
appeal was simple: sensitive people could not fail to be grateful to her for
the beauty she brought into their painful lives. To this day, young actors
and actresses revere Sarah as the bar to which they must aspire, the pinnacle of the art, the perfect summation of all the magic and artifice in
human performance.

Her effect on the development of the art of motion pictures was no less
profound. Adolph Zukor, on the occasion of the 10th anniversary of the
founding of the Famous Players Company, sent a message to Sarah signed
by 22 leading stars of the film industry: "This invitation is addressed to you
because you were the first great artist to lend her genius to our art. Your
example, ten years ago, gave to the motion picture industry the impulse

that has raised it to the place of the most important spectacle in the world. Your appearance in *Queen Elizabeth* was a priceless boon to the cinema, just as your appearance on the stage has always been an inspiration for the theater."

Sarah wanted more than anything else to leave behind a lasting legacy, to achieve some measure of immortality. This desire haunted her early youth, an unknown calling to a destiny greater than other women of her day.

She was born in Paris on October 22, 1845, the offspring of her Jewish mother, Judith Van Hard, and a Dutch father who absented himself completely from her. However, she was baptized at the age of 12 and deposited in a convent by her mother who was unable to control the tempestuous, sickly girl. On rare occasions her mother retrieved Sarah for brief excursions to the Paris night life. The night she attended her first play, *Britannicus,* sitting in a highly visible box with her mother at the Comédie Francaise, Sarah was so moved she reacted in a violent display of weeping, causing audience members to crane their heads in pique at the disturbance. Her mother was humiliated, and quickly yanked the distraught girl into a waiting carriage, spiriting her away from the scene of her embarrassing emotional display. Later, Sarah wrote in her memoirs, "When the curtain slowly rose, I thought I should have fainted. It was as though the curtain of my future life was being raised. That night the actors were performing in *Britannicus.* I heard nothing of *Britannicus* for I was far, far away."

She entered the Conservatoire at the age of 13 and won the second prize for tragedy in 1861 and for comedy in 1862. Her debut was on August 11, 1862, in Racine's *Iphigénie en Aulide.* She later became a member of a group of actors in a theater called the Gymnase, and in 1867 joined the company at the Odeon. Her first prominent success bloomed in Victor Hugo's *Ruy Blas,* and soon after, she struck a phenomenal success as Zanetto in François Coppée's *Le Passant.* The first seeds of fan hysteria were planted in the Parisian students who latched onto Sarah's character in this play, an obsessive love of her spirit and voice that carried her to rapid fame in contemporary and classical works.

Sarah became widely admired and criticized for her capricious, offstage antics, including morbid revelations of sleeping in a rosewood coffin and outrageous attire. She attracted attention usually shown for circus freaks, and did little to discourage the prying fascination of curiosity seekers. She seemed to encourage their fanatical obsessions, and theaters filled with ticket buyers. Her reputation steadily increased with performances of Phédre in Racine's play of the same name, and Dona Sol in Victor Hugo's *Hernani.*

She became a great box office attraction and brought to the theater managers more ticket revenues than any other person. She knew her own drawing power and felt limited by the choice of roles prescribed by those lesser minds controlling her performances.

In 1878 Sarah had felt the growing pains of her talent, and unable to vent her need for expression in the theater, tried her skills with forays into the arts of sculpture, painting, and writing. She attempted daredevil stunts such as descending into an octopus garden in the sea and ascending into the clouds in a balloon. The floating Dona Sol wafted high above Paris on a wild adventure, soaring beyond the city and into the windy clouds. "It was splendid! It was stupefying! The spectacle became fairylike," she wrote. "Large fleecy clouds were spread below us. Large, orange curtains fringed with violet came down from the sun to lose themselves in our cloudy carpet."

The Comédie Francaise managers, far below on the ground, were not amused at her dangerous escapade. The following day they fined her 40 francs for traveling without the consent of the management and for her unbridled temper. Sarah was sick of the pomposity of their tradition-steeped theater and the limited roles she was forced to play. She refused to pay the fine.

A remake of *Ruy Blas* was as successful as the production at the Odeon, but her strained relations with the theater's management were continually agitated by her personal behavior. Years later Sarah recalled her thoughts about the unceasing cries of indignation against her: "I had a continual thirst for what was new. This is how it is," she reasoned. "I have a wild desire to travel, to see something else, to breathe another air, and to see skies that are higher than ours and trees that are bigger. In short, some-thing different." The explanation fell on unconvinced ears. They refused the letter of resignation she sent. "My fame had become annoying for my enemies, and a little trying, I confess, for my friends," Sarah stated, "but at this time all this stir and noise amused me vastly. I did nothing to attract attention; but my fantastic tastes, my paleness and thinness, my particular way of dressing, my scorn of fashion, my general freedom in all respects, made me a being set apart. I did not recognize this fact." She did realize it was time to break entirely from the stuffy theater.

Timely fortune brought an elderly Englishman to her door. "I am Mr. Jarrett, the impresario," he revealed. "I can make your fortune. Will you come to America?"

Mr. Jarrett helped Sarah become the first international star, touring her personally directed plays through Europe, Russia, and America during 1880 and 1881. Her first appearance on the American stage was at the

Booth Theater on Twenty-third Street, the time was 8:30 on November 8, and the play was *Adrienne Lecouvreur*. Having already conquered London and Paris, she was 36 years old. Her arrival in the New York harbor was picturesque—boats flying the French flags came out to meet the liner—replete with reporters. She rarely left her cabin during the voyage, and when she was routed out of her cabin, she was so overcome by the swarm of welcoming strangers that she fainted and had to be revived with smelling salts.

Her managers whisked her behind a pair of horses to the Albemarle Hotel where, as she told it, she barricaded the door and went to sleep on the animal skin rug, while her managers banged on the door panels in vain. When she later emerged, she admitted the press and was duly interviewed, behaving like a baited tigress.

For seven months she remained in this country, playing 27 times in New York and 156 more on the tour of principal cities. She captured the love of the American public as she had captured France and England.

She had one conspicuous success after another for the next 19 years, and later made several extended tours of North and South America.

Sarah made prodigious use of photography, circulating prints, postcards, and cigarette cards in massive quantities, tangibly cementing her image with hundreds of thousands of pictures in every city she played and in remote villages where she was legendary. In 1900 she was in one of the first sound motion picture films, a presentation of her famous duel scene from *Hamlet*.

Daniel Frohman, a prodigious producer of theatricals in the early twentieth century, conveyed an attitude about stage stars venturing into films that was atypical of the time. In his autobiography, *Daniel Frohman Presents,* he wrote:

> I can't see why a dip into the moving picture business should hurt any good actor. This outcry against the new business seems to me much like the fuss made over vaudeville when it was a new thing, fifteen or twenty years ago. When the old time variety acts were baptized vaudeville—a good name because nobody knew what the world meant then and most people have respect for what they don't understand—it was said that no real artist would ever descent to vaudeville. Look at the situation now. Almost any artist will now go into vaudeville if the terms are big enough, and when the player wants to, he or she may return to the legitimate stage work and find as warm a welcome as ever. Miss Rose Coghlan, Messrs. W. H. Thompson, Robert Hilliard and a lot of others here, with Mme. Sarah Bernhardt, Mme. Rejane and Lady Beerhohm Tree on the other side, have played in vaudeville and some day may play in pictures.

Sarah Bernhardt and Lou-Tellegen as Marguerite Gautier and
Armand Duval, in *Camille (La Dame aux Camelias)*.

As time passed, Frohman's prophecy proved true. Sarah delighted in
mystifying the world with her wonderful portrayal of favorite characters
on the screen. Sarah's appearance in motion pictures was proof the film
industry was a vital component of the amusement world. High-class, legitimate managers as well as the agencies began taking the same attitude.

The movies gave her the chance at immortality she craved since her
early youth. Eleven films brought her art to audiences that could never
afford to see her in the live theater. Her 1912 film, *Queen Elizabeth,* pioneered feature-length films in an era when most productions were of 10–12
minute lengths. The phenomenal success of this film achieved the status of
a milestone, and is largely noted in every film history book for its signifi-
cance. But her earlier film, *Camille* (1911), was the match that struck the
flame of *Queen Elizabeth's* success.

Sarah Bernhardt won acclaim as Marguerite Gautier in the tragic story
of the Lady of the Camellias. She played this role more than 3,000 times,

and when the chance came to record her signature role in motion pictures, Sarah accepted the challenge. She defied both age and the muting of her acclaimed voice, performing a silent film condensation of the well-known play, proving her talent could transcend the limitations of the new art. She personally supervised the production, crafting the scenario to fit the peculiar expression and techniques of the silent cinema.

The motion picture of *Camille* is a condensation of the story. It skips over the opening scenes establishing the name and character of Marguerite and her introduction to Armand Duval, and begins the action after the two of them have retired to a country home where the fresh air and rural environment were to be a healing force on the ailing health of poor Marguerite. She is visited by Armand's father, who arrives at the cottage to beg Marguerite to give up her affair with Armand for the good of his future. Understanding only too well the effect her low reputation could have on his success, she consents to leave him, even though doing so breaks her heart. She ends the relationship in the coldest way possible, writing Armand a note renouncing her love for him and leaving. Then the scene changes to the party at the apartment of her friend, Prudence. Armand comes in and is startled to see Marguerite, and then publicly debases her by throwing a deck of playing cards at her face. Marguerite pleads with him to understand why she was forced to give him up. They reconcile in each others arms, but it is too late. In the following scene in Marguerite's apartment, she suddenly dies. Armand lowers her to the floor, and the film comes to its tragic end.

The motion picture was made in two reels, running about a half an hour in total length. The original prints were hand colored, and the film was accompanied with a carefully arranged score fitting the varying moods of the action.

The stars went to Neuilly-sur-Seine in 1911 for the filming. Sarah had studied the art of motion pictures with many of the leading film companies in Paris and did not come before the cameras unprepared. By the time filming started, she believed herself to be an encyclopedia of information on the art of filmmaking. A few rehearsals were necessary so the timing might be accurate, and the film was then made in a single day with each scene filmed in one long take.

Most films made prior to 1912 did not reveal the names of actors. With Sarah's appearances, the selling value of a star name became valuable. There was a chaotic scramble to sign prospective favorites to exclusive contracts. Biograph discovery Florence Lawrence was still the most valuable actress in America at the box office when she succumbed to an offer to leave IMP and join Lubin. In turn, Mary Pickford began to gain renown and left Biograph to join IMP.

Sarah Bernhardt attracted the attention of viewers in every major city, even when many of those viewers were of the lower income population and had not been able to afford to see her on the stage. Her name was already legendary, and as her face began to appear on advertisements for *Camille,* other films with renowned actors followed in an endless tidal wave. The market was highly competitive, and the producers calculated the name of Bernhardt and a film of her most famous role would find a place amid the relentless number of releases.

In 1911 Wallace Reid was gaining legions of fans at Vitagraph in a popular series of films. The same studio boasted the release of comic John Bunny in a new film each week. D. W. Griffith directed *Enoch Arden* for Biograph, while Selig made a three-reel film of *The Two Orphans.* Norma Talmadge was emerging as a noticeable talent in Vitagraph's *A Tale of Two Cities,* while Lionel Barrymore and Blanche Sweet were appearing in a number of Biograph dramas. 1911 was the year film magazines prospered and blossomed onto newsstands, sheet music bore the faces of actresses and the titles of outstanding films, and audience attendance was skyrocketing. In the middle of this explosion of activity and popularity, the Éclair Company simultaneously circulated dozens of prints of Sarah Bernhardt in *Camille.*

Before the prints were released, the studio put each print through the laborious process of hand coloring. This process involved placing stencils over each individual frame of film and coloring the various people and props with an appropriate hue, adding a beauty to the print that enhanced its dramatic effect. They even prepared a careful music score, selecting old chestnuts appropriate to the mood of each scene that most pianists would have readily available or know from heart. This musical cue sheet was sent out with each reel of the film, prompting a uniform presentation in each city that lifted the drama with supporting arias, dictating the emotional theme of the story and affecting audiences with the tragic story.

On April 11, 1911, *The Moving Picture World* wrote,

*Éclair* Presents Mme. Bernhardt in Pictures. [The article stated that] Time and again it has been suggested that the last word in motion picture enterprise would be to induce Mme. Sarah Bernhardt to pose for the motion picture camera. While it has been noticed that the Divine Sarah appeared before the camera, it has not been generally announced that the Éclair Company was the fortunate company to secure her services. That, however, is

A GLORIOUS RECORD OF GENIUS

**OPERA HOUSE** 4 DAYS Beginning WED. Mar. 27 (Afternoon and Night)

Your Only Chance to See

*THE MARVEL AND MIRACLE OF THE STAGE*

— M A D A M —

# SARAH BERNHARDT

In Duma's Emotional Masterpiece:

## "Camille"

NOW in her 71st year, the Divine Sarah will be seen in all her glorious splendour, enacting her finest role, assisted by her

### All-Star Company

A Marvellous Motion Picture

Recording the Personality of the Greatest Actors in the World

ALSO

### Madam Rejane

The Pride of Europe

The most celebrated comedienne before the public, in "Madam Sans Gene," a comic incident in the life of Napoleon.

Seat Sale Opens Monday

**Prices:** Evenings—50, 35, 25, 15c
Afternoons—Adults, 25c Children, 15c

This advertisement for the motion picture of *Camille* appeared in the Saturday, March 23, 1912 *Saint John Globe* newspaper.

the fact about the matter and that fortunate company now announces that it will soon release the picture in which Mme. Bernhardt appears which will be *Camille*. It is also announced by the same company that Mme. Réjane has been secured for a motion picture revival of Sardou's comedy, *Madam Sans Gene*. In both pictures the stars are supported by a distinguished cast.

*The Moving Picture World,* February 10, 1912, reviewed the finished film with these comments:

Mme. Bernhardt has always regarded her rendition of *Camille* as her best character portrayal. But it was with great difficulty that she was induced to

The death of Marguerite. Sarah Bernhardt played this scene more than 3,000 times on the stage in every major country in the world.

repeat her performance for motion pictures. She did consent, however, and entered into the task with such enthusiasm that it was only with great difficulty that her efforts were made to conform to the limitations of the camera. The result is a remarkable motion picture, through the agency of which thousands who have never before witnessed her performance on the speaking stage, will be able to see the world's greatest actress in her favorite roles.

Bernhardt's performance was a suitable record of her stage rendition. All the grand gestures—hands flailing, chest beating, and eye rolling were used in abundance. Sarah played in front of the camera in a fashion that was probably well suited to the stage, but appeared exaggerated on the screen. There is one notable exception: In the moment of Marguerite's death, while held in Armand Duval's arms, with her hands entwined around his neck, Sarah simply lets her hand go limp. Her face is completely turned away from the audience, and she telegraphs the moment of death with this simple, elegant gesture. Armand loosens his embrace for a moment, and Sarah nearly falls, but is caught back in an instant by Armand and gently lowered to the floor.

In a review in *The New York Dramatic Mirror,* 1912, an anonymous reporter stated,

Madame Bernhardt proves in this production, as had been anticipated, her wonderful adaptability to the peculiar forms of expression required for finished picture acting. It is the mark of the great artist, demonstrated more vividly, if anything, than is possible on the theatre stage. With the art of which she is so much the master, she appears in the picture to be the living embodiment of *Camille,* unconscious of camera or of supposed spectators and conveying, not by pantomime, but by natural and significant actions and expression the progress of the story. The culmination comes in the death scene, which Bernhardt's art renders in a way distressing, but tremendously impressive and convincing. She is standing in Armand's embrace with her face hidden from view. By her hand drooping and falling like the flower from which Marguerite's sobriquet was derived.

Fortunately, the picture adaptation of *Camille* was modeled with considerable success after the technique of the photoplay, as developed by the experience and genius of those who led in the growth in this new art. Had the adaptation been merely a reproduction of the action of the stage play minus the words it would have been disappointing, even with Mme. Bernhardt's great ability and prestige. But this pitfall was avoided. The story was told by the method of the cinema and told quite clearly, although it could have been more forceful perhaps and certainly more explicit in some of the scenes. For instance, the fragment of the duel scene, which may have been cut down to avoid the possible interference of troublesome censors, could have been enhanced. There is also a regrettable lack of close-ups of the actors. In this, however, the producers were probably too cautious at the expense of the picture's art—a thing that was hardly necessary in a production of such distinction. In one other respect, the picture failed to realize the most advanced development of the photoplay, which was already being practiced by other producers. There were too many subtitles announcing in words action plainly visible on the screen. At times these advance explanations of what is to follow rob the picture story of its interest. This fault was not uncommon in 1911. Directors were soon to learn the beauty of pictorial depictions and were to strive to avoid unnecessary titles in films made in the following years.

All this, however, is no fault of Mme. Bernhardt, and did not prevent the motion picture record of her interpretation of *Camille* from being one of the masterpieces of the photoplay in the early years of its development as an art form. It succeeded in its destiny to preserve for posterity the world's greatest actress in her greatest role. The settings were realistic and the supporting actors excellent. Lou-Tellegen emerged as a startlingly handsome leading man, his blonde, youthful good looks and athletic physique contrasting well opposite the aging Sarah Bernhardt. The photography was also of the best French quality.

*Moving Picture News,* March, 1912, reviewed the film under the headline "Sarah the Divine in Moving Pictures." The reviewer claimed,

*Camille* was never more pitifully eloquent than in this dumb record. Sarah Bernhardt played with wonderful fire and expressiveness. Great genius that she is, she suited herself to her medium and the result is a long series of photographs that are staccato in their expressiveness. The story is revealed as plain as print. *Camille* is a perfect photoplay. The story lends itself to the purposes of the camera, and Bernhardt is eloquent in every movement. Someone has said that the pictures fairly crackle with life and projects wireless messages to the spectators. All over Europe the photoplay *Camille* is a sensation and Americans are eagerly awaiting the release of these reels, which are now in the control of the French-American Film Company which is rapidly disposing of State rights.

The Film d'Art Company began production of films in 1903, presenting literary figures and the leading actors of the Comédie Francaise in films made of famous plays, exact duplications of the stage performances. Innovative in concept, the effort ultimately failed because their stage-celebrity pictures did not make use of any of the techniques of cinema that were utilized by many other producers at the time. Their only redeeming quality is the excitement of seeing a legendary figure on screen and watching a dead theatre period come to life before our eyes. As records, they are precious for theatre historians. As films, they were woefully lacking in the techniques of cinematic construction already widely used by other directors.

W. Stephen Bush wrote in *The Moving Picture World,* March 2, 1912,

It may well be doubted whether money would have induced Sarah Bernhardt, the greatest of living actresses, to play *Camille* before a moving picture camera. To such a passionate lover of her art, it must have seemed glorious to defy the limitations of space and time and have the whole world as her audience. The cinematograph is indeed a monument more enduring than brass and it is far more ornamental and useful as well. The immortality conferred by the motion picture is well worth having.

It is not the smallest tribute to the genius of Sarah Bernhardt to say that her art loses nothing in its transmission to the little strips of celluloid. The gifts of other noted artists do not shine as well in the motion pictures as they do on the speaking stage, just as some talented singers please us in opera, but are heard to poor advantage in the gramophone. The splendor of Sarah Bernhardt's art remains undimmed in the photoplay.

To paint the lily, or throw perfume on the violets is no more of a wasteful and ridiculous excess than to pile up new adjectives in praise of the genius of Sarah Bernhardt. It is true of her, indeed, that age cannot wither, nor custom stale her infinite variety. To body forth Dumas' conception of *Camille,* an exuberance of youth is needed. *Camille* first wins our sympathy and stirs our profoundest pity because her youth is cast in endless shade, though, of course, her noble sacrifice deepens the feeling. She possesses all the gayety of her kind: the animal joy of living, but not untouched by a certain womanly grace and sweetness. Until she meets Armand, her finer nature has lain dormant, she was a beauteous butterfly and the sins she committed were of the kind which Christian charity is most ready to forgive. Sarah Bernhardt, by a splendid display of her genius, makes us understand the profound change that came over *Camille* after Armand entered her life. With consummate art she shows the ennobling and sobering influence of a sincere love. We see how the careless and frivolous demimondaine of the better sort becomes a true woman, whose soul grows stronger as her body turns chaste. One who patiently bears suffering and humiliation and sacrifices her happiness for the sake of others.

It is, however, in the portrayal of the tragic element that the divine Sarah rises to the most dazzling heights of the mimic art. How subtle is the touch by which she gives us the first hint of the fatal nature of her malady, when the first reel has scarcely begun. This marvelous power in developing the tragic element is finely sustained throughout until it culminates in a veritable triumph of acting in the last scene.

To see these two reels is to realize to the fullest extent the art and power of Sarah Bernhardt and no greater boon could be offered to the theatergoer of today. Every audience looking at these films will be stirred as deeply as those who saw Sarah Bernhardt act in the flesh. It goes without saying that these pictures will gain new friends for the motion picture by the thousands and that directly or indirectly every branch of the motion picture industry will have its benefit from them. I only hope operators everywhere will be kind to the pictures and not try to run them at a Saturday night rate of speed. There is no room anywhere for effects, but music of the right kind will be most acceptable. Pathos should be its dominant note.

Sarah Bernhardt proved advancing age and inexperience with a new art could not prevent her from achieving success. She overcame all obstacles, and created a work of art that stood the test of time. *Camille* is still being shown today.

*Adrienne Lecouvreur* (1912) was Sarah's next film, an adaptation of one of her most popular plays. The story was based on the true-life legend of a famous, French actress and her romances. Again, as in *Camille,* Sarah constructed the scenario and deported her cast in a quickly filmed version of the play. Reviewers noticed the wonderful play of her features, indicating there were many close-ups. *Adrienne Lecouvreur* appears to be lost, until a print resurfaces from some unknown storage vault.

*Sarah Bernhardt a Belle-Isle* (1912), also known as *Sarah Bernhardt at Home,* was a documentary of her life on the private island she purchased and to which she retreated each summer. As her advancing years made touring travels more tiring, Sarah longed for the respite gleaned from her several months spent each year on the island. The documentary film captures her life among the few local natives. She was shown visiting the ocean home of an octopus, catching shrimp with the natives, venturing forth on early morning hunting exhibitions, and relaxing with her beloved dogs. Also featured in the film was her son, Maurice, and his daughters. The documentary was useful for Sarah as a publicity tool, often sent into towns just prior to her arrival on their local theater stages for a live performance of a play, creating advance awareness of her. The film also offered an intimate glimpse of her personal life, for which the legions of admirers she cultivated over the years were rabid.

Adolph Zukor, an enterprising immigrant, imported Sarah's film, *Queen Elizabeth* (1912), and widely circulated it on a State's rights basis in the United States and abroad. This four-reel film was one of the first to use a length later known as feature length and galvanized the industry to accept the longer playing time as a standard. The richly produced saga of Queen Elizabeth and her ill-fated love affair with Lord Essex was made from her play of the same name. Sarah again arranged the scenes to fit the requirements of the silent picture drama, and personally supervised the production. Louis Mercanton, credited with directing the film, seemed to do little more than operate the cameras and lights, as the film is bereft of any camera techniques already used by other directors of the same era. An enormous success, making millions for Zukor and starting the operation of his Famous Players film producing company, *Queen Elizabeth* also showed to great advantage the tall and handsome Lou-Tellegen, whose blond, athletic appearance won many female hearts in America. His connection with audiences was so great in this film that Lasky offered him a contract to come to America and make pictures exclusively for his company. Upon the completion of his four-year contract with Bernhardt, Tellegen came to California and began a career that would catapult him to the top of the ranks of leading men for the next 15 years.

Sacha Guitry, an important figure in the French theater, strongly felt motion pictures should capture the image and essence of the famous persons of the day while they were still living. *Those at Our House* (1915) was his documentary capturing the great artists of France in work and in repose. Sarah was briefly filmed sitting on a park bench with her son, full of the joy of life, and radiating the charm for which she was renowned.

Sarah injured her knee in a stunt fall some years before, and as time passed, her knee grew increasingly worse. By 1912 she could barely walk, and by 1915 the knee developed gangrene. Her entire leg had to be amputated near the hip. She had just completed a role in a play written by Tristan Bernard, *Jeanne Doré,* and after returning from her operation, the world speculated she would never be physically able to work in the theater again. Films were her immediate answer to their challenge, and within weeks of her amputation, unable to walk and still in great pain, Sarah filmed a detailed adaptation of her last play. *Jeanne Doré* (1916) was a heartwarming film of a determined mother and her sacrifice for a son condemned for murder. Because of her infirmity, she was forced to remain seated or standing, and the camera focused on her close-up interpretation to great effect.

Sarah's last visit to America was in 1916 when she was 72 years old, had only one leg left to stand on, could no longer walk, and had to be carried on the stage in a chair. As with all her previous tours, she traveled the length and breadth of the land and carted along, as part of her luggage, her art collection and her coffin. On this final tour, which had to be broken in two by a critical operation at Mount Sinai Hospital, she played on the vaudeville circuit and gave her last performance in this country in October 1918, at B. F. Keith's Hippodrome in Cleveland.

For the final decade of her life Sarah continued to appear in one sumptuous production after another. She became the living symbol of France, and to the end she was borne up by the prodigious vitality and unconquerable spirit which were the essence of her genius.

*Mothers of France* (1917) was Sarah's gallant contribution to the World War I effort. This was her only film made originally for the medium of motion pictures and not based on a previously performed play. Filming took place so close to the front lines that actors could hear the bombardments bursting, and one scene, taken at the foot of France's statue of Joan of Arc, actually involved the cooperation of the French military. Shelling was halted for 15 minutes and the area sandbagged so Sarah could approach the statue and perform a scene with a bedraggled soldier. She was filmed in the trenches with the soldiers in the middle of combat, transported on a litter hoisted by four men. The powerful film told the tale of a French mother losing her husband and son in the heated exchanges of battle. Footage of Geraldine Farrar in Cecil B. DeMille's *Joan the Woman* was double exposed over some of the battle scenes. The film was widely circulated to rave reviews, an inspiration to those suffering family losses in the war effort.

*It Happened in Paris* (1919) featured Sarah in a personally produced film. She appeared in a prologue, discussing the project with the director and star, Mme. Yurska. The actress was Sarah's protégé, and the turgid melodrama introduced the young actress to the world by way of Sarah's careful supervision. The film is among the lost, and no prints are known to exist.

In 1920, Sarah again went on a lengthy, worldwide tour of a one-act play, *Daniel.* She portrayed a male dying from morphine addiction, seeking reconciliation with his one true love. In (1921) a film was made of the final death scene, photographed in careful detail and with camera set-ups designed to take the viewer intimately close to the character's tragic demise. Sarah is seen in several ghastly close-ups as she succumbs to the ravages of drug abuse.

Within two years, uremia was slowly killing Sarah Bernhardt. After a lifetime of reaping millions of dollars with her endless tours of the world and spending each of those dollars she was desperate for money. As the poison steadily worked its deadly course through her body, she bravely signed a contract with an American firm to star in a motion picture as a clairvoyant. In *La Voyanté* (1923) she fulfilled her desire to die on the stage. Her final days were spent making the motion picture of *La Voyanté,* filming up to her final hours in a makeshift studio constructed inside her home. She had to be carried downstairs from her bedroom to pose in front of the camera, valiantly taking scenes as rapidly as they could be rehearsed and photographed. When she became too weak to be carried to the set, cameras were set up in her bedroom and she was filmed in bed with her chimpanzee hopping about the room. She collapsed in between camera set-ups and was restricted for several hours to her bed. She never rose again. As the night wore on, her mind began to replay her greatest roles, and her son observed her lips moving to whispers of the famous speeches she gave a thousand times in *Phédre* and *L'Aiglon.* A priest was rushed in to administer the last rites, and Sarah died on March 26, 1923.

Another actress, dressed in Sarah's costume, played her remaining scenes with her back to the camera, and *La Voyante* was finally wrapped and released.

Sarah Bernhardt proved that neither beauty nor youth were required for making oneself into a motion picture legend. She gave her talent, determination, and sense of adventure to the medium, lifting it up from the one-reel melodrama and positioning it as a compliment to the legitimate theater. Because of her, uncountable millions of people who thought of the movies as a lower-class and often dangerous form of amusement, discovered the rich experiences waiting to be enjoyed in the dark. She led the way for all the other big name stars of the theater, opera, and music industries to bring their talent into films.

## SILENT FILMOGRAPHY OF SARAH BERNHARDT

Le Duel d'Hamlet (1900) ★ La Tosca (1908) ★ Camille (1911) ★ Adrienne Lecouvreur (1912) ★ Sarah Bernhardt a Belle-Isle (1912) ★ Queen Elizabeth (1912) ★ Those at Our House (1915) ★ Jeanne Doré (1916) ★ Mothers of France (1917) ★ It Happened in Paris (1919) ★ Daniel (1921) ★ La Voyanté (1923)

# CAROL DEMPSTER

Carol Dempster was a curious actress, and a very promising one, earning a place in the development of motion pictures by way of her association with D. W. Griffith. When at her best, she was coached by Griffith to be intensely moving and completely convincing. The famous director similarly inspired Florence Lawrence, Mary Pickford, Lillian Gish, Dorothy Gish, Mae Marsh, and Constance Talmadge. In turn, each ultimately left him to follow the lure of more lucrative contracts, and as Griffith magnanimously allowed each to pursue their destiny, another pliable girl would slip into the embodiment of his ideal woman. Carol Dempster found the door of opportunity opening to her when Lillian Gish, Griffith's most prominent muse, succumbed to offers with other producers and more money.

She was born on January 6, 1902 in Duluth, Minnesota, the youngest of four children. When her father decided to change careers and leave his position as a captain on the Great Lakes, he moved to California. Carol was dancing at a school entertainment one day, and her vitality was noticed by premier danseuse, Ruth St. Denis. "I began as a dancer, you know, out in California with Ruth St. Denis," Carol recalled in an interview with W. Adolphe Roberts in *Motion Picture Magazine*. "I was the youngest pupil to graduate in her first class."

Griffith hired Ruth St. Denis to stage the dancing scenes in the Babylonian scenes of his epic, *Intolerance*. Carol was recruited to appear as one of those dancers. Griffith noticed her standing out from the others and invited her to appear in a small role with Robert Harron in *A Romance of Happy Valley.*

*A Romance of Happy Valley* (1919) paired Carol with the popular team of Lillian Gish and Robert Harron in a simple romance reminiscent of the short stories of his Biograph days. The film harkened back to his own days in Kentucky, and told the story of a farm boy who made his fortune in New York. It is one of the most-coveted lost films from the Griffith-directed canon.

*The Greatest Thing in Life* (1919) featured Carol in what Lillian Gish called "one of the best Griffith ever did." The theme was love, the greatest thing in life, and the daring plot focused on Robert Harron as an intolerant snob, unworthy of the heroine, but whose prejudices were shattered by comradeship in the trenches of World War I. Many said this film was Griffith's answer to those who criticized the racist element of *The Birth of a Nation.* One memorable scene showed Robert Harron, a white soldier, taking refuge in the same shell hole as a Negro soldier. As the dying Negro hallucinated, believing his mother to be nearby, Harron comforted him and kissed him on the cheek.

When the film had its premier, Griffith hired a dancer who was gaining attention appearing in a Dorothy Gish film to dance with Carol in a prologue to the screening. The presentation was such a hit it was extended for three weeks. The dancer, who called himself Rudolpho Di Valantina, managed to get a lead role in 1918's *All Night,* but after this he went back to playing bit parts. In 1920 he appeared in six films under his new name, Rudolph Valentino: *The Adventuress, The Cheater, Passion's Playground, Once to Every Woman, Stolen Moments* and *The Wonderful Change.* He continued to be cast as Italians, heavies, and other roles as he could obtain them. Several years later, the Italian immigrant found international fame in *The Four Horsemen of the Apocalypse,* and went on to become an icon of the silent cinema in *The Sheik.*

*The Hope Chest* (1919) featured Carol in a comedy film produced by Griffith and starring Dorothy Gish, the second in her series of Artcraft specials featuring her burgeoning laugh-getting knack.

The Strand Theater in New York premiered the seven-reel film in which Carol Dempster first replaced Lillian Gish as the heroine of Griffith's *The Girl Who Stayed at Home* (1919). Richard Barthelmess rapidly became one of Hollywood's most-loved leading men in this and other films of the Griffith organization. War footage shot but unused for *Hearts of the World* was incorporated into the picture, telling the story of a young man drafted into the army despite the efforts of his father to have him declared essential to the family shipping business. The boy, portrayed by Robert Harron, became a hero on the battlefields of France, while Carol is threatened with rape by a brutal German officer.

*True Heart Susie* (1919), a six-reel film of young lovers in a small village in rural America, cast Carol as the friend of Bettina, a rival for the attention of Lillian Gish's boyfriend, played by frequent co-star, Robert Harron.

Richard Barthelmess again starred opposite Carol in *Scarlet Days* (1919). The western tale of a good/bad man in the California Gold Rush and his encounters with an Eastern girl also featured Walter Long, the villainous Gus of *The Birth of a Nation,* as an evil dance hall proprietor.

Carol played Stella Bevan, a childlike heroine raised on a South Sea island who lives alone with her father, a fugitive from a crime. In *The Love Flower* (1920) an idyllic romance develops when Richard Barthelmess, wandering the sea in his sailboat, comes ashore on the island, unknowingly bringing the man who is looking for her father. For Richard's growing legion of women fans, Carol seemingly fulfilled many a female fantasy. She was shown beautifully in some underwater sequences, emphasizing her lithe, dancing body and her swimming skills. A title describes her "straining and swaying in youth's hot madness." She is shown again later in the film, using her swimming skills for the deadly purpose of drowning the detective plotting to arrest her fugitive father.

*Photoplay* reviewed the film and noted Carol particularly: "If Mr. Griffith wishes us to become well-acquainted with his latest discovery he will not be disappointed. We have seen Carol Dempster through the misty close-up and under water; we have seen her outlined against the sky, the wind whipping her filmy costume about her."

*The Love Flower* was completely overshadowed by the thundering arrival at the same time of Griffith's blockbuster, *Way Down East.* The plot is less complicated and made splendid use of its South Seas location. Richard Barthelmess again appeared opposite Carol as a wandering sailor. *Way Down East* enjoyed such profound success it was exhibited as a road show, an arrangement that increased its earnings and prompted an avalanche of publicity that obscured *The Love Flower.*

It would be six years later when sound films completely supplanted silent films, yet Griffith, consistently innovative in his work, used an experimental sound system in *Dream Street* (1920). The system was remarkably similar to the Vitaphone process so heralded six years later as an achievement of the Warner Bros. The process synchronized records by way of an attaching device. A love song by Ralph Graves was recorded and performed in the film. A prologue to the film presented Griffith speaking an introduction to the audience about the evolution of motion pictures. The experiment was ambitious, and the story solidly drew materials from another Thomas Burke story, similar to that used in his *Broken Blossoms.* An evil Chinese man lusts after Carol, who later betrays the man to the police. The film was rich with allegorical poetry and atmospheric photography.

Once again, the effort was overshadowed by a stupendous Lillian Gish film. *Orphans of the Storm* opened in Boston on December 28, 1921, a few months after the release of *Dream Street.* The saga of two orphans lost in the middle of the French revolution usurped audiences' attention from *Dream Street.*

Carol was urged by Griffith to take part in the John Barrymore vehicle, *Sherlock Holmes* (1922). "I wouldn't do just *any* picture," she declared to Gladys Hall in the July, 1922, issue of *Motion Picture Magazine.* "I didn't even care, at first, to play in *Sherlock Holmes* with John Barrymore. But Mr. Griffith approved it, and all of my friends argued in favor of it, and now I am glad that I did it. Curiously enough, I had never seen Mr. Barrymore either on the stage or the screen. I told him that when he telephoned me about the picture and he said, "Perhaps you have *heard* of me!" I thought he might not want me after that, but he did. He had seen me, it seems, in *Dream Street* and thought that we were much the same physical type. Built long, I suppose he meant!

*One Exciting Night* (1922) was an entertaining, modest film Griffith made with Carol, a murder-mystery thriller complete with sliding walls in a haunted house, characters who are not what they seem to be, and a real-life hurricane finale that rivaled the ice floe sequence in *Way Down East.*

Mae Marsh was recruited to carry the lead role of Bessie Williams in Griffith's 1923 film, *The White Rose.* Carol played Marie Carrington in the story of a clergyman involved in a crime related to sex. Mae Marsh again proved herself capable of a moving performance as a young woman having an illegitimate child. The film was banned in some cities because of the sex theme.

Mae Marsh had a good perspective on Griffith and his vision for Carol's work. To those who criticized Griffith for molding Carol into an actress of merit and a muse for his vision, Mae Marsh explained his penchant for pliable ingénues in her book, *Screen Acting:*

Can he make anyone a star? So far as I know Mr. Griffith possesses no magic lamp by which he makes a star out of anyone. It is not any one quality—unless it be patience—but a combination of many that make him the foremost of our directors. Mr. Griffith is extremely human. There is no unnecessary flourish, or blowing of trumpets, about his manner of direction. That has the simplicity of true greatness. He never lords it over his players as I have seen some directors do. He is kindly, sympathetic and understand-

D. W. Griffith, director of *America* (1924).

ing. Perhaps we are about to do a very vital scene. Mr. Griffith tilts back in his chair—he has a manner of directing while seated—and may say to the actress, "You understand this situation. Now let us see what you would do with it." Here is a direct challenge. The actress is put upon her metal. After giving the matter careful consideration she plays the scene after her own idea. If she does it well no one is quicker in his praise than Mr. Griffith. If otherwise, no one is more kindly in pointing out the flaws. In other words, Mr. Griffith gives the actress a chance. How different from other directors I have seen.

When Robert Welsh of *The New York Dramatic Mirror* asked Griffith for his secret for making stars, he replied, "There is no secret," he says. "I did not 'teach' the players with whom my name has been linked. We developed together, we found ourselves in a new art and as we discovered the possibilities of that art we learned together."

Carol beautifully and precisely achieved the effects Griffith desired. She was loved by many filmgoers but reviled by others, often unfairly criti-

Carol Dempster, the lovely D. W. Griffith discovery.

cized as a pale imitation of Griffith's earlier heroines portrayed by Lillian Gish, Mae Marsh, Blanche Sweet, and Mary Pickford. Many of her admiring fans came to her defense. In *Photoplay,* August, 1919, an anonymous writer said, "The prime reason Miss Dempster has become identified with the list of Griffith players is because she is: First, probably the most graceful in movement of any young woman now in pictures. Second, she has a peculiar type of beauty that appeals to many people. Third, she has a case of real inside sincerity that the camera does not fail to register."

From 1908 to 1930 Griffith developed motion pictures from their humble beginning as a peep show amusement to a level of excellence comparable to the films of today. He was instrumental in the implementation of the dramatic use of devices such as the long shot, flash back, close-, and montage for dramatic effect. He was the first to bring into pictures realistic acting, replacing the exaggerated techniques of the nineteenth-century theatrical stages. "Doubtless this sorry spectacle would have continued through many decades had not Science come to the rescue of these typical Americans in the small places," Griffith later wrote in an article called "Pictures vs. One Night Stands," published in *The Independent,* December 11, 1916. "Science looked askance on the poor actor man and told him his one-night stands were over. Science made an end of a chilly theater and a backward play, It made an end of inadequate scenery, magically, as it were, snatching the faithful from the old, old interiors off to beautiful hours in the glorious spots of the earth. Already the motion picture is the world's chief form of entertainment, the greatest spiritual force the world has ever known. Here in America it has worked in the course of seven years or so a phenomenal change and it is expanding by leaps and bounds."

*The Birth of a Nation* (1915) and *Intolerance* (1916) are the motion pictures for which D. W. Griffith is best remembered. *Way Down East* and a few other films continue to be shown, along with many of the outstanding Biograph films that cut the pattern of motion picture techniques still in use today.

Carol became an important asset to Griffith after three films in a row failed to make large returns on their investment. Griffith decided he would have to recoup his losses by returning to the large-scale pictures for which he was famous. He resurrected *War,* his play about the American Revolution, and commissioned a novelist, Robert Chambers, a specialist in historical romances, to rewrite the story for the film to be titled *America.* Carol was cast in a pivotal role. He believed she was capable of the technique of communicating through shadows, and rewarded his trust with a lead role in the film he believed would stand the test of time. In the article called "Pictures vs. One Night Stands," published in *The Independent,* December 11, 1916, he stated,

> Acting itself has been improved with this development of the technical means of the play. Many actors have told me that they thought that acting on the old stage was difficult, but that it is nothing compared with acting in the new. Not often, in fact, do we find an actor or actress trained in the old school who is successful in the new. Those who succeed are those whose art is simplest and finest. Mrs. Fiske was very successful in her *Tess.* Leo Dietrichstein would be successful, I am sure. Irving or Mansfield would be wonderful. Two years ago there was hardly any real actor depending upon the motion pictures. We paid very little attention to the old-stage actors. And when at last we took them and tried them we found they were far beneath in real acting power the ones we had trained.

Griffith trained Carol to express to the audience what he wanted to convey. The result was vastly more effective than in the old, and audiences were satisfied with the result. In the article "Pictures vs. One Night Stands," published in *The Independent,* December 11, 1916, Griffith claimed:

> I use the word satisfying deliberately as descriptive of the needs of civilization. We have little time for art. We make no pilgrimages to its shrines. Art, in short, satisfies a passion that we Americans are prone, the great mass of us, to satisfy in the form that is nearest to hand because we have so little time between the swift stretches of our increasingly busy life. I have observed often that hunger for beauty in the forms of any particular art is usually appeased by gratification in another. I have observed this particularly in Americans. Few indeed of us go from a motion picture play to a theater, or from a theater to an opera, or from an opera to a circus. Surely most of us would not feel after seeing whole reels of beautiful color pictures the passion for paintings that we felt before seeing them. I think this observation has point. It makes clear, I believe, that from reasons of time no less than of money most of us likely to select the art that satisfies us most and is most convenient and least costly. I should be little surprised, to illustrate, if many devotees of the Metropolitan Museum of Art in New York City have discovered that they can get at a neighboring theater for ten cents, with little expenditure of energy, of time and with as little loss of money as they would spend in carfare to reach the museum, something that satisfies their hunger for beauty and for entertainment.

Griffith was growing desperate. The stars he was credited with creating had all moved on to enjoy the benefits of the fame gleaned from his films: Lillian Gish was making austere dramas for MGM, Richard Barthelmess formed his own company called Inspiration Pictures and was grinding out one hit after another with Henry King. Even Mae Marsh, who few thought could act without Griffith's Svengali-like direction, signed a lucrative contract with Samuel Goldwyn. Griffith was living on the returns from the reissue of *The Birth of a Nation* in 1920. He was beginning to hear people talk about him as if he was an icon of the days gone by. The exhibitors were losing faith in him. And then the idea came to him to make another spectacle like *The Birth of a Nation,* something very American like that film was, only bigger. He would tell the story of the forming of the great nation, not just the South, but the entire country. The passion, the struggle against the British, the Revolution, Paul Revere's ride, Washington praying in the snow, and the intrigue that fomented into the eruption of America. The more he pondered the possibilities, the more his brain fired with ideas.

One-sheet poster for D. W. Griffith's *America,* starring Carol Dempster and Neil Hamilton.

Carol Dempster was available and perfect for the love interest around which he could ignite all the history of the making of the nation. He would create the love story, since one didn't exist. It was just like when he threw Lillian Gish and Dorothy Gish into the tired, old play, *The Two Orphans,* and dumped the whole story into the middle of the French Revolution in *Orphans of the Storm.*

Griffith pored over the historical documents available about the Revolutionary War in America. He was determined to bring Carol into the story with as much accuracy to historical detail as possible.

In *America,* a story of love and romance during the American Revolutionary War, Carol faced the formidable task of sharing the screen with the scene-stealing Lionel Barrymore and handsome Neil Hamilton, and she succeeded.

In 1923 Griffith began filming *America,* arousing tremendous enthusiasm among local people on the actual sites of the Revolutionary War. The populace brought out their treasured heirlooms and mementos from the war to assist in the accuracy of the reproductions. Vivid recreations of Paul Revere's historical ride were performed along with the battles of Valley Forge, Bunker Hill, and the Cherry Valley massacre.

The filming of the Revolutionary War in America was done in the full glare of publicity and with research assisted by historians and historical societies. The accuracy of the details in *America* made the film an ideal tool for teaching school children about their heritage and the winning of freedom from oppression. The film was made with painstaking care and the battle scenes were brilliantly staged. Large numbers of army troops were deployed over the original battlefields and vignettes of action were cut into the scenes to enliven the show. As an historic record *America* is unsurpassed. It is a thrilling spectacle with a last-minute ride to the rescue. Griffith handled the historic battles of Lexington and Concord with the rhythmic editing pace for which he was justly famous.

Not everyone thought as highly of Carol as Mr. Griffith. Karl Brown, his assistant cameraman on all his films from the days before *The Birth of a Nation,* said in his book, *Adventures with D. W. Griffith,* in his opinion, "Lillian Gish and Dorothy Gish and Mae Marsh were far and away the finest actresses on the screen, dependably so at any and all times, because they had mastered the great art of making Griffith's dreams come true. And yet they too were sidelined, waiting indefinitely while Griffith was spending all his time and energy trying to do what was even for him the impossible: making a silk purse out of a—but no, I'd better not say that. He was trying to make the hopelessly inept Carol Dempster, with her bump-tipped nose, into a superb actress of the quality people were in the habit of seeing in Griffith pictures."

Karl Brown's opinion of Carol did not strengthen as he worked on several films with her. Brown said:

> Miss Dempster. She was a newcomer, but then Griffith was always bringing in newcomers, so that was no novelty. But Carol Dempster herself really was a novelty, at least to me. She was pretty enough, if you like them narrow-faced and with close-set eyes, and she behaved herself with what seemed to be over proper decorum on the set. She had but one defect that I could see and that was a little protruding bump at the tip end of her nose. Griffith used to bewail this bump during his characteristic monologues, delivered to himself through the small megaphone he now had the habit of carrying. "To think that perfect beauty can be marred by one little bit of misplaced flesh. What a shame, what a crying shame. Otherwise ... perfection." I thought to myself, "Perfection, my Aunt Aggie's aspidistra! Oh sure, she's fine if you like 'em slip-faced, but what ever happened to the lush Rubensesque beauties of yesteryear, like Blanche Sweet or Seena Owen, who had curves enough for a roller coaster? And why play kindergarten teacher to this inexperienced snip who might be very good to her mother but who had no business being thought of in the same reverie with Lillian Gish, who could be as placid as a mirror lake in repose, but who could become heartbreakingly tragic under dramatic stress? Or for that matter, Dorothy, who could be anything from a dimpled angel to a volcano of hate at one word from Griffith?"
>
> All I could think was that this was Griffith's way, as expressed in the popular saying of that day, "Catch 'em young, treat 'em rough, tell 'em nothing." It had worked before. It would work again. He loved to find new talent, sixteen or under, and mold them into something new and strange. I couldn't fault him for this. Otherwise I'd have been out on my bumper long, long ago.

Carole's nose was not the only concern plaguing Griffith. In the middle of the production Griffith ran out of money. The Central Union Trust Company loaned him $500,000 at 6 percent against the negative of *America*. Filming was immediately continued. To keep the help from the War Department, Griffith arranged an appointment to present some of the finished scenes to President Coolidge. The President was so impressed that arrangements were firmed to continue the cooperation of the government in the production of the film.

*America* was constructed in two parts. The first sketched the background of the Revolution, and the rest of the film concentrated on the evil campaign of Butler. Harry Carr wrote in "Griffith: Maker of Pictures," *Motion*

*Picture Magazine,* August, 1922, about the day he witnessed a scene being filmed for *America:*

> To see a Griffith rehearsal is a marvelous experience. It is to sound the most subtle depths of acting. Griffith goes over the play—over and over, until the actors are ready to commit suicide—but each time it grows a little under his hands. The gorgeous little touches of art which have been planned there in the old dining-room with a couple of kitchen chairs for stagecoaches and a chalk-line for a mountain chasm, are among the masterpieces of American drama.
>
> In a few minutes we were inside the old mansion watching Mr. Griffith at work. He was standing in a prison dungeon with a cobble-stoned floor, discoursing in low tones with Lionel Barrymore, who was sitting on the jail cot. Mr. Barrymore plays the role of Walter Butler, a character without a single redeeming attribute. Griffith was in modern clothes, and Barrymore in boots and breeches and shirt of gloomy hue. Holding his cigarette between his fingers, Griffith stepped back to the firing line of the three cameras, and then called out 'Lafayette' just loud enough to be heard in this unusually quiet studio. The Marquis de Lafayette, with his aide, stepped through the oaken door into the dingy-looking cell, his sword clanging, his tri-cornered hat set off by a red ribbon, and cream-colored lace protruding through the gap left by his graceful cape that hung in folds down to the calves of his high boots.
>
> They had a second rehearsal. "Allow me to present the Marquis de Lafayette" came from Griffith. "Now the sympathy, Lafayette" instructed Griffith, who calls his characters according to the name in the story. "This place is bad for—you," urged Griffith. "That is enough." Even the electricians were interested in the scene, a minor one in this production, regarding which Lionel Barrymore is extremely enthusiastic. It seemed strange that this actor, then seated on the cot in a cell, would be seen that night in the stage success, *Laugh, Clown, Laugh.*

Griffith proceeded with the filming. "Your lights," ordered Mr. Griffith. There was silence, only broken by the words from the director and the buzz of the winding of the cameras.

The film completed principal production in December of 1923, with one scene remaining to be photographed. Griffith had been waiting impatiently for a great snowstorm in which to shoot the Valley Forge sequence. Like many of the famous last-minute rescues of his films, the weather came with all its fury, giving him the final sequence he had been waiting for. The industry, impressed by the advance publicity, was eager to see if the Griffith magic would flame again as it had with *The Birth of a Nation, Intolerance,* and *Way Down East.*

There was already a great deal of competition among the motion picture theaters. In the postwar year of 1920 Mary Pickford, Douglas Fairbanks, and Charles Chaplin were the three biggest names in the industry. Griffith joined them in the formation of United Artists with Hiram Abrams as its president. On March 27, Pickford and Fairbanks were united in marriage, and they reigned as the king and queen of Hollywood. Their home in Beverly Hills was called "Pickfair" to blend both their names into one.

*America,* as an historical drama, had to find a place among filmgoers in the middle of a tremendous schedule of jazz-age releases. Titles already bringing in crowds during the week of the film's release included Rudolph Valentino in *A Sainted Devil,* Rod La Rocque in *Feet of Clay,* Leatrice Joy in *Triumph,* Glenn Hunter in *Merton of the Movies,* Gloria Swanson in *Manhandled, The Humming Bird, A Society Scandal,* and *The Wages of Virtue.* It was the year boxing legend Jack Dempsey starred in a movie called *Fight and Win.* Baby Peggy was a phenomenon of popularity, and appeared in a large-scale version of *Jack and the Beanstalk.* Rin-Tin-Tin was an unlikely candidate for stardom, but Warner Bros. was finding gold with the canine's ability to wring adoration from the public with *Find Your Man.* Buster Keaton had audiences in stitches with both *The Navigator* and *Sherlock, Jr.,* while Harold Lloyd was gaining legions of fans with *Girl Shy.* Into the fray of this diverse outpouring of titles grasping at any public whim of popularity or notoriety, Griffith released his detailed, sumptuous production of history.

Though *America* is discussed less than his other more highly visible films, it is vastly superior in many ways to most of his other films. It is an incredibly fluid, superbly edited and graphically accurate detailing of the formation of America, an impressively staged epic, magnificently photographed in richly textured tones.

The film was an instant hit with critics, if not with audiences. *The New York Times* described the film in February of 1924 as one that would "stir the patriotic hearts of the nation as probably no other picture ever has done." The newspaper went on to say the following:

> The showman and the artist are combined to a certain extent in David Wark Griffith's latest film achievement, *America,* which was presented with due pomp last night before an extraordinarily interesting gathering in the Forty-Fourth Street Theater. We say, to a certain extent, because in the latter half of this production the artist got the better of the showman and insisted on length, which failing will undoubtedly be remedied by generous cutting.
>
> Mr. Griffith is a staunch adherent to drama in his pictorial efforts and to him there can be no drama unless there is suspense. To obtain the lat-

ter it is necessary for him to cut from one scene to another, then to a third scene and eventually back to the first episode. He proved that he could lift his audience by this means, and in the first half of this picture his methods succeeded like a charm. He has then something of overwhelming interest to give his audience, and they lifted their voices in great appreciation. In the latter reels of this production the villainy of Walter Butler is shown in far too much detail, as is the fighting and also in the striving for a far-reaching effect. Time appears also to be taken to give the orchestra its chance in these episodes, in which undoubtedly the musicians acquitted themselves with marked effect, even to making one think that the film was actually going faster than it was. The death by a mere couple of shots for such a brutal specimen as Butler (Lionel Barrymore) seemed to us much too tame an end. He is one of those blackguards without any redeeming attributes.

But the first reels of this photodrama, which incidentally was sponsored by the Daughters of the American Revolution, are something to be remembered, something greater than even Griffith has ever done himself. Nobody who views this marvelous section of the production will ever forget his rendering of Paul Revere's historic ride. The audience was filled with suspense, as the man on horseback tore down the roads, dodged the British officers, spring over stone walls and hedges, leaped clean of crashing ravines and ducked in and out among trees. There was subdued joy in the audience when he outwitted his pursuers, and then came clamorous applause when one of the Royalist riders was chucked off his horse, and quick as a flash Paul Revere was shown clearing a far more difficult jump. The chest and legs of the horse were pictured, and with the crashing music the audience possibly reached its highest pitch of enthusiasm over this marvelous sequence.

Audiences could not help but be impressed in the scene where the body of Charles Montague was brought into the room where his father was ill in bed. Nancy Montague, the character played by Carol, wanted her father to think that her brother died for the British flag, and she took from an old chest the Union Jack and spread it over her brother's body, having concealed her manipulations from her father. The audience at this point, in spite of the enemy father and the British colors, was said to have been silent and breathing quietly.

No other director could have been able to obtain such effects as Griffith had in his depiction of the Battle of Bunker Hill. The uniforms are splendid, and the clockwork precision of the Royalists drilling is a splendid contrast to the efforts of the men in rough, everyday clothes who sped to the call of liberty. In these scenes Griffith has made wonderful shots: medium shots and others taken with a six-inch lens giving an idea of the whole battlefield with the apparent midgets in conflict. In all these scenes, and for that matter, throughout the whole production, Griffith's photography is something to compel the admiration of all. In many shots he softened the contours of the frame, as if partly vignetted, and through this means there appeared something in the nature of relief in the exterior scenes. "The Spirit of '76 was keenly and cleverly brought out, and audience after audience seeing the picture were aroused by this mere photographic effect, as they may not have been with sound and color," observed *The New York Times* reviewer.

*The New York Times* reviewer also noted,

> Tears were drawn last night, and sighs and sobs came from trembling women. And if we criticize the length of the latter portion of this artist's work, we must admit that the woman sitting next to us was clenching her hands with frenzied fear that the two Americans who had entered a house would be discovered by Captain Butler and his murderous crew. We thought for an instant that when they were caught she would scream. And, after all, if it affects one woman that way, it may have impressed scores of others, in spite of the drawn-out portions of the later half.
>
> Griffith as showman came in very strongly in scenes when Butler smiled at her evilly, tantalized her, grasped her by the arm, and then tore part of her gown away. The photography took the most telling parts of this struggle. Neil Hamilton, as Nathan Holden, the handsome hero, gave an excellent performance. Miss Dempster was admirable in her difficult part, and in the scene where she had to cover her mother's body with the British Flag, her acting was all that could have been asked for.

Lionel Barrymore gave a vigorous idea of the villain, Captain Walter Butler. The treatment of this character reflected the point of view that he—not the British—was the real enemy responsible for the Cherry Valley massacre.

Louis Wolheim made an emphatic arch-fiend with naked body and painted face. The cast was one of the best seen in a picture of such historical importance.

The Battle of Bunker Hill and Paul Revere's ride ably made up for all the superfluous detail in the latter half of this picture. For those who saw it in 1924, it stirred patriotic hearts as probably none other picture ever has done. In this, the film was reminiscent of the effect his earlier film, *The Birth of a Nation,* had on audiences.

The film opened at the 44th Street Theater in New York on February 21, 1924 with a twelve-reel length. The film was a critical success in its initial release, but at the height of the Roaring Twenties costume films were not the vogue. In spite of this, his reputation as a director of such epics superceded any wane in the popularity of these kind of films, and the box office returns were relatively good. Unfortunately, the film initially lost money because it did not recoup the high production costs of $795,000 until many years of distribution, reissue and sales of stock footage tallied a final gross of $1,750,000.

When the film was finished, and as meager receipts trickled in after the release, Griffith owed six month's salary to nearly everyone in the company. He was forced to close his Mamaroneck studio. In July, 1924, Adolph Zukor hired Griffith as one of the staff of directors at Paramount. He had finally lost his gamble for independence.

Lillian Gish was invited by Griffith to his Mamaroneck studio to see *America*. She was not one who shared the critic's glowing raves of the film. She expressed in her autobiography, *The Movies, Mr. Griffith, and Me,*

> Apart from a few scenes, the film was a heart-breaking disappointment. Time and again the film seemed to verge on the mastery one expected from Mr. Griffith, only to sink back into the commonplace. Slowly the sad truth emerged. There was no one left among his staff to say "no" once in a while. He needed the gently abrasive minds and personalities of those who had once been close to him. He thrived on the tactful suggestion, the quiet hint that some other director had done as well, that a better effect could be found. Secretly he knew that he needed this help. His constant questioning and his endless appeals for advice had been his way of admitting it. As scene after scene in *America* fell short of its promise, I could almost hear his deep voice ring out, as it had in the Biograph Studio: "Well, what do you think of it? What would you do?" Perhaps he no longer sought opinions. Or perhaps he was surrounded by people who did not want to incur his displeasure.

Neil Hamilton, best remembered today as Commissioner Gordon in the 1960's TV series *Batman,* gave one of his best performances in *America*. The characters played by Hamilton and the female star, Nancy Montague, were woven through the historical recreations in a romantic subplot, allowing the camera to focus intimately on their personal struggles.

The public may have lost their faith in Griffith, but he never lost his belief in Carol or her ability to radiate a spirit worthy of stardom. She continued to be the focus of his next four films.

*Isn't Life Wonderful* (1924) premiered at Town Hall, New York, on December 4, 1924 and the following day at the Rivoli Theater, New York. The 9-reel film was genuinely inspired by the deprivations of the defeated Poles. The picture was shot on the streets of old Berlin, the forests of Crampnitz and Sacrow, and the shipyard at Copenick. Carol was at her best in this story with her hair pulled back while wearing shabby clothes.

It was Griffith's last great film. He went to work for Adolph Zukor as a contract director.

*Sally of the Sawdust* (1925) was based on W.C. Field's popular play, *Poppy*. Carol played the title role of Sally, the daughter of a circus con man with a heart of gold. Fields later remade the film in sound as *Poppy*.

W.C. Fields in his second appearance on the screen made a standout characterization within a story that had mystery, jazz, comedy thrills, romance, and a cyclonic drama. *That Royle Girl* (1925) centered on Carol as a girl of the Chicago slums who clings to the ideals represented by Abraham Lincoln while moving through jazz, jail, and the Chicago underworld.

*The Sorrows of Satan* (1926) starred Carol as Mavis Claire in a film of Marie Corelli's novel. She played opposite Ricardo Cortez in a love story Griffith was compelled to make against his wishes. For many people, this film had Carol's most touching performance as Griffith recreated his youthful love affairs.

According to Anthony Slide in his book, *The Griffith Actresses,* Carol found Griffith one day in the middle of directing a scene of his current film, *Drums of Love,* in which she did not appear.

"Mr. Griffith, I have something to tell you. I hope you will take it right. I'm going to be married."

Griffith was shocked, but as always, he was a model of calm sensitivity. He felt the life being squeezed out of him as Carol went on to explain she was marrying a New York banker, Edwin S. Larson. She left as suddenly as she had come into his life. He quietly returned to directing the scene spread out before him on the stage. He had featured her in twelve pictures, and her defection must have hurt him deeply.

"I don't care to work for anybody but Mr. Griffith," Carol was said to have bluntly stated. "When he has a part which he thinks is my type I suppose I will play it. I wouldn't worry if I never played in another picture."

It was the end of the silent era. Carol retired to happy obscurity. She said, "I just never think about my days in pictures. I am always surprised that anyone remembers me. It was so long ago. So many of my movies were so sad. Maybe my fans would like to know that in real life Carol Dempster had a happy ending."

Carol achieved a lasting place in film history with a performance in *America* that has stood the test of time. The film and the star were appreciated in their time, but as the decades have passed, it is the film and the performance that stand on their own. Carol Dempster shines through the last dozen of the films of D.W. Griffith with as much power as the other young women he shepherded. She was the last star created by the man credited with creating the motion picture as we know it today.

## SILENT FILMOGRAPHY OF CAROL DEMPSTER

Intolerance (1916) ★ The Greatest Thing in Life (1918) ★ The Hope Chest (1919) ★ A Romance of Happy Valley (1919) ★ The Girl Who Stayed at Home (1919) ★ True Heart Susie (1919) ★ Scarlet Days (1919) ★ The Love Flower (1920) ★ Way Down East (1920) ★ Dream Street (1921) ★ Sherlock Holmes (1922) ★ One Exciting Night (1922) ★ The White Rose (1923) ★ America (1924) ★ Isn't Life Wonderful (1924) ★ Sally of the Sawdust (1925) ★ That Royle Girl (1925) ★ The Sorrows of Satan (1926)

# PAULINE FREDERICK

Pauline Frederick was born as Pauline Beatrice Libby in 1883. "My birthday is—or rather was, for I have had my last—August 12," she later stated in an interview published in *Motion Picture Magazine*. "On that date, according to records, I joined the other little beans in Boston. I had four nationalities from which to choose my temperament—first my good old United States; second my mother's ancestors, who were Scotch; and third, my father's who were French and English. Such a combination I realized beforehand would be essential to the making of a picture star and acted accordingly." As a girl she was fascinated with show business, and determined early to place her goals in the direction of the theater. She reminisced, "As a child there were several things besides some well-known young medicines that I disliked to take, and one of these was a dare. When one of my playmates, whose favorite pastime was running off to the theater whenever we could save money enough to buy tickets and reproducing what we had seen on an elaborate home scale, said: 'Polly, I dare you to go on the real stage,' of course I just had to go. I had been studying singing, and succeeded in persuading the manager of a vaudeville house in Boston to hear a couple of my songs."

"I'll put you on for a week," the manager agreed, "and pay you fifty dollars."

That was the first money she earned, and to Pauline, it seemed like a fortune. "My chums were there in full force that night waiting to see 'Polly take her dare,' and for their sakes I had to be brave about it, though

I can remember to this day how I quaked inwardly when I stepped out on the stage and saw the hundreds of eyes turned toward me. I thought each eye was saying: 'She never did this before,' and in companion I was answering: 'No, she never did.' Well, I managed to get through my three songs some way or another, and after that it wasn't so bad. That first week gave me the courage to go further and, of course, further meant New York."

Her parents bred her for a career in music. She was said to have sung in a vibrant, soprano voice, and soon caught the attention of James T. Powers. Her next engagement was playing the fairy queen in *The Princess of Kensington*. She watched three performances of the play in New Haven before her opening in New York. When she walked down the stage on the night of her first performance, her eyes froze on the spotlight as it bore down on her frightened face. For several moments she simply stared at it while audience members wondered if she had forgotten her words. During rehearsal she had been trained to ask questions of the 12 chorus girls and feign interest in their answers, yet all she could do was gaze at the spotlight with a mixture of horror and fascination. When the girls saw her plight they stepped in and commented on themselves without having a question put to them, filling the gap until Pauline could snap out of her immobilized state. She recovered and, like a veteran trouper, began to pummel the chorus girls with the appropriate questions for the remainder of her stint. Three months later she played a comedy part in the same production; her career launched with ample enthusiasm if not with a firm direction.

After engagements in *The Little Gray Lady* and *The Girl in White,* she was given her first lead in *Twenty Days in the Shade.* Pauline had the good fortune to next appear with Francis Wilson in *When Knights Were Bold,* and then supported John Barrymore in *Toddles* at the old Garrick Theater.

Pauline's career accelerated wildly when William Gillette, a star renowned in the role of Sherlock Holmes, began casting actors for a new play, *Samson.* In *Samson* Pauline first played a villainess. She later recalled, "I need no further proof that it is easier to form a habit than to break one, for the heavies have stuck just, well, just as heavily as they should. My advice to embryo actresses is 'if you don't want always to be a heavy, never be a heavy.' "

Benjamin Teal, a theatrical manager, guided her through several stage productions in theaters along the East Coast of America. After her critically heralded appearance in *Samson,* her name became synonymous with quality. The biggest role of her career came with a role in *Joseph and His Brethren,* starring Brandon Tynan and James O'Neill.

By 1915 she attracted the attention of the burgeoning film industry, especially Adolph Zukor. He offered her $1000 a week. The producer of her current play released her on the condition she would ask Zukor for $2,000 the second year and $3,000 for her third. She did as advised, and Zukor agreed with a long-term contract. *The Eternal City,* filmed in Rome, was the film debut of the 32-year-old actress. Her reputation preceded her, and her name was a strong drawing card for the enormously successful film. Zukor's company, Famous Players, reaped a fortune. "I had no test in the studio and the first time I heard the grinding of a camera was when I walked near the gardens of the Vatican," she recorded in *The Story of My Life.* "Since that time I have made over twenty-five pictures for Famous Players, but even now when I see myself upon the screen I regard myself from the strictly impersonal point of view. It is always, 'Now, why did she do it that way? I think the effect would have been better if she had done it this way.' Unless you have been through the experience it is impossible to realize how peeved you get with yourself."

She appeared in three dozen feature-length films during the next five years, a tremendous output of titles, and became one of the most popular stars of the early cinema, specializing in playing commanding and authoritative women. Many of her most successful films were adapted from sensational French plays, a few of which had already been adapted into Italian operas. Unfortunately, few of her Famous Players films survive. Only two atypical roles have not been lost, *The Moment Before* (1916) and *The Love That Lives* (1917) in which she plays a scrub woman who ages to an old woman.

Samuel Goldwyn, a prominent figure in the Lasky film company, struggled with Zukor for power and branched out on his own with his independent production company. Goldwyn was actively seeking the great beauties of the stage and came into fortuitous contact with Pauline. In his 1923 autobiography, *Behind the Screen,* he recalled Willard Mack, Pauline's husband, a playwright and actor, approaching one night at the Directors' Ball at the Biltmore.

"See here, Sam, Polly's contract with Famous Players is just about to expire," he challenged Goldwyn. "How about it, anyway? Now I'd like to see her go with you, for you're a young company and I'm sure you would take a bigger interest in her."

Goldwyn fell in immediately with Mack's proposal, and phoned him some evenings later from the Lyceum Theater where he was then appearing with Lenore Ulric in *Tiger Rose.* When Goldwyn got to his dressing room he found Pauline waiting, and the three discussed transferring her film work to the Goldwyn Company. The possibility crystallized into a fact some weeks later.

Adolph Zukor was furious; for Pauline's large American following was greatly reinforced by her popularity in other countries, especially in England, where she was as much a drawing card as was Mary Pickford. He was emphatic in his praise of Pauline. "Now, there's a girl that anybody could get along with," he said in his autobiography, *The Public is Never Wrong*. "Easy to handle, likes her stories, always on time on the set." A bitter battle ensued. Zukor accused Goldwyn of treacherous conduct in weaning his star away from him. Goldwyn countered that the advance had been made from her side. A discussion on the issue one night at a party became so heated that Alice Joyce came to the arguing gentlemen and physically separated them.

"Gentlemen, gentlemen!" she laughed. "I don't know anything in the world worth so much discussion—especially a motion picture star!"

Goldwyn anticipated a smooth production schedule for Pauline. He was in the middle of moving his studio from Fort Lee, New Jersey, to California. Although the Fort Lee facility was adequate, the summer months were stifling, the ferry journey to and from New Jersey was a smelly pilgrimage that wore everyone's nerves to a frazzle, and the choice of extras and second part roles was not so wide as in Hollywood where the movies were becoming a recognized industry.

Pauline was unwavering in her devotion to Willard Mack. She refused to separate herself from him and move to California. Goldwyn later recalled:

> I am not overrating the emotional pressure of this situation. She would never desert Mr. Mack—not for an hour. I have related that the first time I talked to her regarding a change, I found her in her husband's dressing room. This was no coincidence. It was a habit. After working hard all day on the Zukor set, she spent every evening behind the scenes with Mack at the Lyceum Theater. In consideration of such strongly marked feeling on her part I obviously was compelled to do something about Mack. The fact of it is that, far from wanting him on the basis of agreeable surroundings for his wife, I was most anxious to shift him from theatrical work to our organization.

To lure her into the relocation, Goldwyn was forced to offer Mack a position as head of the scenario department of his company in California. Mack left *Tiger Rose* to accept the appointment at $500 a week, and started his duties at the Fort Lee studio before transferring together with Pauline to the new California facility.

"I don't like this story," Pauline said to Goldwyn upon her arrival in California.

"What don't you like about it?" the producer asked.

Goldwyn listened to her vague protestations, but underneath her words he sensed the real source of her prejudice: the rejected scenario had not been written by Willard Mack. In addition to this infraction, Goldwyn had engaged the famous star of opera, Geraldine Farrar, and the diva's presence on the same film lot sparked an intense professional rivalry.

"Of course, this story is nothing so good as the one you've given Geraldine Farrar," Pauline lamented.

"Very well," Goldwyn retorted, "we'll give it to Miss Farrar. She wants it badly."

Goldwyn saw Pauline not only take the story, but mysteriously run away with it. A few days later more protests met his ears when Pauline approached him with a very injured expression.

"I'm not pleased," she announced.

"What's the trouble now?" asked Goldwyn.

"Why, it's this: how can you expect me to do my best work—I ask you—how can you expect it? I have only one violin, one poor little violin—"

"But, Miss Frederick," Goldwyn interrupted, "you had no music at all while you were with Zukor. How about that? Yet you were doing your best work there."

She was reflecting on the orchestral accompaniment provided for her inspiration on the set. Silent films offered the opportunity for off-set comments, director's instructions, and mood music to be sounded while the cameras turned, and Geraldine Farrar's set boasted the unprecedented luxury of a small orchestra for her inspiration. Goldwyn pointed out that Farrar's operatic tradition demanded the excessive string stimulation, but his approach was not successful. The number of pieces each actress would have became a bone of contention on which he was compelled to throw away much vital energy. The studio soon became a three-ring band. "When I entered it in the morning," Goldwyn later recalled, "I wandered from the jazz selections which were toning up Mabel Normand's comedy to the realm where sad waltzes deepened Pauline Frederick's emotional fervor. The circle was surrounded by the classic themes enfolding Geraldine Farrar. It was hardly strange that outsiders used to gather every day to share in these free airs." In spite of the petty conflagrations of the opposing stars, Goldwyn found Frederick to be the most delightful of women. He was often amazed at her compulsion to work long hours with very little sleep. Vitality sparkled in every look of her eyes. Every sentence she uttered betrayed her deep interest in literature. She was known to her friends to be one of the best-read women they had ever known, altogether a bracing, magnetic, and colorful human being.

The marriage of Pauline and Willard Mack soon dissolved into an unpleasant, nightmarish experience, while Geraldine Farrar and Lou-Tellegen were having similar difficulties with their alliance of marriage and work. Geraldine Farrar recalled in *Such Sweet Compulsion,* "The unwise effort toward domestic and professional alliance always results in trouble for the wrong person. I happened to invite myself to be that one, and realized it all much later. Pauline, too, was having the same unpleasant experience with the aggressive Mack. No wonder Goldwyn was uneasy with his stars. One never knows what fools women will make of themselves when they place heart loyalty above pride and monetary interests." Mack was not only an alcoholic, but also a drug addict, and showed violent tendencies when under the influence. They divorced in 1919. In an interview with *Photoplay Magazine,* Mack ungallantly explained the cause was "too much mother-in-law." No doubt, the omnipresence of Pauline's mother contributed to the demise of their relationship, but Mack's problems were the prominent factor. Pauline apparently considered remarrying him in the 20s, but in a magnanimous gesture of honesty, Mack showed her his needle marks and declared that he didn't want to ruin her life again.

Her first film for Robertson-Cole was *A Slave of Vanity,* illuminating her as a beautiful woman carried by her love of luxury to the brink of ruin. The story mirrored her personal life all too closely. She almost did not make this film. Goldwyn finally soothed Miss Frederick, and production on *A Slave of Vanity* moved quickly and efficiently.

*A Slave of Vanity* was the first of a series of four new films she made in California, based on Arthur Wing Pinero's play, *Iris.* From the standpoint of artistic and commercial values, it was an unusual attraction.

The story was set in England and its characters were drawn from exclusive circles of British life. Morality issues that were known to rise from the leisurely lifestyle of the rich were explored in the characters and their relationships with each other.

The year 1920 was the year Babe Ruth, Jack Dempsey, and Georges Carpentier, already known as outstanding sports figures, made their film debuts. Comedy stars Constance Talmadge, Mabel Normand, and Dorothy Gish continued as the screen's most delightful laugh-getters. It was the year Roscoe "Fatty" Arbuckle's career was finished by a sex scandal.

Pauline's new film had to compete with several other titles bringing huge crowds into film theaters. Among the preeminent attractions were D. W. Griffith's *Way Down East, Passion* with Pola Negri, Lillian Gish

Pauline Frederick in a studio portrait ca. 1920, during which time she was filming *A Slave of Vanity.*

in *The Greatest Question,* Dorothy Gish in *Remodeling Her Husband,* Mae Murray in *On With the Dance* and *Right to Love,* Alla Nazimova in *Madame Peacock,* John Barrymore in *Dr. Jekyll and Mr. Hyde,* and Pearl White in *The White Moll.*

*A Slave of Vanity* premiered near the end of a pinnacle year in film production. Pauline played Iris Bellamy, introduced as a luxurious, pleasure-loving woman. The pegged, pampered wife, a martyr to selfish love for her husband, was showered with luxury. Upon the death of her husband, she suffered as the victim of the capricious circumstances of his last will and testament. His written wishes forbad her to remarry unless she sacrificed every penny of her fortune and her social prestige.

When she met and fell in love with an upright young chap, she hesitated to marry him, feeling unfit to live as the helpmate of a poor man. Her

*Moving Picture World* published this full-page advertising poster for Pauline Frederick in *A Slave of Vanity.*

struggle was a keen one, the more so because of the temptation to accept the love of an attentive, wealthy merchant, Laurence Trenwith. He offered youth, breeding, and sincere affection. Frederick Maldonado, a banker, offered a fortune in excess of that which she would lose when disinherited by marriage. The choice of men weighed heavily on her personality as she agonized under the pressure to choose between the two. The trustee of her estate absconded with her fortune, leaving her utterly penniless. Trenwith moved to America to seek his fortune, after she refused his impassioned plea to travel with him. Maldonado placed a deposit at her disposal, ostensibly as a friendly loan, but foreclosing heavily when the fund was exhausted, and sought to press his claims. At first she resisted, but eventually yielded to the point of accepting the hospitality of his home. Trenwith returned to find her as Maldonado's guest, and departed sadly. The banker,

Nigel Barrie and Pauline Frederick in *A Slave of Vanity* (1920).

stung both by the contempt she showed for him and her love for Trenwith, turned her again into the streets from which he rescued her. She reconciled with Trenwith and agreed to go to America with him to seek a new fortune.

The production had a broad and telling appeal on its own merits, and glowed with the force of Miss Frederick's performance and the directorial handiwork of Henry Otto.

In a review in *Moving Picture World*, November 6, 1920, the film was noted for "the finer instincts and qualities of womanhood that served as the dominant theme for the development of the story."

In another review from *Moving Picture World*, October 30, 1920, Epes W. Sargent wrote,

> Offering a combination of a powerful emotional star and thoroughly competent support in a really gorgeous production of one of the best of Sir Arthur Wing Pinero's plays, *A Slave of Vanity* leaves little that can be desired.
>
> The story of Lady Bellamy has become a part of dramatic literature and this production follows the original script closely. The ending which defers to the exhibitor's convention requiring that all stories must end happily, is

shown to have been only a dream. To those who know the drama, this time-worn expedient comes in the nature of a shock, but otherwise the production, from all angles, is remarkably good.

The photography is better than good; it is artistic and the cameraman has been given a succession of unusual interior sets, sometimes bizarre, but always in keeping.

Miss Frederick leaves little to be desired in her interpretation of her role, responding fully to the emotional demands. Willard Louis overtops Nigel Barrie because of the greater strength of his part; which he handles with admirable discretion. Arthur Hoyt is excellent in a minor role, which he forces to stand out in the brief opportunities offered him, and the others are all wholly within keeping; an unusually excellent ensemble.

Pauline's stunning beauty stayed with her as she aged into her best remembered roles as self-sacrificing mothers and 40-ish society women having a last fling at youth and romance. Then, suddenly, at the height of her success, in the prime of her genius and beauty, she slipped into a series of lesser pictures and voluntarily left the screen, returning to the stage.

When questioned by Adela Rogers St. Johns in a 1926 *Photoplay* interview about her defection from the screen, Pauline recalled,

> Just let me tell you what happened to me the other night. I made a picture not long ago. I won't tell you its name, that wouldn't be fair. I made it because I loved the story. It had tremendous dramatic possibilities. It was sound, honest, big. The woman was a fine woman, a big part. I loved her, I understood her. I don't think I ever worked so hard in my life. I always work too hard. I tried to save myself, but I couldn't. I don't mind telling you that I gave my very heart and soul to that picture. I used to crawl home at night, crawl into bed, sleep like a child.
>
> The other night, I saw that picture. And I came home and cried for three hours, and then I went down the next morning and signed a long-term contract to go back to the stage. [She went on to explain why] In pictures, it's entirely different. You do your work as well as you know how, and then it leaves your hands. For instance, when you've played a scene from a careful beginning, when you've worked it up through the middle part and built to what you believe is a climax, then to go and find the beginning and end cut off, rather hurts your feelings. Or to find the character of a society woman you were playing changed by titles to an adventuress from the Canadian wilds makes your characterization a bit of a disappointment to you.

Pauline later confessed that the move to Robertson-Cole was a mistake, and admitted to her lack of sense in business. She apparently got little help from her dominating mother or her weak husbands, and after the wide disapproval of her 1922 feature, *The Glory of Clemintina,* she returned to

Broadway. Audiences, eager to see a film star in the flesh, flocked to the theater and to her cross-country tours. She was mobbed in Australia. She was off the screen for two years, and her film career seemed to be at an end. A 1924 comeback appearance for Vitagraph with Lou-Tellegen in *Let Not Man Put Asunder* brought her days as a leading lady to an end. The demise of this phase of her career seemed fortunate, for she began a whole new phase with a role as an aging woman fighting the ravages of time and troublesome children in *Three Women* (1924). *Married Flirts* (1924) and *Smouldering Fires* (1925) presented Pauline in memorable fashion, successfully carrying off the role of a woman business executive.

Director Clarence Brown remembered in Kevin Brownlow's book, *The Parade's Gone By,* "Pauline Frederick, who took the lead in *Smouldering Fires,* went through the worst attack of stage fright I ever witnessed. She had been a great Broadway star and had made a number of pictures. Her last real success had been *Madame X.* The first two days on this one I thought she was going to give up. But she was a great artist and she pulled through bravely."

She was one of the earliest stars to try talkies with Warner's *On Trial* (1928), and was as successful in sound films as she had been in silent films. Her warm, throaty voice sounded good coursing through the early microphones, and her striking resemblance to Joan Crawford earned her a role in the 1931 talkie, *This Modern Age,* playing Crawford's mother. *Thank you, Mr. Moto,* (1937) was her final film. The roles she received in the 1930s were not as important as her silent work, though she often managed to dominate films—generally playing an angry matriarch. She usually stole any scene in which she appeared.

During the depression she remained in demand and constantly toured in a demanding schedule of roles, including *Mary of Scotland* with Helen Hayes. In 1936 she had an important part in Henry King's film, *Ramona.*

Her personal life seemed to be as knotted with drama as the makings of one of her film scenarios. Her domineering mother lived with her most of her life. She suffered five unhappy marriages, one of which was to a terminally ill man and one to an alcoholic and drug addict. Her fifth marriage to Colonel Joseph Marmon brought a desire to settle down on Governor's Island and restrict her acting to roles with special appeal, but her asthma began to limit her activities. She collapsed while on tour in San Francisco in *Suspect.* While resting from film work in 1938, Pauline died on September 19th.

Pauline Frederick was a brave and honest actress who was willing to take on parts that other actresses feared. She created some of the most memorable portraits of the silent screen, proving that a woman could be mature and worldly, yet remain feminine.

## SILENT FILMOGRAPHY OF PAULINE FREDERICK

The Eternal City (1915) ★ Sold (1915) ★ Zaza (1915) ★ Bella Donna (1915) ★ Lydia Gilmore (1915) ★ The Spider (916) ★ Audrey (1916) ★ The Moment Before (1916) ★ The World's Great Snare (1916) ★ The woman in the Case (1916) ★ Ashes of Embers (1916) ★ Nanette of the Wilds (1916) ★ The Slave Island (1916) ★ The Slave Market (1917) ★ Sappho (1917) ★ Sleeping Fires (1917) ★ Her Better Self (1917) ★ The Love That Lives (1917) ★ Double Crossed (1917) ★ The Hungry Heart (1917) ★ Mrs. Dane's Defense (1918) ★ Madame Jealousy (1918) ★ La Tosca (1918) ★ Resurrection (1918) ★ Her Final Reckoning (1918) ★ Fedora (1918) ★ Daughter of the Old South (1918) ★ Out of the Shadow (1919) ★ The Woman on the Index (1919) ★ Paid in Full (1919) ★ One Week of Life (1919) ★ The Fear Woman (1919) ★ The Peace of Roaring River (1919) ★ Bonds of Love (1919) ★ The Loves of Letty (1919) ★ The Paliser Case (1920) ★ Madame X (1920) ★ A Slave of Vanity (1920) ★ The Woman in Room 13 (1920) ★ The Mistress of Shenstone ★ (1921) Salvage (1921) ★ The Sting of the Lash (1921) ★ The Lure of Jade (1921) ★ Roads of Destiny (1921) ★ Two Kinds of Women (1922) ★ The Glory of Clementina (1922) ★ Let Not Man Put Asunder (1924) ★ Married Flirts (1924) ★ Three Women (1924) ★ Smouldering Fires (1925) ★ Devil's Island (1926) ★ Her Honor, the Governor (1926) ★ Josselyn's Wife (1926) ★ The Nest (1927) ★ Mumsie (1927) ★ On Trial (1928)

# GENE GAUNTIER

"Through August, September and October I alternately worked in Kalem pictures and haunted managers' offices," Gene Gauntier remembered in *Blazing the Trail.* "For the stage bee still buzzed in my head. Nor did I dare speak of my screen work. Pictures had captured some of their dependable actors and theatrical managers were beginning to fear this new rival. An edict went forth that no one who worked in pictures would be employed, so I kept my dark secret."

Gene was a remarkable writer, director, and actress in films from early 1906 to 1920. Born on May 17, 1885 in Kansas City, Missouri, Genevieve Liggett was literally thrown into her first screen assignment in the summer of 1906. The Kalem company hired her for a daredevil stunt, filming her as a damsel thrown into a river. She was a writer and actress in films from the early days of 1907 on into the 1920s. As a writer, she penned 31 films. She performed in 28 films and is credited as the director of *The Grandmother* (1909).

She first appeared in films between acting jobs with stock company tours. "My funds were running low, and in a vague way I thought of the new opening for actors—moving pictures," she remembered in *Blazing the Trail.* "But, like the rest of the legitimate profession, I looked on them with contempt and felt sure that my prestige would be lowered if I worked in them." She quickly realized the enormous potential of the movies, and began adding to her small salary as an actress by writing screenplays for at least 40 films.

Sidney Olcott, an actor emerging from stage melodramas, had stepped into the lowly profession of the moving pictures. Gene met him at the home of a friend while he was working at the Biograph Company in 1906. Olcott inquired if she would join the cast of a film being made the following day. He explained it was a water picture and, if she could swim, the job was hers for the taking. After explaining she could not swim, Olcott soothed her worries with a promise she would only get her feet wet. With trepidation, Gene joined the intrepid troupe at Grand Central Station and took a train to Sound Beach.

The director led her down a dirt road to a 50-foot-wide river dammed for an abandoned woolen mill. A great pool, 30 feet deep, waited at the edge of the dam, and on the other side, a sheer drop into raging depths extended about 40 feet downward.

The director asked Gene if she was ready to fall into the mill's dam. After she cheerfully informed him of her inability to swim, he railed at Olcott for hiring the wrong girl for the job and threatened to call production to a halt for the day. To save the film for the benefit of the other actors, Gene agreed to the plunge into the 30-foot-deep water, and rescuers were positioned to drag her quickly out of the water before she drowned.

Cameras were readied, and as the director shouted for the action to begin, Gene and a male actor feigned a fierce struggle at the edge of the dam. The actor lifted her bodily into the air, ordered her to hold her breath, and heaved her head downward into the swirling water. As the rescuers poised to leap in after her, the director held them back. Gene's body rose to the surface, then disappeared beneath the water. The cameras continued to grind, and Gene felt herself submerging to the bottom of the river. Her lungs were near to bursting as she flailed herself back to the surface. She gasped for air, frantically glanced for the promised rescuers, then sunk again. She began to drown, when suddenly, the arms of Gordon Burbe, the actor playing the hero, gripped under her and shot the panic-stricken actress into the air as the camera ground its last feet of film past the lens. *The Paymaster* was Gene's exhilarating entrance into the world of film. She earned five dollars for the day's work.

Frank J. Marion, a sales manager for the Mutoscope, a subsidiary of the Biograph, joined the Kalem company in 1907. Olcott and Gene followed him, and when encouraged to try her hand at writing scenarios, Gene began adapting famous works of literature into one-reel melodramas. No thought of copyright infringement entered the minds of the early film makers, and they happily lifted stories from major works including *Hiawatha, Evangeline,* and *As You Like It.*

Marion placed an urgent call to Gene to quickly adapt *Ben-Hur* for a quick picture to be made at the Sheepshead Park racetrack. Pain's Fireworks company, having concluded their summer spectacle at the track, had closed for the season. The film makers seized the opportunity to use the props and scenery still standing from their exhibition. Gene spent two nights reading the massive book and prepared a 10-minute condensation for filming.

A cast and extras were hurried into the track and for three days filmed *Ben-Hur,* complete with climactic chariot race. The footage was rushed into the developing tanks, and within days, the 16 scenes were assembled onto a thousand-foot reel and sold onto the market.

Harper Brothers and General Lew Wallace, publishers of the book, got wind of the little film and promptly filed an infringement of copyright suit against the Kalem Company. For several years the suit became a test of copyright laws, for the new film industry had no precedents to guide it. Moving pictures were deemed neither a play nor a story, and the lawsuit moved from court to court, ultimately landing on the docket of the Supreme Court of the United States. Harper and Brothers won the verdict against the Kalem Company, which was fined $25,000, an enormous sum in its day.

After this painful embarrassment, film producers painstakingly added the disclaimer on every film to the effect: "Any resemblance to persons living or dead is purely coincidental."

By 1909, Gene was widely known as "The Kalem Girl," and became one of the most visible and loved of the early film stars.

Olcott, the company's chief director, traveled with Gene to Ireland in 1909, where they filmed three well-received, short subject melodramas, the first time an American film company ventured that far into a foreign land. Before returning to New York, they made a travelogue in London and filmed another drama in Berlin, Germany, *The Little Spreewald Maiden* (1910).

The following August, 1910, Olcott took Gene and a company to Ireland, England, and Germany. For six weeks they filmed a series of one-reel titles enthusiastically praised by audiences. The following June, Olcott trouped back to Ireland with a larger company and produced his best works, including *Colleen Bawn* and *Arra-na-Pogue* in three reels.

The Kalem Company, for lack of any studio, sent their actors outdoors for location photography on most of their films. This deficiency of resources actually proved to be an advantage, as their films had a realism lacking in most other productions filmed inside studios with fake backgrounds and painted sets.

The films produced on this trip were such a success that Kalem sent a larger company abroad in 1911. Their weekly one-reel release schedule was intense, and to keep up with the demand, actor Kenean Buel doubled as a director and Alice Joyce became his leading lady.

They returned to New York, and on November 25, 1911, Kalem asked Gene and Olcott if they could sail for Egypt on December 22. "It was a wild scramble," explained Gene to W. Stephen Bush of *Moving Picture World.* "We had a picture to finish, packing, two weeks in New York to get our wardrobe, wigs, clothes, passports, and visit the dentist, for we were to be gone at least a year, along with farewell dinners. We did it, of course."

"When we had left New York," Gene related, "Mr. Marion had warned us to take no picture with the Christ in it, unless it should be a mere symbol, a passing shadow. We were soon to be on our way to Palestine."

*From the Manger to the Cross* was the tangible realization of a dream she envisioned while recovering from heat prostration during the filming of a documentary in the heated deserts of the Middle East. Gene suffered a severe sunstroke and passed into a swirling haze of hallucinations in which the entire film played before her mind. "I had a touch of sun at Luxor," she remembered. "March is very hot, and I lay semi-delirious in bed. Alice Hollister sat with me. Suddenly I sat up exclaiming, 'We're going to Cairo and take the Flight into Egypt at the Pyramids. Then the life of Christ in Palestine!' Sid came in and responded to my enthusiasm. As soon as I could be moved, we went down to Cairo...."

Striking out against the orders of her bosses, Gene allied her production team to quietly film the story in secret.

We took a number of scenes on Palm Sunday, then on to Jerusalem. The old city was in such a wonderful state of preservation, even the ablahs worn by the natives were the same as in Christ's time. Our enthusiasm mounted. The story spanned the life of Christ from His birth in Bethlehem and the flight through Egypt, to the return to Nazareth and the meeting with twelve-year old Jesus and the wise men. As a grown man, the film details the calling of the disciples, the wedding at which Jesus turned the water into wine, the resurrection of Lazarus and the woman at the well. The Last Supper, and the agony of Gethsemane. The mock trial and the Crucifixion finish the film in reverent sincerity.

Sid cabled Marion what we were about and that he was returning to London for additional actors. Marion cabled he'd meet him in London. It was a three weeks' trip and, during Olcott's absence, I wrote the script, sets were built on a tract of ground bounded by the Wall of Jerusalem on one side and a convent, the Brides of Christ, on the other, and costumes were made by a costumer we had brought from Cairo. All was ready to start when Olcott arrived with a dozen English actors, including R. Henderson Bland, who

Gene Gauntier, star of *From the Manger to the Cross* (1912),
conceived the film in a sunstroke delirium.

was to be the Christ. Helen Lindroth, too, had been sent from Jacksonville,
Florida to Jerusalem, accomplishing what, I believe, is the longest jump on
record.

Mr. Marion had taken his first trip abroad just to shake hands with Sid
and wish us good luck, taking the next steamer back. It was such things that
made us so loyal. Marion's ability to reverse his decision and see with a
clear vision spurred us on.

Olcott secured additional money from Marion and the approval to film
*From the Manger to the Cross*. They arrived in Palestine in late March and
began filming on the Sea of Galilee at Tiberius.

For the role of the Christ, Olcott hired five persons to portray his different ages from infancy to manhood. Robert Henderson Bland, an English
actor, was hired by Olcott after a telephone interview because he liked the
sound of the actor's voice. This was odd because the film was being made
as a silent. Bland claimed to have been divinely inspired in the making of
the film, and his astonishingly real performance supports this claim. Bland

The Three Wise Men, following the star seen in the East, in *From the Manger to the Cross* (1912).

told Olcott he received a vision during the night in which God told him he was His chosen son. "I felt as if I was being enveloped by some strange power and being led gently on," Bland later commented. "Frankly, we thought he was mad," said Olcott in an article in Charles Foster's *Stardust and Shadows.* "But we didn't argue, he was obviously what we wanted.... Bland needed no direction, he was superb," said Olcott. The actor said that he was totally unaware of the camera and that he performed as though guided by some strange and compelling force. After making the film he returned to England, and only performed in religious plays from that time on. Bland won many medals for heroism during World War I, serving the British Army as an officer. In his book called *From the Manger to the Cross* he declared that Christ had come into his soul during the making of the film, stayed with him during the war, and made him invincible.

Gene described Olcott's interest in philosophy and psychic phenomena. She said, "It was impossible to keep anything from Olcott. He knew what was going on through some sixth sense. Consciously or unconsciously, he used the power of suggestion, or even hypnotism, on his actors. He would stare straight into our eyes with those large blue orbs of his and never shift his glance as he explained the situation or action. No one thought of questioning his instructions or of refusing, no matter how difficult, to do the stunt he demanded."

Gene also remembered the amazing work of their cameraman, George Hollister. He had only one wooden camera with which to work. The intense

Mary, Joseph, and the baby Jesus sleep in Egypt in
*From the Manger to the Cross* (1912).

heat of the desert often caused it to crack, and George would spend his
nights in an improvised dark room, stopping up the cracks with adhesive
tape. Of all the hundreds of scenes taken during those strenuous, stifling
months, not one had to be retaken. So great was the level of confidence
in George's work, Olcott's company returned to England without having
any of the footage from the last reels of the picture. In fact, Olcott took
the last two reels back to New York where they were developed and run
for viewing on a later day. Olcott was extremely pleased with the quality
of the photography. He immediately attended to the details of the preparation of advertising. In those days, copyright was obtained by submitting a
prose version of the scenario as a manuscript, rather than copyrighting the
actual printed celluloid. After rushing through these tasks in three weeks,
he rejoined the company in Ireland.

"It was work in those days—but creative work, blazing the trail," mused
Gene. "We were always discovering new possibilities and each little success or surprise fed our enthusiasm. Mr. Olcott and I had no one over us.
I scarcely ever submitted a scenario and never while abroad. The Kalem
never knew what our picture was to be until they saw the first run in the
projection room. We would have risked our lives (and did many times) out
of sheer love for, and loyalty to, the Kalem. For four years the same friends
were together and we were known as the O'Kalems, and later, during the
oriental tour, as the El Kalems."

In *Magill's Survey of Cinema: Silent Films,* the author quoted Gene: "And it's an odd fact, that it was a film we had not started out to make.... We worked late into the night every night preparing for our work of the next day—and then the next day would be spent under the burning sun on the burning sands....And so *From the Manger to the Cross* was filmed. One hot day succeeded another hot day, and one sticky night was just like the preceding sticky night. But we felt repaid, for we knew the results were good."

Upon their return to the United States, the culmination of the trip was *From the Manger to the Cross.* The film was edited into 4,700 feet, a complete whole story, and revealed to the directors of Kalem. The impact of the film was so powerful and overwhelming they decided to release it as a five-reel feature, virtually unheard of at the time.

The finished masterpiece became the film that made the fortunes of the very men who attempted to defeat its creation. It is one of the few Kalem films to survive the ravages of time, as remarkably impressive today as it was in 1912, the year of its making.

The year 1912 was a year of other great advancements in film making. Sarah Bernhardt set a historical landmark in the field of motion pictures with her multi-reel production of *Queen Elizabeth,* pushing producers to adopt the concept of longer films. Motion pictures were now well established as entertainment and had virtually replaced the resident stock companies and road shows of the legitimate theater, and for many towns, the nickelodeon was a relic of the past. Theaters were built especially for the exhibition of film, and multi-reel productions were the latest craze. It was the same year animated cartoons were becoming a regular feature of a film schedule and, along with a newsreel, preceded the showing of a longer, feature-length production.

*From the Manger to the Cross* had to compete in 1912 with the emerging popularity of comedy films. Mack Sennett left Biograph and D. W. Griffith to strike out on his own, taking with him a definite idea that people would laugh at what he thought was funny. His Keystone Comedies began to play in theaters with a new title each week, bringing clowns like Fred Mace, Ford Sterling, and Mabel Normand into towns to cause uproarious laughter with their high-speed antics.

This year was also a year of great creativity in filmmaking. Mae Marsh appeared in a watershed film dealing with psychological motivations of the caveman. *Man's Genesis* explored the role reasoning and thought played in the development of man. Lillian and Dorothy Gish debuted in films with *An Unseen Enemy.* For Pathé, Pearl White emoted in *Mayblossom,* while Beverly Bayne starred with Francis X. Bushman in *The Magic Wand.* It was the year Mary Pickford quit the movies and retreated to the greater allure of Broadway.

*From the Manger to the Cross* reverently premiered in London on October 3, 1912, at Queen's Hall. The audience included more than a thousand clergymen. Anthony Slide recounted this event in *Magill's Survey of the Cinema:*

> Dr. William Inge, the Dean of St. Paul's, commented, "I thought the exhibition reverent and beautiful. I shall certainly recommend others to see it." A screening at London's Albert Hall followed, and the critic for the *Daily Express* wrote, "So great, it seems to me, are the possible results of a general presentation of this film that I left Albert Hall yesterday longing for its exhibition in all the cathedrals, the churches and the chapels in the land, that is, in the atmosphere of reverence and worship to which it absolutely belongs, and used to quicken the imaginative life which is becoming so woefully stunted in an age of triumphant mechanics.

The film again premiered in the United States at Wanamaker's Auditorium in New York on October 14, 1912. Civic leaders and clergymen reacted enthusiastically to the premier.

At the time this film was made movies were still in their infancy. Many people considered motion pictures to be a low and often indecent form of cheap amusement. The uplifting theme of this film attracted millions of people to the primitive nickelodeons for their first motion picture viewing. They experienced a simple, straightforward and splendid production, performed in a natural style atypical for the time. The actual locations of Egypt and Palestine added authenticity and the appearance of reality, startling audiences with the power of the graphic imagery to move their emotions. The Kalem studio made millions on the film, and it was widely circulated over the entire world in many languages for several decades. It was a sensation in its day. One of the first blockbusters, it was the early inspiration for D.W. Griffith and Cecil B. DeMille to venture into larger epics. Both directors ultimately filmed their own versions of the story of Christ: Griffith with *Intolerance* and DeMille with *The King of Kings.*

W. Stephen Bush described the film in *Moving Picture World* October 26, 1912: "The titles of this production to be classed as the greatest achievement in cinematography are many, but chief among them is the realism of it all. It is not a Passion Play; it is the very story of the Passion and of many incidents recorded by the evangelists. It is indeed a cinematographic gospel. Because of its sublime work it will be easier than it was before to 'go forth and teach all nations.' The film shows four exquisite scenes, one taken from the recorded events and the others either taken from old traditions or constructed out of the probabilities of the known events. The scenes in and about the home at Nazareth are beautifully conceived and full of a sweet and pathetic naturalness. In taking into the film an ancient Christian belief, that Joseph, Mary and the Divine Child were during part of their sojourn in Egypt near Babylon, the producers have added a charming and instructive scene, which will be new and most interesting to many audiences."

In addition to the careful preparation of the print for screening, a musical program was compiled. This early attempt at scoring was not the last word in musical accompaniment, but it orchestrated an uplifting mix of Gregorian chant and classic music of a religious tinge. Synchronization was allowed to vary from performance to performance, but the end result was highly superior to simply singing hymns as the film rolled through the projectors.

*Motography* deplored Kalem's choice of title for the biblical masterpiece,

> because it is held literally. Had it been named "The Life of Christ", the producer would have carried it beyond the crucifixion to the ascension. This beautiful, 5,000 footer stops at the cross, and if I recall my old Sunday school lessons, it might have gone a little farther for a more pleasing ending. However, this is merely suggestion. *From the Manger to the Cross* is splendid. It is the kind of production that will interest a clientele that does not come under the classification of film fan. It is this tremendous clientele that must be reached and every effort to do it should be encouraged. That Kalem sought Palestine for the settings is in itself most commendable.

Olcott began directing films as early as 1907 with primitive, early renditions of *Way Down East* and *Ben Hur* and continued helming moving pictures until the end of the silent era. Mary Pickford's *Poor Little Peppina,* Valentino's *Monsieur Beaucaire,* and several Richard Barthelmess features were but a few of the dozens of excellent films created by Sidney Olcott. Although *From the Manger to the Cross* was filmed in 1912, its ultimate length caused initial exhibitors to loathe booking it. The standard of the day was one and two-reel films, and this hour long film upset the conventional program. Only a few short years later the industry was drowning in a wave of feature length pictures, and it was some time before the Christ film was launched into its release around the country.

Olcott mentioned the treatment American exhibitors accorded the film in gnashing comments in an article called "The Present and the Future of Film" in *The Theatre of Science* by Robert Grau, 1914.

> To a great extent, the splendid advancement shown by the various picture interests during the past year is largely due to the entrance of the gentle-

men who were so late in arriving, but, having arrived, proceeded to make it known in their truly characteristic way. It is well they are here, for it means that each and all must bend their utmost energies to the production of subjects and spectacles that will, in a measure, overshadow the efforts of the past. But of one thing all must be certain; great distinction must be made in the method of exhibiting the various subjects for claptrap and art will no more mix in moving pictures than upon the strictly legitimate stage. Striking examples of what is meant are to be found in those beautiful uplifting subjects, *From the Manger to the Cross,* and *The Miracle.* The exact methods that had tremendously enriched the coffers of the various manufacturers of the country, when applied to other productions, sounded the death-knell for these.

One firm, gentlemen of high ideals, are, I know, heartsick over the manner in which one of their subjects, they so generously financed, was released for exhibition. Not from a monetary standpoint, but from the fact that their admirable effort to give something of sterling merit, was so foully butchered in the hands of those apparently utterly devoid of discerning the difference of placing a biblical subject as against a "give-me-the-papers" melodrama.

The subject in question involved the traveling of thousands of miles by a large company of artists, much laborious research, and a continuous movement through an arid inhospitable country, to the exact, or legendary spots in which the events in the life of the Savior, as we know them, were enacted.

But it understood that in Great Britain, so well were the requirements for managing this masterpiece in a reverential and dignified way understood, that not only did the press and pulpit take it up and almost unanimously advise their hearers to see it, but it was, and is now, a common occurrence for a minister of the gospel to ask, or to be asked, to open the exhibition with prayer. And yet this work, a year or more after release date, has yet to be seen upon the screen in many of the larger cities of the United States.

In such elevating and worthy subjects as these, with their great adaptation for the betterment of all mankind, cannot be successfully put before the masses in this country, then the influence of the motion picture is woefully hampered by a stagnation of ideas relative to the handling of them.

But undoubtedly there are men, comparatively newcomers, upon whom we may depend to show the keen, and judicious foresight requisite in placing before the public in a masterly manner the various productions, in a way peculiar to their needs.

Those who have their ears to the ground know full well that the cry is for better things, and that the influence of the motion picture is a wonderful and absorbing thing, unlimited, and, as yet, unharnessed.

Gene's daring vision, produced against the initial wishes of shortsighted Kalem managers, resulted in one of the most enduring films in the history of motion pictures. Most of Kalem's films have been lost to the ravages of time, decomposition, and neglect. *From the Manger to the Cross* is one of the few to have survived. It was reissued in 1917 and again in 1938 with a musical score and narration by the Reverend Brian Hesson. The film has been widely available in recent years on DVD, VHS, CD, and cable television to millions of new viewers. It is the film for which Gene Gauntier is remembered.

Gene eventually left Kalem to form her own production company. The Gene Gauntier Feature Players made a filmmaking jaunt to Ireland, releasing melodramas with sensationalistic titles such as *In the Clutches of the Ku Klux Klan* (1913) and *In the Power of a Hypnotist* (1913). She gracefully retired in the early 1920s and wrote her autobiography in 1928, appropriately titled *Blazing the Trail*.

## SILENT FILMOGRAPHY OF GENE GAUNTIER

The Paymaster (1906) ★ Evangeline (1908) ★ Way Down East (1908) ★ The Scarlet Letter (1908) ★ Hulda's Lovers (1908) ★ Dolly, the Circus Queen (1908) ★ Thompson's Night Out (1908) ★ The Romance of an Egg (1908) ★ The Man in the Box (1908) ★ The Stage Rustler (1908) ★ Betrayed by a Handprint (1908) ★ The Girl and the Outlaw (1908) ★ The Taming of the Shrew (1908) ★ As You Like It (1908) ★ The Girl Spy (1908) ★ The Wayward Daughter (1909) ★ The Slave to Drink (1909) ★ The Man Who Lost (1909) ★ The Romance of a Trained Nurse (1910) ★ The Stepmother (1910) ★ The Forager (1910) ★ The Castaways (1910) ★ A Child's Faith (1910) ★ A Lad from Old Ireland (1910) ★ The Girl Spy Before Vicksburg (1910) ★ The Little Spreewald Maiden (1910) ★ An Irish Honeymoon (1911) ★ A War Time Escape (1911) ★ The Lass Who Couldn't Forget (1911) ★ In Old Florida (1911) ★ The Fiddle's Requiem (1911) ★ To the Aid of Stonewall Jackson (1911) ★ The Romance of a Dixie Belle (1911) ★ Special Messenger (1911) ★ Rory O'More (1911) ★ The Colleen Bawn (1911) ★ The Fishermaid of Ballydavid (1911) ★ Arrah-Na-Pogue (1911) ★ Hitherto Unrelated Incident of the Girl Spy (1911) ★ The O'Neill (1912) ★ His Mother (1912) ★ The Vagabonds (1912) ★ Far from Erin's Isle (1912) ★ You Remember Ellen (1912) ★ Captain Rivera's Reward (1912) ★ Victim of Circumstances (1912) ★ The Belle of New Orleans (1912) ★ The Fighting Dervishes of the Desert (1912) ★ Missionaries in Darkest Africa (1912) ★ An Arabian Tragedy (1912) ★ Captured by Bedouins (1912) ★ Tragedy of the Desert (1912) ★ Winning a Widow (1912) ★ A Prisoner of the Harem (1912) ★ Down Through the Ages (1912) ★ From the Manger to the Cross (1912) ★ Ireland, the Oppressed (1912) ★ The Shaughraun (1912) ★ The Mad Maid of the Forest (1915) ★ Witch's Gold (1920)

# JANET GAYNOR

Janet Gaynor was born Laura Augusta Gainor on October 6, 1906, in Philadelphia, Pennsylvania. She attended high school in San Francisco and, shortly after graduation, moved to Los Angeles hoping to find work in films. Her life was much like the character she later portrayed in *A Star is Born.* Janet believed she was destined to be a film star, and with no qualifications other than unshakable dreams, she pestered the various film studios for a chance to appear in any role. She worked as an unaccredited extra or bit player in 18 films, finally earning a lead part in a two-reel western, *The Johnstown Flood* (1926). She was signed to a contract with the Twentieth Century Fox Company, who were impressed with her ability to project vulnerability and naiveté.

In 1927 she was teamed with Charles Farrell in *Seventh Heaven,* a film considered by most audiences and critics one of the best motion pictures ever made.

Immediately after *Seventh Heaven,* Fox cast Janet in *Street Angel.* It was not a sequel as-such, but it was a sister film in many ways. An exquisite film, steeped in moody, atmospheric visuals, it was one of the best works Frank Borzage ever produced. The combined efforts of the two stars and the same director were said to have produced a beautifully crafted romance, a visual masterpiece with magnificent, sprawling sets, probing tracking shots, and shadowy cinematography filled with foreboding atmosphere. Ernst Palmer received an Academy Award nomination for his photography. It was also one of the last silent films ever made.

Janet Gaynor as Angela in Frank Borzage's masterpiece, *Street Angel* (1928).

Borzage's unforgettable masterpiece magnified Janet's good soul in one of the greatest films of the silent era. Janet showed that a woman hardened by life could bloom with the restorative healing of a man's adoration. Now considered to be lost for all time, *Street Angel* survives in still photos taken at the time of the filming of the motion picture.

"A powerful drama, unfolding in Naples, Italy, and revolving around a young man and a young woman, who loved each other passionately. From the point of view of direction and acting it is a masterpiece—one that should form a model for other directors," read the introduction to *Street Angel* in *Harrison's Reports,* April 21, 1928.

The opening title read like a synopsis of the film: "Everywhere...in every town, in every street...we pass, unknowing, human souls made great by love and adversity."

Janet played Angela, a wholesome waif, who tended her mother in their little world of poverty. Desperate for a much-needed medicine, with no money, father, or friend, she took to the streets, sacrificing her purity trying to pick up men for cash. Her obvious innocence prevented her from enticing a single male, so she attempted to grab a customer's change from

Janet Gaynor played a waif returning to her home and finding her mother dead in *Street Angel* (1928).

a food vendor's counter. She was caught and sentenced by the police to spend a year in the workhouse. There was a disturbance in the workhouse and, with the inmates in turmoil, she chanced an escape, only to run home and find her mother passed away. The hopelessness of her lonely world was devastating until the arrival of a traveling circus troupe. Her fortunes changed when they hid her from the authorities and carried her away to safety.

In time she became their star attraction, and though her life seemed glamorous, she turned into a hardened, course, world-weary gypsy. Her life had no room for such trivial matters as trust or love. Gino, a young painter, joined the circus to sell his skills to the customers. He knew nothing about her past, and his sensitivity was in contrast to Angela's world-weary mask. The gentle artist, attracted to the fiery star, painted her portrait, seeing in her eyes the longing look of a kindred spirit. He painted her inner being trapped inside a glossy veneer. When he unveiled for Angela the finished portrait, to her astonishment, she saw an image of ethereal, innocent beauty, the opposite of the way she saw herself.

"But I am not like that!" she exclaimed in a subtitle.

"You are... to me," responded Gino.

They left the circus to take up a life living in adjacent apartments. Gino finally secured a big, commercial assignment and proposed to Angela.

Borzage directed the film during the chaotic transition of the industry from silence to sound. In a 1930 article entitled "Directing a Talking Picture," Borzage said:

> The first duty of a director is to tell a story. The art of narration is important. A good director should be able to hold your interest in conversation. Some people are naturally good story tellers. Others are not. I believe it is possible to develop latent ability as a story teller, but it cannot be wholly acquired.
>
> To make a really good picture, a director must have a good story. Players who can act—photography—sound recording—settings are all important, but the story tops the list. It takes a very bad director to entirely spoil a very good story; but a director, no matter how skilled, can achieve little with poor material.
>
> Every good story is based on a struggle. Complications help and better most stories. A character study, or a tableau is not a picture and a director must avoid the false trails that leave such a film product upon other hands. Suspense, clues, dramatic forecasts and all the other arts on the story teller's shelf can be used with good effect. Even with talking pictures I believe that the story should be developed as far as possible through the scenes. Audiences prefer the action of the characters, to a steady exchange of conversation between the players.

*Street Angel* was released in 1928 when producers were tensed over the reaction the public would have to the looming specter of sound films. Throughout the land motion picture theaters were wiring for sound, and many exhibitors were already profiting from the novelty of music and talk. Musical backgrounds were hastily laced into the background of silent pictures, and other titles were rushed back into production to create single scenes with musical performers or dialogue. They were advertised as "part-talkies" and joined the craze for sound. Fox came up with a system that was different from the one used by Warner Bros. The Warner technology utilized sound on disc, 78 rpm recordings spun in synchronization to the projected image, whereas the Fox system used an optical image impregnated into the film itself, images of sound waves that transformed into audible sound with a conversion device. Both systems worked beautifully, and their competing technologies further aggravated the already confused theater owners. Those booking Warner films tended to gear for their sound-on-disc system, while those exhibiting Fox films retooled their projectors to accommodate the sound-on-film system. *Street Angel* was quickly reworked to take advantage of this system in use at the dawn of sound films, and the screenings greatly benefited from the inclusion of a synchronized musical score and strategic sound effects. The whistling between Angela and Gino was said to be a particularly effective use of this early sound recording.

Mordaunt Hall of *The New York Times* made the following comment in his review of the film:

> The story is told in a peculiarly appealing fashion. It is particularly charming when Gino whistles a few bars from "O Sole Mio" and hears the answer whistled by Angela. When she is led away to the workhouse, Gino is in his room. He whistles and at first Angela cannot make a sound with her nervous lips, but finally she succeeds in spasmodically whistling the air. All these scenes are so marvelously photographed, that even without considering the story or the acting; they are always a source of admiration. It is indeed a picture which possibly more than any other reveals the strides made in motion picture camera work.
>
> Miss Gaynor and Mr. Farrell, who were together in the film conception of *Seventh Heaven* are equally clever in this current offering. Miss Gaynor is especially fine in the sequence in which she is having the tearful hour with Gino, who looks upon her tears of sorrow as tears of joy. Mr. Farrell is a fine specimen of manhood, and he, too, acts as well as he did as that very remarkable fellow in *Seventh Heaven.* He is swelled with pride as the artist who has earned an enviable commission and when he is left alone he is doleful, morose, wondering what has become of Angela.
>
> Mr. Borzage, who evidently knows his Naples, has done everything humanly possible to reflect the atmosphere of that blue-skied city, even to having the police going on their rounds in two and in the selection of types.

*Harrison's Reports* said the following of Borzage:

> [He] seems to possess the touch of Murnau; if one, in fact, did not know who had directed it, one would feel positive that it had come out of the hands of director Murnau. There is a feeling in the acting of all the characters, particularly in that of Janet Gaynor and of Charles Farrell. Miss Gaynor, one may be sure, has never done better work in her short screen career. She and Mr. Farrell make an excellent pair of screen players. The scenes where the heroine is shown being confronted with the authorities who had recognized her as a fugitive from justice and followed her to her home to arrest her; the scenes that follow, which show her spending a last hour, granted her by the Carabineer at her pleadings, the hero being unaware of the fact that she was to leave him to go to jail to serve her sentence of one year, which had been imposed on her for attempted robbery while soliciting; the distraction of the hero, who, when he woke up in the morning, found the heroine missing and was unable to explain her absence; their meeting at the waterfront

a year later, when the heroine came out of jail and was unable to find the hero; the hero's overtaking her when she, fearful lest the hero, who did not know the cause of her absence and had taken the wrong viewpoint, ran into the church, seeking sanctuary; the sight of the hero's painting, which represented the heroine as a Madonna, hanging over the alter and bringing about an immediate change in the feeling of the hero towards the heroine—all these are so presented as to leave an indelible impression on one's mind. It is not the direction or the acting alone: it is the combination of both, wrapped up with the soul of the director and of the players.

But of the supporting players, Mr. Armetta stands out the most. As the owner of the circus, Mr. Armetta steals the picture in a few of the situations wherein he appears. He acts in so peculiar a way as to cause laughter quite often. *Street Angel* is truly a big picture.

*Variety,* April 11, 1928, said the following of the film:

Another of those superior program pictures William Fox and Winnie Sheehan are accumulating so rapidly, with each making the heart of the exhibitor playing the Fox stuff beat a little faster every time. That this special exploitation at the Globe at $2 may not do more than break Fox even, if that, for the Broadway run is fine promotion for Fox and those same exhibitors, for it spreads the fame of Fox and the film. Top say that Fox's *Street Angel* is sure box office for any picture theater for a week or longer sums it up for the commercial end.

In *Street Angel* is revealed the rapidly progressing studio ideas. Long and continued shots are in the picture of streets and alleys, that at first glance appear impossible of studio manufacture but doubtlessly were.

*Street Angel* become noted for this newfound power in cinematography. At times the close-ups of Janet were said to be nothing short of startling cameos on the sheet of the screen, almost three-dimensional in design, especially in one where she and Charles Farrell faced each other in medium close shots. The lighting bathed the sets in a wash of wall shadows, adding murky depth and mood to the emotional fervor of the moment.

Technically there was much to admire throughout the splendid production. The picture was merely the illustration of the narrative crafted from the play by Monkton Hoffe, and held so closely to the original thread of the narrative any illusion was submerged. Tension and suspense were missing, and if any was tried for by the director, did not make itself manifest. The film was said to be a fluid panorama of the story told in an almost totally pictorial way.

Borzage forced his camera to see the soul of Janet through the eyes of the painter. The beautiful woman the director mined with the lens of his camera may not have been his secret alone, for someone on the Fox lot must have seen the same thing a long time ago when Janet was signed to a long-term Fox contract. Many a picture was to be made in Hollywood calling for Janet's soul and eyes. Those other films were later arranged, providing an opportunity to explore something else that Janet owned—a sense of acting subtlety permitting her the rare moments in close-up isolation to get over her portion of the director's vision. Janet was the personification of the title role of *Street Angel,* and played it all of the while, though none of the characters drew real sympathy. Instead, they were said to be like an abstract artist's conception of a character, a style that was both haunting and in keeping with the theme of a painter in love with his subject.

Charles Farrell, as the painter enraptured with Angela, was made up as a strangely Italian youth in looks, costumed to appear to be a vagrant artist doing odd painting jobs around the countryside. He was pictured without having his hair combed and adeptly manifested his adoration of Angela by frequently focusing his full attention on his beloved, a primal gaze willingly shifting the attention of the audience to the girl instead of to himself. The *Variety* reviewer noticed young couples in the audience were appropriately fascinated by the young couple and their romance as it played on the screen, marveling at the will power of both. Janet and Charles composed a good team for Fox.

In the opening scenes set in Italy and Naples, Janet as Angela was rescued from the police after receiving a year's sentence and escaped with the touring circus. Through that circumstance she met the young painter who was attempting to scratch out an existence among the denizens of the little traveling wagon circus.

In the beginning the picture was light with some slight mirthful minutes, while the lovemaking of the leading pair was shown in a sentimentally likeable tone. The unreeling of the story was continuously impressive, and since it was devoid of any high-action moments, the presentation seemed to some viewers to be longer than it actually was, though at 9,221 feet or 10 reels, it was considerably longer than the average film.

*The Film Daily,* April 15, 1928, called the film a "beautiful picture, commercially and artistically geared as few pictures are. Carries a universal appeal and is certain to send them out talking about its breath-taking loveliness. Janet Gaynor again proves she is a great actress. Charles Farrell excellent. The performances, acting, delicacy of treatment canvassed against exquisite photographic backgrounds make *Street Angel* extraordinary. The direction of Frank Borzage, magnificent; Photography by Ernest Palmer, incomparable."

The silent film language had reached its zenith, and the Academy of Motion Picture Arts and Sciences was launched in 1929 by leading actors, writers, directors, and producers to celebrate the creativity of its outstanding artists. Janet was the first to win the Best Actress award for her cumulative work in *Street Angel, Seventh Heaven,* and *Sunrise.* In *Street Angel* her transformation from innocent child to worldly cynic and back again to the pure of heart is amazing, exhibiting a personality which is completely at odds with her established image.

Although she stole every scene with her fiery expressions and gestures, Charles is said to have scored with his projection of the fundamental essence of Gino's gentle sensitivity, maintaining a balance between arrogance and congeniality without sacrificing masculine appeal. He apparently succeeded admirably in a performance that was considered as truly impressive as Janet's. He was not nominated for an Academy Award, an oversight typical of his career. That year the Best Actor nominees were Charlie Chaplin, Richard Barthelmess, and Emil Jannings, with Jannings taking home the award.

That same year she married attorney Jesse Peck, and within five years was the top female box office attraction in the country.

Janet and Charles had a special magic and chemistry used to great advantage in 10 films. *Street Angel* was a huge hit of 1928, making *The New York Times* Top 10 List. *My Angel,* the original song by Erno Rapee and Lew Pollack, was a success in sheet music and recordings.

Her charming, gentle voice was ideally suited to talkies and she made the transition to sound films with great success. In *A Star is Born* (1937) she vocally imitated Katharine Hepburn and Mae West convincingly. She received her second nomination for the Best Actress Academy Award.

Gilbert Adrian was the film industry's foremost costume designer during the 1930s and 1940s. His uniquely styled, broad-shouldered suits and coats worn by Joan Crawford became widely copied into American ready-to-wear outfits. *Letty Lyndon,* Crawford's 1933 film, featured Adrian's huge, puffy sleeved dresses. The look quickly translated into another fashion trend.

Janet married Adrian in 1939, and their son Robin was born in 1940. She retired from work in motion pictures and enjoyed being a full-time mother, while Adrian retired from MGM and opened his salon, Adrian Ltd., in 1942 in Beverly Hills, California. His unique designs custom-clothed Hollywood's top stars, and his ready-to-wear lines decorated exclusive retailers in major cities around the country.

He was forced to close Adrian Ltd. in 1952 after suffering a heart attack. He and Janet happily retired to the tropical seclusion of a ranch in Brasilia,

"My Angel," original sheet music of the theme song for
*Street Angel* (1928), was specially composed and recorded
in the early Movietone sound process.

Brazil. Janet busied herself with a newfound talent painting landscapes in
a vibrant, colorful style.

Mary Martin, famous as the perennial *Peter Pan* re-run endlessly on
American television, remembered Janet as her closest friend, in her autobiography, *My Heart Belongs:* "We met in the early Hollywood days and I
have loved her always. For herself, for her intellect, her good common sense,
the way she has lived her life, and the many things she has taught me."

One day she received a letter from Janet and Adrian inviting her and husband Richard Halliday to see their new Brazilian house. "We knew they
had property there but we didn't know just where," she noted. "When we
set forth on our freighter, Hedda Hopper had mentioned it in her column,
and added that she knew Janet and Adrian 'would love to know where in
South America the Hallidays are....' Janet's mother saw the item, clipped
it, and mailed it to her, and Janet and Adrian had promptly written to us."

Mary and Richard traveled the thousand mile journey to Brazil, and then took a plane from Sao Paulo. Adrian and Janet met the couple in a station wagon, bounding them along tracks through the trees to their home set three thousand feet above the red desert. They were supremely taken by the glorious vista of mountains spreading deep into the distance amid surrounding jungle. They soon purchased their own ranch in the area.

Janet worked occasionally, playing a lead role in the 1957 film, *Bernadine,* but continued to enjoy the quieter lifestyle of retirement. After returning in 1958 to design costumes for the film musicals *Grand Hotel* and *Camelot,* Adrian suffered a second heart attack and died on September 14, 1959. She married producer Paul Gregory in 1964. In 1976 her still life paintings were exhibited in a New York gallery and quickly became coveted treasures.

The Academy of Motion Picture Arts and Sciences invited Janet, the first Oscar winner, to present the acting award at the 50th anniversary telecast from the Dorothy Chandler Pavilion on April 3, 1978. She shared the stage with many former Oscar winners from the golden age of Hollywood, including William Holden and Barbara Stanwyck, Bette Davis and Olivia de Havill, and Fred Astaire, Joan Fontaine, Kirk Douglas, Natalie Wood, and Greer Garson. Janet presented the Best Actress award to Diane Keaton for *Annie Hall.*

*Harold and Maude,* a unique and startling low-budget film, became an enormous hit in the early 70s, and by the end of the decade reached cult status. Legions of admirers flocked to midnight screenings of the "May/December" romance between a lunatic youth and an antiestablishment senior citizen. Colin Higgins shaped the tale into a musical scenario and David Amram composed lyrics and sounds for a Broadway production of 1980. Janet came out of retirement to star as Maude in the musical directed by Robert Lewis. On January 19 the cast began a run of 21 previews. The play opened at the Martin Beck Theater on February 7, 1980, and closed four days later.

In 1982 Janet was in San Francisco with Mary Martin and friends. One night they decided to dine at a new restaurant in Chinatown. A taxi was called, and when it arrived, it was about 7:30 in the evening and still light outside. Mary, Ben Washer, Janet, and Paul took their seats. Janet was the smallest of the group, and because she did not like to slide across a big back seat to one end, Mary recalled she got in first, and was followed by Janet, and then they were joined by Washer. She indicated he was always a perfect gentleman, and had paused to shut all the doors before lastly climbing into the car, sitting to the far right side of the rear seat. Paul joined the driver, taking a place to the right side of the front seat. He was the tallest one in the troupe, and needed the slight amount of extra room of the less-crowded front seat.

About two and a half miles from Mary's house, as the taxi entered a busy intersection, a speeding van ran through the stoplight and collided with the taxi. Ben was killed instantly; Paul got whiplash and broke several ribs; Mary shattered her pelvis in three places, broke two ribs, and suffered a punctured lung; and Janet was smashed between her two friends. She was rushed to San Francisco General Hospital with the others and spent months in the intensive care unit. Mary had to learn to walk with the aid of a walker, and pushed herself day by day until she was finally able to walk down the hall to see Janet.

"When I first saw her, I was shocked, because she was absolutely blown up out of proportion because of all the poisons in her system,"

Mary remembered in her autobiography, *My Heart Belongs*. "Her bladder had been injured very badly." She had four operations while she was in intensive care, followed by two more operations at another hospital. Eventually Janet returned to her home. Her recovery was slow, but iron will and determination miraculously brought her partially back to a semblance of her former health. Soon, however, she succumbed to an attack of pneumonia and died in Palm Springs on September 14, 1984.

Janet Gaynor, radiating the warmth of humanity and sincere goodness, led all film actresses by being the first to carry the accolade as the best in the profession, a sentiment echoed by critics and supported by public adulation. She carried the torch passed by Mary Pickford as America's Sweetheart.

## SILENT FILMOGRAPHY OF JANET GAYNOR

Cupid's Rustler (1924) ★ Young Ideas (1924) ★ All Wet (1924) ★ The Haunted Honeymoon (1925) ★ Dangerous Innocence (1925) ★ The Burning Trail (1925) ★ The Teaser (1925) ★ The Plastic Age (1925) ★ Crook Buster (1925) ★ The Beautiful Cheat (1926) ★ The Johnstown Flood (1926) ★ Oh What a Nurse! (1926) ★ Ridin' for Love (1926) ★ Skinner's Dress Suit (1926) ★ Fade Away Foster (1926) ★ The Shamrock Handicap (1926) ★ The Galloping Cowboy (1926) ★ The Fire Barrier (1926) ★ The Man in the Saddle (1926) ★ Don't Shoot (1926) ★ The Blue Eagle (1926) ★ The Midnight Kiss (1926) ★ The Return of Peter Grimm (1926) ★ Martin of the Mounted (1926) ★ Lazy Lightning (1926) ★ The Stolen Ranch (1926) ★ Forty-Five

Minutes from Hollywood (1926) ★ Pep of the Lady J (1926) ★ Seventh Heaven (1927) ★ The Horse Trader (1927) ★ Two Girls Wanted (1927) ★ Sunrise (1927) ★ Street Angel (1928) ★ 4 Devils (1928) ★ Lucky Star (1929)

# DOROTHY GISH

Of all the great silent film stars, Dorothy Gish is most deserving of a chapter in this book because the general populace has completely forgotten her. This vibrant woman, who as an adolescent entered movies in D. W. Griffith's Biograph one-reelers, helped establish the art of silent film acting and motion picture development, enjoyed a career that spanned seven decades, and is barely remembered. She was world famous as a comedienne in an era dominated by male clowns. Were it not for her relation to Lillian Gish and her dramatic performance in D. W. Griffith's *Orphans of the Storm,* she probably wouldn't be remembered at all.

She was born into a broken family after her restless father walked out on his wife and first child, Lillian. Mary, her mother, was desperate to make enough money to support the family, and out of necessity resorted to offering her self-conscious impersonation of an actress to any producer who would hire her. As soon as they were able to walk the two little girls were earning income to supplement their mother's, playing in lurid melodramas and posing for pictures. Dorothy was often forced to go out alone with touring plays, leaving behind her mother and sister to trek the small towns of America under the dubious supervision of various actresses.

In an article titled, "And So I am a Comedienne," Dorothy remembered the old melodramas she and her sister Lillian used to play in, lurid tales primed to give the audience a wide variety of incidents and thrills. In *Her False Step* the child actress made her entrance in the middle of a snowstorm, depicted by a gently pelting shower of fake snow made from paper and cotton. After each performance the debris would be swept up and dumped into boxes to be carted on to the next performance in another town. Again and again the imitation snow would be used until it not only took on a brown tint but also an assortment of nails and an occasional dead mouse. As the tour wore on, the child began to dread the scene in the snow, cringing as the polluted sweepings fell from the rafters onto her shoulders while she spoke her line, "Is it much farther, mother?"

The Gish family crossed paths with their friends the Smith family and, for a time, roomed with little Gladys Smith, her sister Lottie, and brother Jack. The road took them all in different directions and for several years, the two families lost track of each other.

Mary Gish tried to keep her little family together when possible, even going into a partnership one summer operating a candy concession at Brooklyn's Fort George Amusement Park with Charlotte Smith and her brood of three children, Gladys, Lottie, and Jack. The enterprise ended suddenly one day when little Jack fed their entire stock to the family dog. The dog died, and the two fatherless families reluctantly parted to wander the rails again in third-rate touring plays.

One day, a local movie theater proclaimed a bill made entirely of Biograph films, their favorites. Dorothy and Lillian went into the nickelodeon to enjoy the show and were startled to see their friend, Gladys Smith, radiating from the screen in a film called *Lena and the Geese* (1912). When the show ended, they raced to tell their mother. In *The Movies, Mr. Griffith, and Me,* Lillian remembered her mother saying, "The Smiths must have fallen on hard times if Gladys has to pose for pictures. We must look them up when we get to New York." Mary also must have smelled a moneymaking opportunity, for she knew Charlotte Smith recognized a good thing when it came her way. If the Smiths were making pictures there had to be some money in it, she reasoned; wouldn't her two little girls be equally able?

Albert Paine wrote in *Life and Lillian Gish* that the two girls and their mother decided to look up Gladys Smith in the telephone book, to see if she was at the Biograph. On close inspection of the numbers listed they found: Biograph Co., 11 E. 14th St. A hasty phone call was dispatched to the firm.

"Hello, hello! Is this the Biograph Company?"

"That's right. What's wanted?"

"We'd like to speak to one of your actresses, Gladys Smith."

"Sorry—no such person here."

"But we saw her in a picture of yours, in Baltimore."

"What picture?"

"*Lena and the Geese.*"

"Oh, that was Mary Pickford."

"Oh—oh, all right–can she come to the telephone?"

The Gish girls now knew who she was—Gladys ... so much the better. Gladys, who was now Mary, came to the telephone, and after a brief period of greetings, invited them to come to the studio.

"Lillian and Dorothy, at the top of the outer step at 11 East 14th Street, found themselves in a wide hall, confronting a great circular heaven—climbing stairway that ascended to the unknown," wrote Paine. "A tall man with a large hooked nose was walking up and down, humming to himself. A boy took in their names, and presently Mary, brighter and prettier than ever under her new name, appeared and flung herself into their arms. The tall man continued walking up and down, and now added some words to the tune he was humming: 'She'll never bring them in—she'll never bring them in,'—a suggestion to Mary, who declined to take any such hint.

"Mr. Griffith," she said, "these are my friends, Lillian and Dorothy Gish. They were on the stage for years, in child parts, just as I was; I know you'll have something for them, here."

Griffith tested both girls in the roles of sisters for a film to be titled *An Unseen Enemy,* an exciting suspense film he was making that week. He tied a different colored bow on the heads of the girls and then shot a gun into the air to stimulate their terrified reactions. They were truly terrified, and their horror required no acting skill. They got the parts, but wondered if picture work was something they should do. The director appeared to be a madman, but with Gladys Smith in their films and a Barrymore wandering in and out of some of the roles, they figured it couldn't be too bad. The easy money was tempting to the unemployed girls.

Griffith, who was directing a picture at the time, took a moment to look over the two young theater veterans. He found Lillian had an exquisite, ethereal beauty, and Dorothy was just as pretty in a pert and saucy manner, mischief seeming to pop right out of her. She also had a tender, sweet charm noticed by many in the Biograph studio. After questioning them about their acting experience, he immediately hired them to appear as extras in the film he was directing that week. Lillian recalled being seated in an imitation theater audience with her back to the camera and reacting to other actors performing on a makeshift stage. The actors wore a garish, yellow-tinted makeup and were bathed in an eerie, bright blue light, two elements utilized in cameras functioning with orthochromatic film stock in wide use around 1912.

A beautiful portrait of Dorothy Gish, ca. 1915.

Griffith saw to it that they were featured in many films. Dorothy would go on to star in over one hundred one- and two-reel films and features over the years, often appearing with her sister Lillian.

Linda Arvidson, Mr. Griffith's secret wife at the time, remembered in her autobiography, *When The Movies Were Young,* "Lillian and Dorothy just melted right into the studio atmosphere without causing a ripple. For quite a long time they merely did extra work in and out of pictures. Especially Dorothy, as Mr. Griffith paid her no attention whatsoever and she kept on crying and trailed along. She also continued to play in many one and two reel Biograph films, learning the difficult technique of silent film acting, and preparing for opportunity when it came. Dorothy was still a person of insignificance, but she was a good sport about it; a likable kid, a bit too perky to interest the big director, so her talents blushed unnoticed by Mr. Griffith. In *An Unseen Enemy* the sisters made their first joint appearance. Lillian regarded Dorothy with all the superior airs and graces of her rank. At a rehearsal of *The Wife,* of Belasco and DeMille fame, in which picture I played the lead, and Dorothy the ingénue, Lillian was one day an interested spectator. She was watching intently, for Dorothy had had so few opportunities, and now was doing so well, Lillian was unable to contain her surprise, and as she left the scene she said: 'Why, Dorothy is good; she's almost as good as I am.' Many more than myself thought Dorothy was better."

She was also prone to have accidents. The worst occurred when Mae Marsh, Lillian, and D. W. Griffith were in the middle of making *The Birth of a Nation.* On Thanksgiving Day, Dorothy had lunch with a group of actors and Mr. Griffith at a small restaurant two blocks from their studio. As they returned by cab, Dorothy stepped off the curb to cross the street and a speeding car swerved within inches of her. She stepped away just as it passed, but failed to see a second car right behind it. The car struck Dorothy and dragged her nearly 40 feet, injuring her foot so severely the tip of her toe had to be amputated.

"It's funny about my being in an automobile accident," Dorothy was quoted as saying in *The Movies, Mr. Griffith, and Me,* while recuperating from the injury. "I went to a fortune teller a month ago and was warned to be careful about automobiles. The woman told me I was to be hurt by one within a short time. And really, I have tried to be careful ever since, but that didn't save me."

In *Hearts of the World* (1918), a film about World War I and the devastation of France, Dorothy found her first foothold, striking a personal hit in a comedy role that captured the essence of her sense of humor. As the "little disturber," a street singer, Dorothy's performance was the comic highlight of the film, and her characterization in this role catapulted her into a brilliant career as a star of comedy films.

They completed work in Europe during the bombardments, and the return voyage was particularly harrowing. The war increased in ferocity, and the German military dispatched U-boats throughout the oceans, sinking everything from rowboats to battleships. The studio workers left behind in America to grind out program films for his studio were tensed with fear. With each passing day, the tension grew as concern over their return voyage heightened. For a time their boat disappeared. There was no trace of her by way of the early tracking methods, as these depended on the actual ship radioing their whereabouts. Communications from the Griffith voyage ceased. Widespread opinion among his studio began to creep toward the unthinkable: the ship had sunk without a trace, taking with it Lillian and Dorothy Gish, their mother Mary, Robert Harron, Billy Bitzer, and a number of others in the crew.

Camera man Karl Brown, in *Adventures with D. W. Griffith,* recalled their tension: "I tried to divert myself by coming to grips with the only phase of music left open to me. Performance was clearly not for me. I could play the piano, yes, but not in such manner as to impair the appetite of Josef Hofmann or to cause Sergei Rachmaninoff to be plunged into despair. So I went to Blanchard Hall, our music center of the time, and began to butt my head against the unyielding walls of harmony, theory, and composition. No go..."

Lillian Gish recalled in her autobiography the draining experience of their return from war-torn Europe: "Our ship bound for home had six eight-inch guns to protect us from the enemy. We awakened one morning to the sound of gunfire. Rushing into our life suits, we hurried on deck—to discover another boat nearby. It hadn't answered our signal to hoist its flag. Fearing it was an enemy boat shielding a submarine, our ship had opened fire across its bow." The ship's captain determined the boat had put on its brakes so fast it skidded in the water. When the first volley of assault fired from the actor's ship, the intruding vessel quickly ran up a Scandinavian flag, and all hands on both ships waved friendly white handkerchiefs, bringing the harrowing episode to an end.

Then the word was flashed that Dorothy, Lillian, and Griffith had arrived safe in New York with his little group. The film was completed with additional interiors in his studio on a frenzied, day-and-night schedule.

*Hearts of the World* had its premiere at Clune's in March 1918, and opened a few weeks later in New York. Its success was great, and Dorothy found her salary raised to $500 a week. Dorothy's "Little Disturber" role in *Hearts of the World* was an enormous success. She stole the film with her comic face and movements. No one was more pleased than her sister, because she was instrumental in persuading Griffith to use Dorothy rather than Constance Talmadge, who was his original choice. As a comedienne, Dorothy was a revelation. Griffith inadvertently gave vent to Dorothy's innate sense of humor and her ability to convulse audiences with laughter. This role opened the door to an entirely new dimension to her career.

Griffith did not use Dorothy in any of his earliest epics, but while he spent months working on *The Birth of a Nation* and *Intolerance,* Dorothy was featured in a vast number of Triangle and Mutual releases directed by young Griffith protégés such as Donald Crisp, James Kirkwood, and Christy Cabanne. Elmer Clifton directed a series of seven Paramount-Artcraft comedies with Dorothy that were so successful and popular, the

Dorothy Gish and Harold Vizard in flight in *Flying Pat* (1922).

tremendous revenue they raked in helped to pay the cost of Griffith's expensive epics. These films were wildly popular with the public and the critics. She excelled in pantomime and light comedy while her sister appeared in tragic roles. Dorothy became famous in this long series of Griffith-supervised films for the Triangle-Fine Arts and Paramount companies from 1918 through 1920, riotous comedies that put her in the front ranks of film comediennes. All of these films have been lost, victims of the unbelievable neglect of the studios that made them.

*Flying Pat* was one of these comedies, made when Dorothy was at her height of her popularity and it showcased her pioneering role as a comedienne in films. The story of *Flying Pat* follows Patricia Van Nuys as she takes a hint from her husband and starts out on a career of her own. As an Aviatrix, she survives the test of a machine which determines whether she may aspire to sail in the air; thereafter, she goes up with a skilled aviator, Endicott, and does stunts until she uses the wrong throttle and brings the machine to earth in a nose dive.

Both escape unhurt, but they go to a neighboring roadhouse to fully recover. Pat telephones her husband. When he reaches the roadhouse, Pat is again herself, but her husband, who advised her to seek a career

Harold Vizard helps Dorothy Gish, as Patricia Van Nuys, attempt a career as an aviatrix in *Flying Pat* (1922).

of her own, drags her home in a fit of jealousy. Pat soon pursues another career, and takes a train for Albany. She falls into bad company and is fleeced of all her money. She returns home at a time when the family cook has quit and arranges with the butler to do the cooking herself. She succeeds in passing herself off as a Swedish kitchen maid, convincing her husband with the impersonation, but her cooking is so bad he discharges her.

Meanwhile a policeman and Endicott have both entered the kitchen. Pat hides one in the bin and the other in a laundry basket. Her husband finally recognizes her. He becomes suspicious and discovers Endicott. When he proposes to arrest Endicott, Pat provides the policeman by opening the laundry basket. All is forgiven and the young wife decides to give up her career as Flying Pat.

The year 1920 was a great year for comedy motion pictures. Among the titles convulsing audiences were Colleen Moore in *Dinty* and *A Roman Scandal,* Louise Fazenda in Mack Sennett's *Down on the Farm,* Will Rogers in *Almost a Husband,* Wallace Reid in *What's Your Hurry?, The Dancin' Fool, Double Speed,* and *Sick Abed.* Douglas Fairbanks mastered light comedy in *The Mollycoddle,* while his wife, Mary Pickford, brought hilarity to *Pollyanna.* The top comedy star of them all, Charlie Chaplin, was releasing one classic each month from Mutual, memorable, side-splitting films such as *The Pawnshop* and his feature-length film debuting Jackie Coogan, *The Kid.* Even Dorothy Gish had a huge following with three other laugh-provoking films that year: *Mary Ellen Comes to Town, Remodeling Her Husband,* directed by her sister Lillian, and *Little Miss Rebellion.*

Louise Reeves Harrison reviewed the film in *Moving Picture World,* December 25, 1920:

> *Flying Pat* starts out with a bright conception, one which arouses high expectations. These are fulfilled in the early scenes, particularly where the lively young star trains to manage an airplane. From the moment of her downfall in company with her teacher, the comedy drifts away from the subject into a series of inconsistent scenes apparently devised to give Dorothy Gish the opportunity to be amusing, but so little related to each other and to the anticipated line of action that interest sags. This is particularly true when old material is used to fill in the required number of reels. The absence of definite characterization and of anything like a story that could stand on its own merits puts a heavy burden on the charming young star.
>
> Dorothy does her little best with her opportunity, but it is overworking her to depend so entirely upon her quaint and really delightful personality in such an obvious vehicle. There are other actors with automatic roles, but they cannot be expected to get beyond them. There is nothing objectionable about the story. As shown at the Rialto Theatre it pleased those who are content to see Dorothy Gish and be amused by her antics regardless of the story's standard, but *Flying Pat* can only be designated as fair entertainment.

*Variety,* December 17, 1920, said *Flying Pat* was "a substantial comedy feature, with all the elements of good, fast, harmless yet delicious nonsense.... the picture has been given a good production and the photography is skillfully handled by one who should be, but is not programmed. The titles are appropriate, although they do compare unfavorably in instances to similar captions associated with slapstick films. It is a hearty, good picture for those who care for the star's work."

Linda Arvidson Griffith said in *When the Movies Were Young,* "Dorothy was that rare thing, a comedienne, and comediennes in the movies have been scarcer than hen's teeth. She proved what she could do when she got her first real chance as the bob-haired Marinette in *Hearts of the World.*

Mae Marsh recalled in *Screen Acting,* "Some actresses have set styles of hair dress which they seldom vary. I think of Dorothy Gish's black wig. Dorothy had tried many styles of hair dress and found none of them to her liking. She experimented with a black wig and was delighted with the result. It contributed something to her expression, brought it out, as it were, which she felt had been lacking. Since *Hearts of the World,* she has never stepped before a camera without her trusty black wig!"

"And then I slammed the door on a million dollars," Dorothy said in *The Movies, Mr. Griffith, and Me.* Lillian Gish wrote about a Paramount representative visiting Griffith and telling him the company wanted to sign Dorothy to a contract. By the terms of the new contract to be made with Paramount, she would star in seven films that would earn her a total of a million dollars. Lillian recalled her Mother did not go with Dorothy to the conference at which the contract was to be discussed, thinking it would be good for her daughter to handle it on her own. Dorothy attended the conference, listened politely, and then just as politely turned down their offer of a million dollars. When she reported her response to her family, they were startled and asked why she turned it down. "A million dollars—at my age," Dorothy replied blithely. "Why, it would have ruined me."

*And So I Am a Comedienne,* an article published in *Ladies' Home Journal,* July 1925, gave Dorothy a chance to recall her public persona: "And so I am a comedienne, though I, too, once wanted to do heroic and tragic things. Today my objection to playing comedy is that it is so often misunderstood by the audiences, both in the theater and in the picture houses. It is so often thought to be a lesser art and something which comes to one naturally, a haphazard talent like the amateur clowning of some cut-up who is so often thought to be 'the life of the party'. In the eyes of so many persons comedy is not only the absence of studied effect and acting, but it is not considered an art."

The other star of *Flying Pat* was James Rennie, born April 18, 1890, in Toronto, Ontario, Canada. He had success as an actor in stock companies in the United States and appeared on Broadway in *His Bridal Night,* a 1916 farce. After a stint with the Royal Air Force in Britain, he returned to the theater as Ruth Chatterton's leading man in the 1919 production of *Moonlight and Honeysuckle.*

Lillian Gish directed him in his film debut with her sister Dorothy in *Remodeling Her Husband.* She recalled that "Dorothy found a handsome leading man from the theater, James Rennie." While making her directing debut, Lillian remembered having difficulties with Dorothy. She had her own ideas; Lillian had her way of working out a scene. Lillian finally got her interested in the film by encouraging her interest in the new leading man, rehearsing their love scenes over and over, so that she would turn her attention from Lillian's directorial endeavors. Years later she regretted this course of action, for pushing the two young stars together resulted in Dorothy's one attempt at marriage. She and James Rennie were married for almost 15 years, and the two of them starred in several other films together. Rennie's career lasted for more than 20 years.

By the time of her return to the legitimate stage, Dorothy and Rennie had separated. They stalled filing for actual divorce until the year 1935. In those days, couples seeking a legal end to a marriage had to resort to one or the other testifying to some grievous affront. Dorothy refused to testify against Jim. She conceded he was a wonderful man and the failure of their alliance in matrimony was due to no personal fault about which she could hurl accusations. After being grilled by the judge, he finally demanded in exasperation, "Do you want this divorce, or don't you?" Finally Dorothy surrendered the feeble excuse that Jim had driven her into a fit of hiccoughs for six days. The judge granted the divorce.

Dorothy never remarried. She spent much of her next years living with her sister and mother. "I remember trying to teach her to be tidy," Lillian recalled with amusement. "She had exquisite handkerchiefs and gloves, but her dresser drawers were always in a state of confusion. Her best handkerchiefs were lost; there were more single gloves than pairs. 'Let's start with your glove drawer and try to keep it tidy,' I suggested. But my suggestion didn't work. Later, because of her disorderliness, I could not share an apartment with her.... Her room was always a ragbag of discarded dresses, hats, shoes and bags after she finished dressing." Dorothy fretted her sister and mother as she never settled for the first dress she put on. They often watched her progress from the front door as she returned home, making her way to her bedroom, the floor behind her marked by a trail of jettisoned garments she began to shed as soon as she closed the door. Lillian later recalled it was not that Dorothy was deliberately untidy, she just had her mind on so many other things she could not bother with the tedium of orderliness.

D. W. Griffith again used the talents of Dorothy Gish in *Orphans of the Storm,* opening his epic expansion of the "Two Orphans" and the French Revolution on January 3, 1922, at the Apollo Theater in New York. Lillian Gish recalled many critics welcoming it as one of Griffith's best films. The picture contained no outstanding innovations, but was a monumental showcase for all the brilliant techniques he had developed, mastered, and brought through the years to unrivaled peaks. The sequences of the storming of the Bastille and the last-minute rescue of Henriette at the guillotine recalled the ride of the Klan in *The Birth of a Nation* and the climax of the modern story in *Intolerance*.

*The Bright Shawl* (1923) brought Dorothy into a beautiful Richard Barthelmess film, playing a Cuban dancer persuaded by Barthelmess to gain information for the rebels against the Spanish army. She pays for her deception with her life.

*Romola* (1924) featured Dorothy with her sister Lillian in director Henry King's stunningly beautiful picture set in Renaissance Italy. Dorothy played Tessa, a hoydenish rake who had to die in the story. One of the most difficult scenes was that in which Dorothy's lover, Tito, was to throw her into Lake Arno. After repeated attempts, Dorothy simply would not drown. Lillian and her mother were nearby, watching with binoculars from a window in the Grand Hotel as the struggling photography ensued. At the time, the Arno was dirty and filled with debris. When they pushed Dorothy's head down, her other end would pop up. She could not swim, and instinctively would not submerge either. After much wasted film, Henry King, the director, finally gave up and called an end to the day's wasted effort.

King was required by Metro to work on another project immediately after the principal production had been made, and Lillian Gish was left with the task of supervising the final cutting of the film. As the footage was assembled into a final whole, the remaining scene of Tessa's death was still not photographed. By late October, well after the weather had turned icy, Lillian and a small camera crew went to the waters off Mamaroneck determined to drown Dorothy. An expert diver was stationed just out of the camera range, poised to pull her under. Dorothy had a bad chest cold, and to add to the misery of the moment, she was terrified of the water. Lillian insisted the reluctant drowning victim fortify herself with a strong drink before going into the water, in spite of the fact Dorothy had an aversion to alcohol since the age of three, an attitude begun when she had the measles and was compelled to swallow medicine imbued with a strong percentage of alcohol. The liquor had the intended effect on the actress. The hidden diver dragged Dorothy under the water and held her just long enough for a simulated drowning, after which he released her, gasping, to the surface. After the successful staging, Dorothy was made to run up and down in her wet clothes to get her circulation going. By the next day she was over her cold, and the completed footage was assembled into the finished film.

Dorothy busied herself in 1925 completing *The Beautiful City* with Richard Barthelmess and William Powell and *Clothes Make the Pirate* with Leon Errol.

*Nell Gwynne* (1926) took Dorothy to England in a magnificent production directed by Herbert Wilcox for British National Pictures. The opening performance at the New Plaza Theater was a great event in the history of British film. Prince and Princess Arthur of Connaught were present and a host of celebrities in the realms of art, letters, industry, and sport attended. The film, based on Marjorie Bowen's famous story, gave Dorothy an opportunity to exhibit a meteoric performance, said to be vivacious, "roguish, and captivating," according to the *London Morning Post,* March 2, 1926.

*London* (1927), Dorothy's second film for Herbert Wilcox, used a story from author Thomas Burke. The film was retitled *Limehouse* in England.

*Tip Toes* (1927) brought Dorothy's wit and humor into a pairing with Will Rogers. The British comedy also featured well-known English comedian, Nelson Keys, and the film rocked with laughter. It was a splendid production, and Dorothy looked more beautiful than ever.

Another made-in-England production, *Madame Pompadour* (1927), was a sufficiently entertaining film, not quite up to the standard of *Nell Gwynne,* but better than the average British film product. Dorothy again stole the whole show, and proved to be very popular in the United States.

Sound films were appearing on theater screens, and as the conversion chaos and panic began to spread, Dorothy wisely chose to take a respite from film work and return to the American stage where she spent her childhood in innumerable roles. George Cukor directed her in *Young Love,* and the light comedy found success with New York audiences as well as those on the road. A London production followed with equal success. Audiences loved seeing the great star in person, and for Dorothy, it was a timely opportunity to reacquaint herself with the rigors of spoken dialogue.

The great depression affected all of the entertainment field. Radio was making inroads as a cheap form of amusement, and film theaters instigated "bank nights" to boost box office returns. It was also the era of marathon dancing, the tragedies of the great dust bowl, and Shirley Temple, the number one attraction in motion pictures. Both Dorothy and Lillian ventured into separate experiments with the new sound film technology, Lillian with *One Romantic Night* (1930) and Dorothy with *Wolves* (1930).

*Wolves* was again directed by Herbert Wilcox, but it was made without a full understanding of sound technique. In spite of the great cast which included Charles Laughton, it was not a success in Europe. The film was later released in America in 1934 as *Wanted Men.*

The year 1931 brought Dorothy into an amusing satire that was an instant hit on the New York stage. *The Streets of New York or Poverty is No Crime* opened in 1931. That same year she also appeared in *The Pillars of Society, Getting Married,* and *The Bride the Sun Shines On.*

The following year she starred in the play, *Foreign Affairs* with Osgood Perkins, and *Autumn Crocus* with Francis Lederer.

In 1934 Dorothy starred in *By Your Leave* and *Brittle Heaven;* she starred in *Mainly for Lovers* in 1936. The following year, *Missouri Legend* featured Dorothy in a play based on the Jesse James legend. The sterling cast included Jose Ferrer and Dean Jagger in roles near the beginning of their careers.

The year 1939 brought both sisters another role of a lifetime. "Dorothy and I went to see the New York Production of *Life With Father,* starring Howard Lindsay and Dorothy Stickney," Lillian remembered joyfully in her autobiography. "After the performance I said: 'This is the play we've been waiting for to take through America.' " Lillian predicted the popular play would be a perfect showcase for all the people who had seen the hundreds of films featuring Mary Pickford, Dorothy, and herself. She was introduced to Lindsay backstage, and immediately surprised the producers with her enthusiastic desire to head the first company to go on the road, with Dorothy taking the same part for the second road company, and the movie rights for Mary Pickford. Regrettably, Pickford did not make the film version, but the Gish sisters did take the two road companies on extensive tours.

Lillian opened in Chicago with the play in 1940, and Dorothy began a two-year tour with another road company of the same play. Mary Pickford regrettably passed on the opportunity to appear in the film version. The role of Vinnie was played by Irene Dunne and William Powell played Father.

After several more plays in the following years, Dorothy was asked to play in a delightful comedy film, based on the reminiscences of Emily Kimbrough and Cornelia Otis Skinner. *Our Hearts Were Young and Gay* (1944) took Dorothy into the Paramount studios with a charming cast. She acquitted herself well, and the film was a hit for Paramount.

*The Magnificent Yankee* (1946) presented Dorothy at the Royale Theater in a beautifully sentimental comedy. Lillian noted in her pictorial book, *Dorothy and Lillian Gish,* John Chapman's review of the film: "Miss Gish and Mr. Calhern give the finest performances I have ever seen them in. She is a delight and a darling." The play was about Mr. Justice and Mrs. Oliver Wendell Holmes, telling about a man who was appointed a justice of the Supreme Court of the United States in 1902; a man who was so noble a person that, 31 years later, a new President paid the homage of making a call one scant hour after the President's inauguration.

Director Otto Preminger cast Dorothy in his 1946 film, *Centennial Summer*, and she was said to have been amused that she and some of the other stars were allowed to sing Jerome Kern's beautiful music. Even Mae Marsh appeared in the film in one of her many bit parts.

*The Whistle at Eaton Falls* (1951) was a documentary-style film produced by Louis de Rochemont. Dorothy was filmed as the widow of a mill owner.

Television in the 1950s offered many actors the opportunity to appear in plays broadcast live. Dorothy eagerly ventured into the new medium, appearing on NBC's Lux Video Theatre on the night of November 24, 1955, in a production of *Miss Susie Slagle's,* a charming story about a lady who ran a boarding house for struggling medical students. The play had been a film in 1945 with her sister, Lillian, made for Paramount Pictures Corporation.

*The Chalk Garden* featured both Lillian and Dorothy Gish, together for the first time on a live stage since their childhood. Dorothy played the grandmother's role, and Lillian played that of the governess. They went on to a successful summer tour.

One night, shortly after Lillian was closing in a play called *I Never Sang for My Father,* a summons from overseas alerted her to the collapse of Dorothy. A few days after Lillian reached her, Dorothy died of bronchial pneumonia.

"The truth is, that she did not know what she really wanted to do," said her sister, Lillian. "She had always had trouble making decisions and assuming responsibilities. In some ways she had never grown up.... She was such a witty and enchanting child that we enjoyed indulging her. First Mother and I spoiled her and later Reba, her friend, and her husband Jim. Reba called Dorothy 'Baby' and so did Jim. With the best intentions in the world, we all helped to keep her a child."

In a tribute and retrospective of Dorothy's career, The Society for Cinephiles published the remarks in 1986 of Helen Hayes, The First Lady of the American Theater: "The name Dorothy Gish brings a smile to your lips and conjures up such joyous memories of her merriment and wit. One cannot mourn her, but be thankful of the time she was with us to provide such happiness. A poet I particularly like once wrote, 'A bard of passion and of mirth, Ye have left your soul on earth.' While we may have lost Dorothy's lovely body, her soul is definitely still here, especially for this magnificent tribute."

There is a photo showing Dorothy Gish holding aloft the black wig she wore in many films, glowering at it; the picture is captioned, "You made me what I am today." In *Flying Pat,* Dorothy Gish played a girl searching for her place in the work force. Dorothy found her niche as a comedienne in a lengthy series of popular films in an industry dominated by male clowns such as Charlie Chaplin, Harold Lloyd, and Buster Keaton. She worked extremely hard and achieved worldwide fame for her efforts. In her few surviving films, she was an outstanding example for millions of girls in her era to follow.

## SILENT FILMOGRAPHY OF DOROTHY GISH

An Unseen Enemy (1912) ★ The Painted lady (1912) ★ The Musketeers of Pig Alley (1912) ★ Gold and Glitter (1912) ★ My Baby (1912) ★ The Informer (1912) ★ Brutality (1912) ★ The New York Hat (1912) ★ My Hero (1912) ★ A Cry for Help (1912) ★ The Burglar's Dilemma (1912) ★ Oil and Water (1913) ★ The Perfidy of Mary (1913) ★ The Lady and the Mouse (1913) ★ Just Gold (1913) ★ Her Mother's Oath (1913) ★ The Widow's Kid (1913) ★ The Vengeance of Galora (1913) ★ Those Little Flowers (1913) ★ Pa Says (1913) ★ The Lady in Black (1913) ★ The House of Discord (1913) ★ Almost a Wild Man (1913) ★ The Adopted Brother (1913) ★ Judith of Bethulia (1914) ★ The Mysterious Shot (1914) ★ The Floor Above (1914) ★ Home, Sweet Home (1914) ★ The Wife (1914) ★ The Warning (1914) ★ The Sisters (1914) ★ Their First Acquaintance (1914) ★ The Tavern of Tragedy (1914) ★ The Suffragette's Battle in Nuttyville (1914) ★ Silent Sandy (1914) ★ The Saving Grace (1914) ★ Sands of Fate (1914) ★ The Rebellion of Kitty Belle (1914) ★ The Old Man (1914) ★ The Newer Woman (1914) ★ The Mountain Rat (1914) ★ Liberty Belles (1914) ★ A Lesson in Mechanics (1914) ★ Her Old Teacher (1914) ★ Her Mother's Necklace (1914) ★ Her Father's Silent Partner (1914) ★ Granny (1914) ★ A Fair Rebel (1914) ★ A Duel for Love (1914) ★ Down the Road to Creditville (1914) ★ The City Beautiful (1914) ★ The Better Way (1914) ★ Back to the Kitchen (1914) ★ The Availing Prayer (1914) ★ Arms and the Gringo (1914) ★ How Hazel Got Even (1915) ★ Minerva's Mission (1915) ★ Bred in the Bone (1915) ★ Old Heidelberg (1915) ★ The Warning (1915) ★ Jordan Is a Hard Road (1915) ★ Victorine (1915) ★ Out of Bondage (1915) ★ An Old-Fashioned Girl (1915) ★ The Mountain Girl (1915) ★ The Lost Lord Lowell (1915) ★ The Little Catamount (1915) ★ Her Mother's Daughter (1915) ★ Betty of Greystone (1916) ★ Little Meena's Romance (1916) ★ Susan Rocks the Boat (1916) ★ The Little School Ma'am (1916) ★ Gretchen the Greenhorn (1916) ★ Atta Boy's Last Race (1916) ★ Children of the Feud (1916) ★ The Little Yank (1917) ★ Stage Struck (1917) ★ Her Official Fathers (1917) ★ Hearts of the World (1918) ★ The Hun Within (1918) ★ Battling Jane (1918) ★ The Hope Chest (1919) ★ Boots (1919) ★ Peppy Polly (1919) ★ I'll Get Him Yet (1919) ★ Nugget Nell (1919) ★ Nobody Home (1919) ★ Turning the Tables (1919) ★ Mary Ellen Comes to Town (1920) ★ Remodeling Her Husband (1920) ★ Little Miss Rebellion (1920) ★ Flying Pat (1920) ★ The Ghost in the Garret (1921) ★ Orphans of the Storm (1921) ★ The Country Flapper (1922) ★ Fury (1923) ★ The Bright Shawl (1923) ★ Romola (1924) ★ Night Life of New York (1925) ★ Clothes Make the Pirate (1925) ★ Nell Gwynne (1926) ★ London (1926) ★ Tiptoes (1927) ★ Madame Pompadour (1927)

# MAE MARSH

Millions of people see her on television every year and do not know the name of the striking woman with the haunting face. In *The Grapes of Wrath* (1940), when the destitute Joad family inch their wrecked jalopy into a refugee camp, a woman walks directly into the path of their car, staring at the beaten family as if they were creatures from another planet. That woman is Mae Marsh. In *Titanic* (1953) she is the woman to whom Norman gives up his life preserver. In *Julie* (1956) she is the hysterical, white-haired woman who senses trouble onboard an airplane, stalks to the cockpit, flings open the door, and in a shocking close-up, gasps in horror at the sight of the pilot slumped dead in his seat.

Her angular face and liquid eyes peered out from the movie screens of at least one hundred and fifty films. She was the central star of 80 titles, and suddenly appears for a few startling seconds in at least 70 other films.

Mae was born on November 9, 1895, in Madrid, New Mexico. Her father, a railroad auditor, died when she was four. Her family moved to San Francisco where her stepfather was killed in the great earthquake of 1906. Her great aunt then took Mae and Marguerite, her beautiful, older sister, to Los Angeles, hoping her show business background would open doors for jobs at various movie studios needing extras. For the little schoolgirl, watching her older sister wear costumes and pretend to be the heroine of a melodrama was imaginative fun.

Mae loitered around the sets and locations while her older sister worked on a film, playfully observing the fascinating progress of her sister's performance. "I tagged my way into motion pictures," Mae recalled in *The Silent Picture.* "I used to follow my sister Marguerite to the old Biograph studio and then, one great day, Mr. Griffith noticed me, put me in a picture and I had my chance. I love my work and though new and very wonderful interests have entered my life, I still love it and couldn't think of giving it up."

Linda Arvidson, the director's secret wife, was employed at the Biograph while Griffith was their resident director. In *When the Movies Were Young* she remembered a beautiful actress known as Margaret Loveridge who was present in some of their films. "For Miss Loveridge had also a little sister. And it was some such situation that led little sister to the movies and to Redonda at this time. Little sister was a mite: most pathetic and half-starved she looked in her wispy clothes, with stockings sort of falling down over her shoe-tops. No one paid a particle of attention to the child. But Griffith popped up from somewhere and spied her, and gave her a smile. The frail, appealing look of her struck him. So he said, 'How'd *you* like to work in a picture?'

"Oh, you're just fooling—you mean *me* to work in a picture?"

"Yes, and I'll give you five dollars." No stage bashfulness in the hanging head, the limp arms, and the funny hop skip of the feet.

"Oh, you couldn't give me five dollars."

"Oh, yes I can."

"You sure you're not fooling?"

"No, you come around some time, and you'll see, I'll put you in a scene. What's your name?"

"Mae Marsh."

"I'll remember, and I'll put you in a movie some day."

Margaret Loveridge, as soon as sister Mae's star began to rise in the movie heavens, changed her name to Marguerite Marsh. Griffith worked hard with little Mae after she followed the Biograph troupe from their California filmmaking excursion back to their home in New York.

Lionel Barrymore, a member of the cast of one of the single-reel Biograph dramas, observed the little girl and remarked to his co-stars her astounding resemblance to the famous New York stage actress, Billy Burke. Griffith was impressed by the resemblance and found a part for little Mae in the film being made that week. To the surprise of everyone, Mae was quite good. She had never acted before, and proved to be pliable under the direction of Griffith, soon earning roles in a number of his one-reel films. These films made in the first decade of the twentieth century pioneered every cinematic technique in use today. Mae also played an integral part in the formation of film acting technique, the peculiar acting style of *looking* rather than *speaking, thinking* instead of *gesturing,* and *being* as opposed to *acting.*

Mae and her mother followed the Biograph players to New York where her sister was in the company. The day they reached the East the company was working outside. The two Marshes were so excited when they got off the train in New York they drove immediately to the location and fluttered onto the scene. She did some extra work for several weeks, learning the rudiments of film acting, and reading poems by Tennyson within sight of Griffith. She impressed him as the type of heroine so glorified in the poet's poems, the ethereal type he liked to idealize in his films.

One morning in 1912, Griffith called his stock company together and told the stories of two films to be made that week: *The Sands of Dee,* a lyrical allegory based on a famous poem, and *Man's Genesis,* a tale of two cavemen and their jealousy over the affection for a girl, Lily-White. The picture was to show the accidental discovery of man's first weapon. The actors were first prepared wearing animal skins. As Griffith pondered the outfits, he thought of the film's theme, and discerned the folly of the animal skins. They would have to have been torn by hand, an impossibility, as weapons had not been discovered prior to the story beginning. He changed his mind and opted to have them wear clothing made of grasses. Bobby Harron came out dressed in his grassy outfit, and the female costume was displayed for the company to see.

Mary Pickford was the resident star of the Biograph lot, and Griffith assigned to her the bare-legged, grass-skirted role of Lily-White. There are several varying accounts of this momentous day in the writings of Mary Pickford, Mae, and several others who were present at the Biograph when Mae earned her first opportunity to work as an actress before the cameras. They all begin with Mary's refusal to play the part of Lily-White after donning the revealing grass costume.

"Well, I don't think I care for this. That shows all your legs," Mary complained.

"Is that so?" Griffith said, eyeing little Mae playing a few feet away.

"Yes. I'm not going to go up there on the screen and show all my legs and body, practically. It's indecent. Give it to that kid; give it to her. She doesn't care. Give it to her. She doesn't care if she shows her legs."

Mae didn't care. She was just a kid, as Mary stated, and it was understandable to her that a married woman like Mary Pickford would feel embarrassed to show all of legs.

"No, I don't," little Mae interjected. Griffith then announced that if Mary would not play that part in *Man's Genesis* she would not play the coveted title role in his next film, *The Sands of Dee.* All the actresses on the payroll stood behind Mary, each refusing in turn to play the part, citing the same objection. Mae was willing and eager for an opportunity to advance in the ranks.

Years later, Mae recalled in *The Silent Picture,* "...and he called rehearsal, and we were all there and he said, 'Well now, Miss Marsh, you can rehearse this.' And Mary Pickford said, 'What!' and Mr. Griffith said, 'Yes, Mary Pickford, if you don't do what I tell you I want you to do, I'm going to have someone else do *The Sands of Dee.* Mary Pickford didn't play *Man's Genesis* so Mae can play *The Sands of Dee.*' Of course, I was thrilled, and she was very much hurt. And I thought, 'Well, its all right with me. That is something.' I was, you know, just a lamebrain."

"I thought, 'It serves him right', recalled Mary, 'she'll give a bad performance.' "

Griffith assigned the Lily-White role to the relative newcomer, and rewarded her with the sought-after role in *The Sands of Dee.* The Biograph actresses secretly hoped she would fail, but *Man's Genesis* became a watershed film in the history of motion pictures, one of the first to explore psychological motivations in a character's development. When seen today, these two films show Mae appearing to have the grace usually reserved for experienced actresses. She is confident, poetic, and vivid.

Later, when Mary Pickford and the other Biograph players filed into the projection room and watched the first screening of the two films, they were astounded at the transformation of the little schoolgirl into an actress to be admired. Mary graciously congratulated Mae on her performances in the films.

"You did it better than I could," she said. Later, Mary confided to others her thoughts after this incident: "She had no experience; she had previously worked in a department store. And I thought, 'This does it. I've spent ten years in the theater, and if she can do that without any experience, I don't belong in pictures.' "

To Griffith, Mary said, "I'm going to tell you something now, Mr. Griffith. You can take these amateurs. I'm going back where I learned my métier, my profession. One year from tonight, I will be on Broadway." A year later she left movie work to return to the theater, and true to her vow, starred on Broadway in *A Good Little Devil.*

*Man's Genesis* was originally filmed under the title *Primitive Man*, and Griffith had difficulty convincing the Biograph owners the film was going to be a drama. They could only see it as a comedy. Griffith was determined it should be a serious story. The little film was taken seriously by the public, as it was meant to be. It was a highly praised picture and prompted a spate of imitation films from many other picture studios.

*The Sands of Dee,* Mae's second film of importance, was reviewed by *Moving Picture World* in 1912. Epes Sargent of *The New York Times,* complained about Griffith's single-reel films, lamenting the increasing number of shots and accelerating pace of the films, playing the nerves of the audience to the breaking point. He actually took a stopwatch and counted the number of shots in *The Sands of Dee:* "In the Stockton list the Biograph takes top notch with 68 scenes, but they are not quick sands alongside the same company's *Man's Lust for Gold.* This contains 107 scenes...."

Griffith adopted Mae frequently in many films, as she was a pliable muse for his idealized vision of femininity and a good replacement for the departed Mary Pickford.

*The Escape* (1914) was one of the films Mae listed as being among her personal favorites. George Blaisdell wrote about going to the Broadway studio of the reliance Company to have a talk with Henry Walthall, an actor in the film, and Mae. "Near the Broadway end of the building Jim Kirkwood was seated in a comfortable chair, his long frame sunk into its depths as he meditatively watched and guided the rehearsal of the players under him. We wandered to the Sixteenth Street part of the studio. Under lights fiercer than any that ever beat on a throne stood Blanche Sweet and Mae Marsh rehearsing a scene in the forthcoming feature production of Paul Armstrong's *The Escape.* In the play the two are sisters. Miss Sweet uttered no word. Her lips did not move. She looked. You felt what she was thinking. Miss Marsh, a slip of a girl, looking even younger than she actually is—and she is in the teens—indulged in pantomime. Her lips moved, but she spoke not. A slight cough indicated the tuberculosis taint of the character she was portraying. It was all very interesting. For a quarter of an hour we stood by the camera just behind a tall man seated comfortably, a big brown fedora hat pulled over his eyes serving as a shade from the lights. He was talking into a megaphone. It was a mild, conversational tone. At times there would be a lull. Then again there would be advice, but the voice was not raised. So this was the man who so thoroughly inspires his players that they in turn may penetrate and stir the hearts of their audiences; who by his magnetism binds to him with hoops of steel these same players. It is a rare trait, this secret of commanding unbounded loyalty, an unusual equipment, especially in one of pronounced artistic temperament. It is a cordial handshake Mr. Griffith has for a stranger."

*The Birth of a Nation,* produced by Griffith in 1915, presented Mae as The Little Sister of the film's hero. Her moving portrayal, especially the wrenching death scene after plunging to the bottom of a mountain peak, firmly set her face and name into the minds of movie goers.

Mae Marsh as The Little Sister in *The Birth of a Nation* (1915).

She made many films in the wake of the success of *The Birth of a Nation,* including the historic *Intolerance* (1916). Called "the first film fugue," *Intolerance* told four stories of injustice simultaneously. The first, a modern story, depicted Mae as the wife of a young man wrongly sentenced to death for a crime he did not commit. The film wove around this story the tale of the death and crucifixion of Jesus Christ, the fall of ancient Babylon, and the massacre of St. Bartholomew's day in France during the reign of Charles IX. The story threads are interwoven in an increasing panorama of action and tension.

Of her work in *Intolerance,* Julian Johnson said in *Photoplay Magazine,* "The finest individual acting accomplishments are Mae Marsh's." Frederick James Smith, in *The New York Dramatic Mirror,* said: "Mae Marsh stands pre-eminent for her touching playing of the girl of the modern story." In spite of this critical acclaim, by the late teens her popularity had begun to wane.

After *Intolerance* (1916), Sam Goldwyn signed her to a contract at $2500 per week, but her films made without Griffith were lacking the spark for which she was known, and by the late 'teens her popularity began to fade; she retired on the eve of her marriage in 1918.

*The Birth of a Nation* was re-released in the year 1920, and Mae found a resurgence of her popularity. When Mae returned to the screen in the 1920s, her acting skills had refined with maturity. Her persona, without the guidance of Griffith, finally crystallized in *The Little 'Fraid Lady,* a Robertson-Cole super special, based on Marjorie Benton Cooke's novel, *The Girl Who Lived in the Woods.* The story was adapted for the screen by Joseph Farnham and directed by John G. Adolfi.

The film was released in 1920, and *Moving Picture World,* December 4, 1920, reviewed it: "The picture has dramatic and artistic qualities which are worthy of the return of an artist whose popularity has not been diminished by her absence. The experts who made the film presented not only the atmosphere of the Great North Woods, but contrasted it with society life. Greenwich Village scenes were used to great effect."

The picture dealt with the adventures of a little girl who, with her dog as her sole companion, flees the city and its shams, taking refuge in an old hunting shack on a large estate owned by Judge Carteret. There she tries to earn her own living with her paints and brushes. She exchanges her paintings at the village store for groceries and dog biscuits for herself and Omar, her canine companion. Though a squatter, she resents the intrusion of the new country home Judge Carteret is building. When she can no longer exchange her paintings for supplies, she invades the new mansion in an effort to sell her work and attracts the attention of Saxton Graves, an interior decorator, who has charge of the construction. She flees from him, but her reserve is broken down when Bobby, the son of Graves' widowed sister, is injured near her home, and she comes to the Graves house in response to Bobby's urgent appeals.

She is engaged to decorate the library of the judge's new home and is given a check for one thousand dollars. Later this is taken from her by her father, Giron, after he has vainly sought to play upon her supposed intrigue with the judge to get himself clear of a murder charge. He seeks to smear her reputation, using the check as a weapon, but the girl turns upon his accusation of improper relations with Carteret. Giron accidentally shoots himself, clearing the way for her marriage to Graves, while the judge wins Grave's sister.

*Moving Picture World* published this two-page spread of Mae Marsh in *The Little 'Fraid Lady* (1920).

Mae was surrounded by a supporting cast including Tully Marshall and Kathleen Kirkham. In the cast was Mae's nephew, George Bertholon, Jr., who played a large part in the story. His fall down a hill, pushed by his pet dog, served as one of the motivating forces of the action.

Of interest were the mural decorations on the walls of the set, done by Mae herself, during the course of the play. She was shown actually painting the decorations, and her work in this line came as a surprise to her many admirers. Familiar with her skill at screen playing, fans were unaware of her additional talent with brush and palette.

The scenes of Greenwich Village, New York's Bohemia, were taken on a specially constructed street resembling every detail of the famous section around Washington Square.

More than 200 people, costumed in masquerade regalia and evening dress, thronged in the scene of the artists' ball, creating a storm of paper with their confetti and dusters that rivaled the Mardi-Gras. There were novel dancing effects, and the story was said to be carefully advanced through the action.

Mae offered a technique ripened and more finely developed in this film, not only regaining but surpassing her former popularity. The quaint whimsies of manner previously marking her as a star in the old Biograph films were replaced by a more careful playing and an increased tenderness.

There were a number of animals in the picture, but particular attention surrounded a dog named Jacques III. When expressing dislike of his mistress' hat, he not only shook his head, but his expression matched his gesture. Jacques III earned numerous close-ups and he impressed audiences with an ability to feel the emotion he was supposed to depict.

*The Little 'Fraid Lady,* one of several 1920 films with Mae, fought for a position in the middle of a memorable array of other touching, dramatic films of that year. *The Last of the Mohicans* was a moving presentation of the famous story. Otis Skinner made his film debut in an elaborate, highly praised production of his famous play, *Kismet.* Ina Claire also made her attention-getting film debut in *Polly With a Past,* while Pola Negri emoted in a highly stylized version of *One Arabian Night.* Carol Dempster was winning her body of admirers with her work in *The Idol Dancer* and William Farnum maintained his hold on the public with his outstanding work in *If I Were King.* Jack Pickford was touching in *The Little Shepherd of Kingdom Come,* veteran star Clara Kimball Young tugged heartstrings with *Mid-Channel,* and Pauline Frederick wrung tears with her unforgettable role as *Madame X.*

*The Little 'Fraid Lady* was reviewed in *Moving Picture World,* December 18, 1920. Epes W. Sargent wrote,

> Robertson-Cole have spared no expense in the first production in which Mae Marsh is seen since her return to the screen. A cast of unusual excellence, a spectacular production of scenes of revelry in Greenwich Village, and some beautiful exterior locations combine to give real charm to a play abounding in improbable situations.
>
> The story makes a striving effort for suspense through the simple expedient of withholding the obvious, which will not fool the average patron, but the story provides Miss Marsh with limitless opportunities and serves to permit her to display a ripened technique. When the girl's father commands her to persuade her judicial friend to abandon a murder trial the audience knows very well that they are supposed to fear the worst, but they also know that the man must be the girl's father or she could not marry the hero, as she must in the end. Knowing this, the plot is robbed of its intended mystery, but even knowing this, we can still admire the work it gives Miss Marsh. The secondary star is easily a clever dog, with a bright boy, George Bertholom, Jr., a good third. In the adult cast is Tully Marshall who gives a strong performance; Herbert Prior plays with graceful ease, and Charles Meredith is boyish and convincing, if inclined to overact at times.

Sargent also felt the overall production was remarkably good, the settings artistic, and the exterior locations beautiful. He was also taken by the pictorial design of the dazzling splendors of the ball scenes, handled with

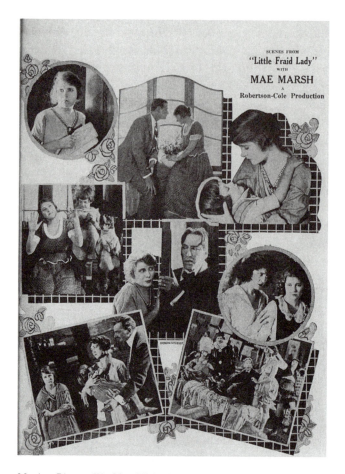

*Moving Picture World* published a composite of photos of scenes
from *The Little 'Fraid Lady* (1920).

an excellence of taste never seen before. By all such accounts, *The Little
'Fraid Lady* was a remarkable film from Mae's Goldwyn period.

Maude Cheatham wrote an article called "The Marsh Flower" in *Motion
Picture,* February, 1921, carefully observing the Mae Marsh of 1920:

> Even California skies sometimes behave like spoiled children, just when
> you want them to show off their prettiest and let the world behold their
> charms, clouds arise and they become dull and uninteresting. It was this
> kind of sky that was casting its somber spell over Hollywood and play-
> ing havoc with motion pictures the morning I had my interview with Mae
> Marsh. However, the famous little star remained serene and unconcerned,

letting her director, John G. Adolfi, do the worrying over silent cameras and loss of precious hours.

Mae Marsh is a name known everywhere that pictures are shown and this means in almost every nook and corner of this old world of ours. Typifying, as she does, all that is sweet and wholesome, dainty and feminine, Mae has won her laurels through consistent and hard work, and she is today one of the best loved of all the film stars.

After a year's absence she is once more at work before the camera, much to the joy of all fans and, she declares, even a greater joy to herself. This day, Miss Marsh was dressed in a funny little calico dress with a gay tam bobbing about on her unruly reddish brown hair.

Sitting on the steps of the country store, the pivotal point of the straggling street, she was childishly digging the toes of her sturdy shoes in the dust, while the remainder of the company lounged about, waiting for the sun to steal through the grey clouds.

A shout from the cameraman brought us back to the present, for the sun had burst forth, flooding the little set with its brilliance.

"Quick, let's get to work," called Director Adolfi, and the next moment Mae was enacting a pathetic little scene. She was in the midst of her new Robertson-Cole picture, *The Little 'Fraid Lady,* adapted from Marjorie Benton Cooke's story, "The Girl Who Lived in the Woods," and in the words of the star, it affords her a perfectly darling part.

Enthusiastically, she went on, "There is everything in it: tender pathos, wholesome humor, and the girl is so deliciously human all the way through that I have become deeply attached to her. This is because I seem actually to live her life." I did not doubt this, as I recalled how completely she merges herself into her screen characters, bringing a wistful and poignant appeal, peculiarly her own, which never fails to grip and hold attention.

"And the future?" I ventured.

"I want to go on and do better things in motion pictures. Some day, I hope to go on the stage. I believe all our experiences combine to make us better actors. We may not need to actually live through everything we act but at least, we must have gained a comprehension of the mental attitude attending such experience and this comes only by touching life at many points. I have always idolized Maude Adams, Julia Marlowe and Mrs. Fiske. They have been my inspiration. All three have lived, struggled, achieved."

Mae appeared in at least 80 additional films after *The Little 'Fraid Lady,* and starred in the next 17 of her pictures. She chose to retire, and played occasional supporting parts and cameos in several dozen sound films for the following three decades.

Sound films were no problem for Mae. She returned from retirement and played a touching role in Henry King's remake of the fine old Mary Carr tear-jerker, *Over the Hill* (1931), wringing tears from audiences with her portrayal. She was a natural for character roles, and worked in this manner for the next several decades.

Some of her most noticeable cameo appearances can be seen in the following films: In *Drums Along the Mohawk* (1939) she played a pioneer woman; in Tobacco Road (1941) she played a County Clerk's assistant; a miner's wife in *How Green Was My Valley* (1941); Floyd's wife in *The Grapes of Wrath* (1940); Leah in *Jane Eyre* (1944); the piano teacher in *A Tree Grows in Brooklyn* (1945); a flower lady in *The Dolly Sisters* (1945); Tommy's mother in *The Snake Pit* (1948); Miss Jenkins in *A Letter to Three Wives* (1949); Father Paul's mother in *The Quiet Man* (1952); a Jerusalem Woman aiding Demetrius in *The Robe* (1953); a party guest in Judy Garland's *A Star is Born* (1954); the Dark Cloaked Woman at Fort Guarding in *The Searchers* (1956); a family council member in *Donovan's Reef* (1953).

Mae Marsh overcame the handicap of inexperience to achieve the admiration of audiences and her peers, and in doing so, pioneered a style of acting technique still in use today.

## SILENT FILMOGRAPHY OF MAE MARSH

Ramona (1910) ★ Serious Sixteen (1910) ★ Fighting Blood (1911) ★ The Siren of Impulse (1912) ★ Just Like a Woman (1912) ★ One Is Business, the Other Crime (1912) ★ The Lesser Evil (1912) ★ The Old Actor (1912) ★ A Beast at Bay (1912) ★ When Kings Were the Law (1912) ★ Home Folks (1912) ★ A Temporary Truce (1912) ★ Lena and the Geese (1912) ★ The Spirit Awakened (1912) ★ The School Teacher and the Waif (1912) ★ An Indian Summer (1912) ★ Man's Genesis (1912) ★ The Sands of Dee (1912) ★ The Inner Circle (1912) ★ The Kentucky Girl (1912) ★ The Parasite (1912) ★ Two Daughters of Eve (1912) ★ For the Honor of the Seventh (1912) ★ Brutality (1912) ★ The New York Hat (1912) ★ The Indian Uprising at Sante Fe (1912) ★ Three Friends (1913) ★ The Telephone Girl and the Lady (1913) ★ An Adventure in the Autumn Woods (1913) ★ The Tender Hearted Boy (1913) ★ Love in an Apartment Hotel (1913) ★ Broken Ways (1913) ★ A Girl's Stratagem (1913) ★ Near to Earth (1913) ★ Fate (1913) ★ The Perfidy of Mary (1913) ★ The Little Tease (1913) ★ If We Only Knew (1913) ★ The Wanderer (1913) ★ His Mother's Son (1913) ★ A Timely Interception (1913) ★ Her Mother's Oath (1913) ★ The Reformers (1913) ★ Two Men of the Desert (1913) ★ Primitive Man (1913) ★ Influence of the Unknown (1913) ★ For the Son of the House (1913) ★ Judith of Bethulia (1913) ★ The Battle at Elderbush Gulch (1913) ★ Brute Force (1913) ★ The Great

Leap: Until Death Do Us Part (1913) ★ Home Sweet Home (1914) ★ The Escape (1914) ★ The Avenging Conscience (1914) ★ Moonshine Molly (1914) ★ The Birth of a Nation (1915) ★ The Outcast (1915) ★ The Outlaw's Revenge (1915) ★ The Victim (1915) ★ Her Shattered Idol (1915) ★ Big Jim's Heart (1915) ★ Hoodoo Ann (1916) ★ A Child of the Paris Streets (1916) ★ A Child of the Streets (1916) ★ The Wild Girl of the Sierras (1916) ★ The Marriage of Molly-O (1916) ★ Intolerance (1916) ★ The Little Liar (1916) ★ The Wharf Rat (1916) ★ Polly of the Circus (1917) ★ Sunshine Alley (1917) ★ The Cinderella Man (1917) ★ Field of Honor (1918) ★ The Beloved Traitor (1918) ★ The Face in the Dark (1918) ★ All Woman (1918) ★ The Glorious Adventure (1918) ★ Money Mad (1918) ★ Hidden Fires (1918) ★ The Racing Strain (1918) ★ The Bondage of Barbara (1919) ★ Spotlight Sadie (1919) ★ The Mother and the Law (1919) ★ The Little 'Fraid Lady (1919) ★ Nobody's Kid (1920) ★ Till We Meet Again (1920) ★ The Flames of Passion (1920) ★ The White Rose (1923) ★ Paddy the Next Best Thing (1923) ★ Daddies (1924) ★ Arabella (1924) ★ Tides of Passion (1925) ★ The Rat (1925) ★ Racing Through (1928) ★ Over the Hill (1931)

# MAE MURRAY

Mae Murray was called "the girl with the bee-stung lips." She was a fascinating, beautiful dancer, the living image of the new woman of the Roaring Twenties. "Once you become a star, you are always a star," was the lofty attitude Mae Murray clung to for most of her life. She was a popular star of early films, yet her name has slipped out of the consciousness of popular culture. Erich von Stroheim's *The Merry Widow* is the film for which she is best remembered, but it was not typical of most of her work. She walked a long road to success before gaining immortality in this one film. Ironically, *The Merry Widow* is the film she reportedly had the most unpleasant experience making. According to Kevin Brownlow in *The Parade's Gone By,* Von Stroheim extracted from Mae an unequalled performance, taking minute pains to probe from the depths of the woman's feelings nuances never before realized. Most of the directors for whom she emoted were satisfied to let Mae simply romp, dance, and freely express her lighter nature.

Mae Murray was born May 10, 1889, in Portsmouth, Virginia, as Marie Adrienne Koenig. Little is known about her childhood, but by her teenage years she was already in New York. She made her professional debut singing *Comin' Through the Rye* as Vernon Castle's partner in 1906 on Broadway in *About Town,* and soon appeared in the 1908, 1909, and 1915 *Ziegfeld Follies* as a featured dancer.

Mae stunned the opening night audience at the 1915 *Ziegfeld Follies* with two specialty numbers, making show business history in a single night. The first number, in a Persian harem setting, presented her in a seductive dance beside a lit pool, a bedazzling enchantress tempting a handsome prince. The second had her enter the darkened theater house and take a seat beside comedian Ed Wynn, excitedly telling him about her new movie role. On the stage, a huge screen descended, and an actual motion picture began starring Mae as Merry Pickum, a satire of Mary Pickford, in long, golden curls and antebellum hoop skirt in a travesty of a D. W. Griffith-style civil war story, the type of film audiences of 1915 had seen. Strangely, this skit created the impression that Mae was already working in films. Adolph Zukor quickly hired her and produced her film debut, costarring with Wallace Reid in *To Have and To Hold* (1916.)

"You know the story, don't you?" asked Mae of Grace Mack in a 1918 interview. She busied herself with the tea things spread out on a table of her garden behind the little Hollywood bungalow. Miss Mack came to learn why the beautiful star left her imminent position with the *Ziegfeld Follies.* She was surprised to see the movie giant was only a few inches over five feet in height, an elfin creature.

"No. You were one of the brightest luminaries of the *Follies.* Why did you leave for the golden West?"

"Well, in those days I usually got home with the milkman in the morning," Mae revealed. "There was a one o'clock closing, and dancing kept up until around three, and then by the time I had my makeup off and started for home, it was nearly four. One morning I was later than usual. The sun was about to rise. I made the taxi driver take me to Central Park, the air was so cool and sweet and fresh. It promised to be a very pearl of a day. And then, all in a second, I resolved to spend the day out of doors and in the country. I did spend all day long in the country in an old-fashioned country garden. I went to sleep in a flower bed, with an old hen and her chickens picking all around me. And that day I resolved to leave Broadway and the bright lights for the life I loved—the open country and God's own sunlight.

"I went into pictures not because of the money I could make as movie star, for when I first went in I was paid only a modest salary, much less than I had received as a stage dancer. But at last I had the chance to dance out of doors in the sunshine, and I was so much happier that the dollars couldn't make any difference one way or another.

"My real pay began when the postman started bringing to me letters telling me how this little girl and that one loved Mae Murray in the pictures. Then their mothers would write, saying that the kind of pictures I was doing were good for little girls to see. Oh, but that did make me happy! My public is made up of little girls and big girls and their mothers. The postman brings me many letters from them every week, but it is very seldom I have a letter from a man.

"Why?" asked the writer.

"Oh, I don't know," bantered Mae, tipping her muslin halo of a hat so the sun didn't shine in her eyes. "Don't you think that the people you start out to interest are those who pay the most attention to you?"

"Do you work as hard as you did in the Follies?"

"Work hard? I should say so," she exclaimed. "Only it's so much nicer to be working in the daytime and the sunshine, instead of all night. I am up before seven in the morning and ready for work at eight o'clock. All day I'm before the camera, whether it is in the studio or out on location, but I don't mind it a bit. At sunset the day is done and my stint is finished. Then I can come home to my little bungalow and sit out here in my little garden and near the muffled night noises. And then when it is time to turn in—and I do it awfully early—guess what?"

The writer couldn't.

"Why, I just curl up right on that swinging hammock in a corner of the porch. Sometimes the wind blows it a little, and that's heavenly. And when it rains, see, I can let down that waterproof flap and still be comfortable out of doors at the same time. I just cannot bear to be under cover a minute, since I started to live out of doors. Perhaps I am making up for lost time—the time I danced away under artificial lights all night long."

Her films were often made outdoors, and frequently lit with diffused sunlight on open-air stages. Each story usually featured her in at least one dance scene, making great use of her powerful and effective manner with dance.

Adela Rogers St. Johns observed her instinct for the theatrical in 1924:

I have seen her dancing at the Montmartre with some dark-haired youth. She comes quietly from her table, her golden hair hidden beneath a twisted black turban. Her famous figure is clothed so demurely, so simply, in black velvet. No jewels. No make-up. The floor is packed with couples mad to dance. Unobtrusively she slips in among them, the music sways her, the pretty head flings up, the black velvet whirls about her, revealing unexpected shimmerings of silver and tiny shoes with diamond buckles and sheer stockings that make you think of slender, nude legs. In ten minutes, she and her partner have the floor to themselves and the dancers are watching, although apparently Mae Murray hasn't noticed either their departure or their attention. And yet I swear to you that Miss Murray has done nothing that the most perfect lady might not do, worn nothing that a perfect lady might not wear, and danced nothing that many debutantes cannot dance.

Joan Crawford frequently remarked that she spent her free hours as an ingénue at Metro-Golden-Mayer Studios haunting the sets of the great women stars of the day, especially Mae's. She watched the way the star controlled and used every muscle in her body to make a visible drama out of the simple act of walking across the floor.

Her beauty transcended the early years of screen imagery in the teens, a style that reflected the Victorian era's girl-next-door, virginal purity. After World War I, when styles from that era accelerated to a more modern type, she quickly remade her image in the Roaring Twenties' style of sharp hair designs and reconstructive makeup. Her famous bee-stung lips were the vogue in the 1920s, epitomized by many leading ladies of the screen.

She starred in 44 films, from *To Have and to Hold* (1916) to *High Stakes* (1931). Her early image changed from wholesome, virtuous girls to classic vamps, as illustrated by some of the titles of her films: *Sweet Kitty Bellairs; The Dream Girl; The Big Sister; The Plow Girl; A Mormon Maid; The Primrose Ring; Princess Virtue; The Bride's Awakening* were some of her films from 1916–1918. These titles evolved into the dissipations of jazz-age youths, exemplified by their names: *Modern Love; The ABC of Love; A Delicious Little Devil; Jazz Mania; Mademoiselle Midnight; Married Flirts; The Merry Widow; Altars of Desire,* all from the 1918–1925 era.

*Fascination* was one of these MGM films made to showcase Mae Murray, her face, her style of movement, and her personality. The film had no other reason for being. Appropriately titled, the movie-going public was fascinated with her, and her husband, director Robert Leonard, knew well how to capture the essence of his wife's charms.

In *Fascination,* Mae played Dolores de Lisa, daughter of the Spanish-American aristocrat Eduardo de Lisa. Dolores' upbringing in New York fashions her into a typical, carefree flapper with no responsibilities at all. She is whisked away by her aunt to Spain where it is hoped she can be reformed into a lady. But the playful Dolores meets and falls in love with Carrita, a toreador, forgetting about her fiancé left behind in America.

Her fiancé travels to Spain to reunite with Dolores, but she has vanished, having run off to the bullfights. He runs into trouble and Dolores saves him from his difficulties. In the end, she decides to return to her fiancé and subdue her life into one of sedate bliss.

Production on *Fascination* was influenced by Will Hays, a member of President Harding's cabinet, who was hired to head the Motion Picture Producers and Distributors of American, Inc. It was his role to police the content of motion pictures, a measure tantamount to censorship, self-imposed by the industry to stem any governmental interference amount-

MARCH 25¢

CLASSIC

A BREWSTER PUBLICATION

Mae Murray

*Motion Picture Classic,* March, 1923, showcased Mae Murray on the front cover.

ing to Federal censorship. The scandals involving Fatty Arbuckle, Mabel Normand, Mary Miles Minter, William Desmond Taylor, Olive Thomas, Wallace Reid, and others simply reached the boiling point as far as public relations were concerned. The industry could no longer afford to allow the personal lives of men and women of the industry and the content of various films to inflame the moral anger of patrons, many of whom were on the warpath against the perceived wanton ways of the denizens of Hollywood. The Hays office would enforce strict rules of behavior and content. A lengthy list of do's and don'ts were imposed on the producers, and a morals clause was included in every contract. It was a massive bleaching of the industry, aimed to eradicate offenses before they happened.

In spite of the restrictions levied by the Hays office, many a questionable point was included in films, now done with the power of suggestion rather than overt depiction. Writers and directors were forced to resort to creative ways to suggest improprieties, and this often caused points unsaid and unseen to be more powerful than if they had been spelled out in detail. For example, D. W. Griffith's *Intolerance,* made before the Hays office rules, featured two shots of men appearing to have their heads lopped off in battle. A scene of this type in future films would show a soldier swinging a sword, then cut to the horrified reaction of some onlooker, then finish with the lifeless and headless body of the victim. In this manner, the delicate sensibilities of those audience members prone to easy shock would be spared. It also sucked the guts out of many films.

*Fascination* was released in April of 1922. It was the year a Mexican dancer, Ramon Samaniegos, was transformed by director Rex Ingram from an extra into a star in *The Prisoner of Zenda.* The greatest achievement in documentary films came with Robert J. Flaherty's *Nanook of the North.* Alla Nazimova was appearing in her infamous production of *Salome,* Constance Talmadge appeared against type as an oriental girl in *East is West,* and Dorothy Gish starred in *The Country Flapper.* The biggest hit of the year was Douglas Fairbanks' *Robin Hood,* but audiences were also flocking to several Harold Lloyd comedies. Lillian and Dorothy Gish were causing lines to form around the block wherever theaters were showing Griffith's *Orphans of the Storm,* and Rudolph Valentino was packing theaters with *Blood and Sand.*

As MGM shipped crates of reels containing *Fascination* to theaters, an industry screening prompted *Photoplay,* July, 1922, to describe the film: "Mae Murray, as a fifth Avenue flapper with no responsibilities at all, makes glorious promises she fails to keep after the first two reels. She goes to Spain, plays around with a toreador, poses for misty close-ups, and even does a 'lilliangish'. What might have been good comedy-drama degenerates into Spanish love and hate, made in New York. Why does the lovely Mae do it?"

*Variety,* April 21, 1922 said the following of the film:

[The film was] a great box office title, it seems, as was attested by the S.R.O. business Easter Sunday. It is an original story by Edmund Goulding, which affords the star ample opportunity for display of her peculiar personality, pep and dancing, the action starting in America and winding up in romantic Spain. This is enough excuse for Robert Z. Leonard, the star's director-husband, to spread himself on the fandango and castanet hokum, and he has spread it on wisely and well. Taking the situation of Dolores' fascination for Carrita, the toreador idol of Spain, as the central situation, Leonard and the scenario writer have revolved a series of bizarre and colorful situations around it.

Mae Murray was known for wearing outrageously glamorous gowns in
many of her films. *Fascination* (1922) kept her well-suited in a parade
of splendid outfits.

Miss Murray is supported by a high-grade cast, which by no means
detracts from the star's individuality. Robert W. Frazer as Carrita portrays
the matador in a sympathetic light, the audience seemingly disappointed at
his fate in jail for an attempt to avenge his honor, which was falsely sullied
by Parola, a dancer. Helen Ware as the dancer was perfect in the characterization, as was Emily Fitzroy as the aunt, another unsympathetic role.

The production represents real money. The costuming and settings are
lavish and in keeping with the locale and action. The direction is even,
although during the fore section it assumes a farce vein with some of Miss
Murray's alleged flapper retorts.

*Fascination* was one of these hot, jazz-age films, loaded with flaming
youth, bee-stung lips, and prohibition defiance. Mae Murray typified the
emerging, postwar woman of independence, boldly striking through the
morals and manners of the Victorian era and setting the pace for a vibrant,
new style of living.

The Dance of the Bulls stirred up a heated controversy and was criticized by many for the lurid and suggestive movements deployed by Mae.
*Fascination* was also lambasted for its depiction of the Spanish matador,
played in the film by Robert Frazer. After a particularly stinging letter to

*Movie Weekly* by one critic, Mae came in to the publication's office and spent two days with the editors composing her defensive rebuttal, hoping to squelch the criticism. The letter read:

My dear Mr. Gonzalez:

In the August 5th issue of *Movie Weekly,* the Editor publishes a letter answering mine. This letter is a series of retractions and erroneous statements.

Your last letter proves many things. You admit you are not a Spaniard, but a Cuban. Your mother owns a hotel in Havana and is of an old Cuban family, and you, by your criticism, are not a Spaniard. Don't you, yourself, know that Cuba is not Spain and Cubans are not Spaniards? America at one time was ruled by England, and most of the settlers were English. That doesn't make Americans English, nor would they, the Americans, attempt to criticize anything English.

You act in the same manner as a Society calling themselves 'Andalusians,' because Francis Cugat, a Spaniard, did not consult them on arriving in Cuba. The article you sent in regarding scenes taken in Cuba was a copy of an article published by them in a Cuban paper while we were in Cuba, but you did not print the article which appeared the next day, apologizing.

The man in whose paper the article appeared is a gentleman of honor and intelligence and knew how absurd such a statement was and caused it to be retracted. You failed to print this, or, possibly, it did not suit your purpose.

As our story was about Spain, we could not take the ideas of Cubans. This was resented by a handful of people. The Andalusian Society and you have all waited for a chance to air your grievance and bring yourself to notice through my name. It is always a bad thing to hold hatred and to try to hurt anyone, as it only acts as a boomerang. In this case, it makes you ridiculous. You make statements and then contradict them; when you see you are made foolish you try another, as you now try to criticize the matador's attire.

Every custom, every detail, even the collars, ties, shirts, shoes, were absolute and true copies of illustrations found in present-day periodicals from Spain and not Cuba. These periodicals are sent to the Carnegie Library, where we accumulated our data. They were consulted not only by our advisor, but by myself. Anyone who would choose to go to this same library would see that every matador does not wear the same collar nor the same shirt, that in viewing half a dozen pictures of matadors there is a difference not only in the way they wear their hair, but in collars, ties, etcetera. From a month to six weeks was given to just such a simple detail.

As I have been to Cuba and Spain and the difference in the two countries being so apparent, I would suggest that before attempting again to speak of Spain, you pay it a visit, and you will then observe that although you speak the same language, your lives and costumes are totally different.

Your statements regarding a Spanish Consul are untrue as are your other statements regarding information received from the Metro Office. Both of these will be taken care of by those mentioned.

About the Cuban people I met, I can only say the most charming things. They are a lovable and enthusiastic, as well as an appreciative race; but about this handful of Andalusians, who think they know all there is to know of Spain and who are trying to hurt a man who is a scholar and who really does know about Spain—I have only pity. They acted like children. You speak about the majority of people being ignorant. Are you so qualified to judge?

I wonder if by your own work, you will arrive at a place where the world will know your name. This is only done by hard work—not attempting to tear down another's work and purpose. To do these things takes all of one's time, so don't try to bring yourself into the vision of others by trying to criticize others—*do something*—only by our work are we measured.

Very sincerely yours,

(Signed) Mae Murray

Francesco Cugat, Mae's attorney, also wrote a letter in defense of her Dance of the Bulls, in addition to supporting the authenticity of her costuming, saying in part:

As for the dance, that is decidedly Miss Murray's. I don't think any mere trifling words can take away the original and beautiful impression that she, as an artist, created. How could anyone connect such a simple, unique and innocent dance with the Spanish version of 'horns.' When she brought in her conception of the costume she wished to use, I, knowing this legend, would certainly have told her and designed it otherwise if it had impressed me as imitating a 'satyr.' But this conception impressed me as being only a fantastic dance of the bull. It is well to bear in mind *it is not a Spanish dance,* but a dance of an American girl.

Mae starred in seven more films of the same type as *Fascination,* and then made the film for which she was immortalized. *The Merry Widow* (1925) has been exhaustively written about in many motion picture history books. Director Erich von Stroheim created a lavish, highly detailed and sophisticated look at the degradation of a poor working girl, denied the love of an important man by his family, and her later transformation into a sparkling and glib widow of enormous wealth. Von Stroheim elicited from Mae a performance that was superb, her greatest work in motion pictures, and the film was an enormous hit. Still shown today, *The Merry Widow* was one of the best films of the silent era and, oddly enough, one of Mae's least typical. Much has been written about the stormy production and the con-

Mae Murray in a fantasy dance sequence in *Fascination* (1922).

stant clashes between the headstrong star and the equally iron-willed director. It is enough to say Von Stroheim pounded out of Mae a performance of depth and sincerity that, were there an Academy of Motion Picture Arts and Sciences in 1925, she would surely have been nominated for the Best Actress of the year.

Mae immediately reverted back to her formula on completion of *The Merry Widow.* Her three remaining films were silent, *The Masked Bride* (1925), *Valencia* (1926), and *Altars of Desire* (1927). She appeared with dozens of other stars in a cameo appearance in the Marion Davies comedy, *Show People* (1928).

Mae starred in a few early talkie films, *Peacock Alley* (1930), *Bachelor Apartment* (1931), and *High Stakes* (1931), but after the crash of the stock market and the horrors of the depression in the early 1930s, her film career as an exotic fantasy creature had passed its vogue.

Her marriage to Prince Mdivani ended and she lost custody of her son; she was forced into bankruptcy and barely survived the next two decades. When *Sunset Boulevard* was released in the early 1950s, Mae was briefly interviewed by reporters after the premier of the now-classic Billy Wilder film. She was viewed as an example of the Norma Desmond type of deranged, silent film actress. "None of us floozies was that nuts!" she was quoted to have flung to the reporters, according to Jane Ardmore in the biography she cowrote with Mae.

In her later years a sort of dementia seemed to overcome her. Richard Griffith wrote in *The Movie Stars,* "Her appearance eventually became an outlandish caricature of the superstar, rather a dangerous caricature. She would walk down Fifth Avenue with her head bent back as far as it would go, as if she was gazing at the heavens. The concerned observer realized that she was trying to present a youthful chin line to passersby, and he hoped that she wouldn't fall flat on her face at the next curbstone. She was said to have wangled invitations to charity balls, which she attended all the time, she would command the orchestra to play the theme tune from

*The Merry Widow* and waltz to it solo, compelling the paying customers to withdraw from the dance floor."

In *Nazimova,* author Gavin Lambert claimed Alla Nazimova was said to have written an entry in her personal diary quipping: "Mae Murray MUST have $330.00 to pay for her child's operation. I gave her a check. She gave me an IOU." With Mae's career gone and her mind skidding into orbit, the next time she ran into Nazimova she denied having ever signed any IOU. "It must have been someone else pretending to be me," she reportedly claimed. On close inspection of the IOU, the signature was scrawled as "Mary Murray". Nazimova's diary noted on a May 17, 1936 entry: "Mae Murray has vanished." In a later incident, she was found wandering in the park by the Salvation Army.

She cowrote her autobiography in 1959, and spent her last days in the Motion Picture Country Home, in Woodland Hills, California. "And what has become of those beautiful young faces that graced the screen and our lives so long ago—if measured in time?" asked Francis Marion in *Off With Their Heads.*

Year after year the church bells have been tolling.... some lie in mausoleums, flower bedecked at Easter.... others in graves that bear only their names, long forgotten by the public that once idolized them. Many are living, secure in their homes, with children and grandchildren. Quite a few are at the Motion Picture Country Home, where old friends meet to peer at faded photographs or to read aloud their favorable notices, the newspaper clippings yellowed with age. Here there is companionship, not loneliness.... Mae Murray never knew that she had found her way home; her disturbed mind was aware of nothing beyond her pitiful vanity. "Step aside, peasants! Let the Princess Mdivani pass!" she demanded imperiously of the nurses who came forward to help her into the hospital. "Where are the cameras? Where are my flowers? I must be photographed with flowers! Get them before I'm surrounded by cameramen!" A doctor came forward. "If you're a Hearst reporter, be sure to mention that I've just finished my memoirs." She wheeled on the nurses. "Music! I always make my entrance with music! Have your orchestra play *The Merry Widow Waltz.* That's the number I made famous." She held out her hand to the doctor. "May I introduce myself? I'm Mae Murray, the young Ziegfeld beauty with the bee-stung lips—and Hollywood is calling me." He caught her in his arms as she slumped forward. "Poor old thing," said one of the nurses....

She died in 1965.

## SILENT FILMOGRAPHY OF MAE MURRAY

To Have and to Hold (1916) ★ Sweet Kitty Bellairs (1916) ★ The Dream Girl (1916) ★ The Big Sister (1916) ★ The Plow Girl(1916) ★ On Record (1917) ★ A Mormon Maid (1917) ★ The Primrose Ring (1917) ★ At First Sight (1917) ★ Princess Virtue (1917) ★ Face Value (1918) ★ The Bride's Awakening (1918) ★ Her Body in Bond (1918) ★ Modern Love (1918) ★ Danger, Go Slow (1918) ★ The Scarlet Shadow (1919) ★ The Twin Pawns (1919) ★ What Am I Bid? (1919) ★ A Delicious Little Devil (1919) ★ Big Little Person (1919) ★ ABC of Love (1919) ★ On with the Dance (1920) ★ The Right to Love (1920) ★ Idols of Clay (1920) ★ The Gilded Lily (1921) ★ Peacock Alley (1922) ★ Fascination (1922) ★ Broadway Rose (1922) ★ Jazzmania (1923) ★ Fashion Row (1923) ★ The French Doll (1923) ★ Mademoiselle Midnight (1924) ★ Married Flirts (1924) ★ Circe, the Enchantress (1924) ★ The Merry Widow (1925) ★ The Masked Bride (1925) ★ Valencia (1926) ★ Altars of Desire (1927) ★ Show People (1928)

# ALLA NAZIMOVA

Alla Nazimova, the stage's supreme muse of the works of Ibsen, transferred to the silent screen a unique dramatization of her greatest stage success, *A Doll's House.* The studios objected, Nazimova insisted, and the end result proved her vision was right. She won critical acclaim for her work. The reluctant, shortsighted men who ruled the film studio failed to preserve this effort. *A Doll's House* is considered one of the most-coveted lost films.

Alla was born Mariam Edez Adelaida Leventon in the Ukraine and endured an appalling childhood in Russia where she was abused by her father and shunned by her stepmother. At age 17, abandoning her training as a violinist, she quietly studied theater with assorted young actresses with whom she shared a boarding house.

At age 17 she auditioned at the Philharmonic School in Moscow with Konstantin Stanislavsky. Her work with the Moscow Art Theatre led to tours of the United States, where she impressed the Shubert Brothers. The theatrical giants opened her in *Hedda Gabler* in English. For the following several years she established a reputation as the outstanding portrayer of the Ibsen works, *A Doll's House, The Wild Duck, The Master Builder,* and *Little Eyolf.* She became the darling of the New York Theater, alternating between Ibsen's heavy plays and lighter fare.

*A Doll's House,* the famous story of Nora Helmer, has been a role coveted by actresses from Ibsen's first presentation of the play. The story initially concerns a forgery Nora committed many years earlier to save her husband's life. A blackmailer threatens to reveal the shame of her act to Torvald, her authoritarian husband, and ruin his illustrious career. When the truth finally comes out, Nora is shocked to learn where she is held in her overbearing husband's esteem, prompting Nora to walk out on both her husband and her children.

Alla appeared in *A Doll's House* in English for the first time in 1907. According to Gavin Lambert, in his book, *Nazimova,* she commented: "It was the misfortune of Nora that she had been made into a doll through her training first by her father, then by her husband. Nora can change.... but how can her husband change when he thinks everything he does is exactly right? She could not help him, he could only hinder her. That is why she never came back." A particularly noted touch in her performance came at the dramatic climax of the play when Nora leaves her husband. Alla was seen to caress the door with her hands. The simple but moving gesture was noticed by critics, and when expounded upon in reviews, was a surprise to Alla. She had made the gesture, but made it unconsciously. After the effect was brought to her conscious attention, and that of the public, she carefully amended each night's performance by including the telling pantomime.

In February 1908, Alla toured in *The Master Builder, A Doll's House,* and *Hedda Gabler.* The plays were sold out for three weeks in Washington, impressing critics there as her identity with Ibsen spread across the country. D. W. Griffith invited her to visit him at the Biograph Studios. While there, he was said to have advised her not to do pictures at that time as they were not ready for her exotic type. Alla's skill with pantomime, as part of careful gestures in her stage presentation, ideally suited her for the cinema, and Griffith's warning notwithstanding, she made a quiet resolution to ply her craft in the fledgling medium of motion pictures. The gateway to Hollywood soon opened for the star.

During the early years of World War I, she appeared on the stage in a one-act pacifist drama, *War Brides.* The story was set in an unnamed European country, and focused upon a woman, Joan, losing two brothers and her husband in the war. An order resounds from the king of the land for women to bear more children to fight future wars. Joan organizes a backlash, protesting the ungodly requirement. When threatened with jail for disobeying the order, Joan shoots herself. The play was a resounding hit, breaking house records during its twice-daily, four-week run. A six-month tour of the Keith-Orpheum circuit took Alla around the country with *War Brides,* and when the torpedoed ocean liner, *The Lusitania,* sank off the coast of Ireland, audiences rallied to the war effort with unheard of zeal. *War Brides* fanned the flame of pacifism as America shifted from a position of neutrality.

Lewis J. Selznick offered Alla $30,000 to star in the film version of *War Brides,* with an additional bonus of $1,000 for each days schedule overran the planned 30 day production. Herbert Brenon was hired to direct, and some of the play's actors repeated their roles in the film. Richard Barthelmess, the college-age son of her English tutor, was enticed to forgo education and join the cast as Joan's son in the film version of the play. It was the motion picture debut of Barthelmess, who would go on to great success in many films.

Alla also debuted in films in *War Brides* (1916) and immediately created a sensation with her exotic manner, powerful presence, and sincere portrayal. Metro offered her a five-year, $13,000 a week contract, and she had a meteoric career appearing in 17 silent films.

Frances Marion, already a renowned writer within the film industry, recalled speaking to Rudolph Valentino after he appeared with Alla in *Camille.* He was lavish in his praise, and remembered how Alla painstakingly rehearsed him until she actually got him to act, not to strike poses or hang an actor's gesture out as a symbol of an emotion. He expressed gratitude for the important training she generously gave him.

Frances recollected in her memoirs the puzzlement expressed by many over Alla's enigmatic personality. "There was beauty in the irregularity of her features, the depth of her searching eyes, her mobile mouth that could smile with a child's smile, then appear as cruel as a hawk's beak." Alla gave very few people the chance to intimately know her. She was like the Sphinx, silent and mysterious at night, but garish and faulted in the noonday sun.

As her success in films grew, Alla became convinced that she alone could best direct her efforts, and a break with Metro opened the door of opportunity for her to give vent to the extravagant aspirations festering in her mind. She visualized highly stylistic presentations of her stage success, *A Doll's House,* and the Biblical tale of *Salome.* After several major companies refused to finance the projects, she made the unwise decision to produce both films with her personal savings. She wrote the screenplay, assigning the assumed name in the credits to "Peter M. Winters," and recruited her husband, Charles Bryant, to make his directorial debut with *A Doll's House.* Wallace Beery took on the role of Tovald, Nora's husband.

Alla discussed *Salome* and *A Doll's House* enthusiastically with Frances Marion. "They shall rise above these mediocre pictures which I've been forced to accept," she told Frances. "I visualize *Salome* as a Russian ballet, ephemeral, yet imperishable because it is of the spirit. *A Doll's House* must embody the stark realism of Ibsen, for that is of the theater."

She took full responsibility for the success or failure of the productions, guided by a firm belief in the positive reception both films would earn with

Alla Nazimova in her prime, a pensive portrait ca. 1922.

the public and critics alike. For Alla, the effort was more than just a career gamble, it was the realization of her destiny.

After several weeks of shooting it became apparent that photography was not capturing the 42-year-old actress admirably, and Beery felt he was unable to do justice to the role. Alla and Beery parted amiably, Alan Hale stepped into the Tovald role, a new camera man was brought in, and shooting continued. Alla knew little about photography, but the new results gained by the lensing of Charles Van Enger made her look ten years younger, the right age, Alla felt, for her character. The play was slightly opened up for pictures, in the example of the final scene. In the play version, Nora leaves her husband and children by pausing at the door of their middle-class home, caressing the door, and then exiting. In the filmed version, her newfound freedom is accentuated by a depiction of her outside, the camera following her after she slams the door, pulling a fur-trimmed hat and coat close around her body, and walking away into the snow with a suitcase, facing life alone.

A pioneer in the modern technique of acting without elaborate mannerisms, Alla believed that gestures must have some form of inner justification that emphasized thought. This technique was never so apparent than in her film production of *A Doll's House.*

This film production of the popular play is both forgotten and fascinating, forgotten because so few living people have seen it, and fascinating because of its compelling and mysterious star. A legend in the history of twentieth-century theater, her work is known more by reputation than by experience. *A Doll's House* appears to be a lost film, as are most of her silent films, another of the great tragedies of the neglect and carelessness of the major film studios.

*A Doll's House* was not the only film made from a famous play and released in 1922. Among the most outstanding titles, the year also offered *Tess of the Storm Country* with Mary Pickford, *Clarence* with Wallace Reid, Ramon Novarro and

Alla Nazimova in a winter exterior shot from *A Doll's House* (1922).

Alice Terry in *The Prisoner of Zenda,* and John Gilbert and Estelle Taylor in *The Count of Monte Cristo.*

Ibsen's plays had been filmed as motion picture treatments many times prior to 1922. Both the form and substance of his plays were not standard, pictorial material well-suited to the art of the cinema. They were essentially stage plays, and as such, relied heavily on dialogue interaction and character presentation. Henry B. Walthall had presented an early version of *Ghosts,* and *A Doll's House* was essayed by Dorothy Phillips in 1917 and by Elsie Ferguson in 1918, both reputed to have been rather tame adaptations of the play. Alla brought to her version of the film the experience gained from having played the part many times on the stage.

*The New York Times,* in a 1922 review, indicated the following:

> The essential quality of the action, of course, is not pictorial. There is relatively little in it to satisfy the moving camera. But by getting away from the Ibsen form as much as possible, and at the same time keeping close to the Ibsen spirit, a conscientious and intelligent director, aided by a great staff, can make an interesting and at times forceful substitute for words. And this is what has

been done in the present instance. The picture, for example, goes back to the beginning of the married life of Torvald Helmer. And Norma, much of Ibsen's off-stage action is shown on the screen, and the ending, in which the future of Torvald and Nora is not determined, is adhered to. With regard to the latter, perhaps, a stronger sense of the ultimate reunion of Helmer and his wife in the photoplay than in the original play, but it is at no time suggested. The outcome is left to the spectators and to their own imaginations. And for this, as well as for the intelligence and sincerity with which they have done their works, those responsible for the photoplay are to be congratulated.

One of the best things about this version of *A Doll's House* was said to be the way in which the various moments of the play were filmed by the camera with great intimacy. *The New York Times* reviewer noted as a prime example the scene in which the ex-convict and money lender exchanged clandestine dealings.

*Motion Picture News,* February 25, 1922, said the film was undoubtedly the best of the many productions made up to that time. As a silent film, the magazine said, it had been denatured. The review went on to point out,

> The picture is simply the story of a young wife who, after making a great sacrifice to save her husband's life, finds him unworthy of her love and decides to leave him. In evolving a picture play from the original script, no actual liberties have been taken with the plot. Action and incident, even though rather trivial, has been substituted for words and the characters move about and get over effectually and without the excessive use of titles, all that is necessary in unfolding the plot.
>
> How well the picture will please the aggressive, however, is another matter. Lovers of Ibsen may object because the Ibsen touch is missing. Those who know little of Ibsen and considerable about pictures, may think that the plot lacks punch and is rather trite.

The picture was extremely well acted. Though often difficult to subdue, Alla corrected many of her noted film-acting faults by carefully displaying no disposition to strike poses, and was said to be truly effective in her emotional scenes. The supporting cast was rated flawless, being pointedly chosen as types and proving to be excellent counterparts for the star.

*Motion Picture News* concluded their review by stating, "The production as a whole is adequate. Good sets have been provided and the photoplay and camera work are satisfactory. Also considering that the dramatic strength of the plot is not great, an excellent continuity has been evolved. The picture makes no attempt to be foreign in atmosphere and is presented as a drama which might happen anywhere. Every human emotion is pictured, and all the elements of a really great photoplay are to be found in *A Doll's House*."

Alla ran the gamut of emotions from comedy to pathos, even to the point of laughter and tears. Her experience with the role in live theater indicated where there was to be humor in the situations where Nora, the doll-like wife, made her odd and ludicrous mistakes as a housekeeper and as a mother of an infant and two beautiful children. She presented a lesson for all women everywhere in bringing out the big point in the play, namely, that every woman has the right to control her own destiny and develop the full realization of her own individuality and personality.

*Variety,* February 17, 1922, said,

With this picture it is just a question whether or not the coupling of the name of Mme. Nazimova with the Ibsen play in which she appeared on the speaking stage is to draw any money. As a film, *A Doll's House* is entirely lacking in action to make it particularly worthwhile, and the hoydenish acting of Nazimova can hardly be expected to put it over.

As a picture, even with Mme. Nazimova, it is rather tiresome and old fashioned and this particular production is so handled to give it more the atmosphere of a foreign production.

Mme. Nazimova as the star, and her husband, Charles Bryant, as the director, have managed to pick Scandinavian types for the principal roles, and it must be said that the selection of Alan Hale for Torvald was a most happy one, but Mr. Hale was undoubtedly over-directed, unquestionably he was compelled to overact in a couple of the scenes. This is what lends so much of a foreign production atmosphere to the feature.

Mme. Nazimova seemed at all times to be forcing herself in the playing of the role and it is doubtful if her interpretation of Nora will enhance her screen value to any great extent. Photography is of the rather dark sort without any shading as to lights. The sets are adequate, although a couple of storm exteriors showed plainly that it was studio stuff that was used.

The director, Charles Bryant, born January 8, 1879, lived with Alla and directed her in a number of her silent films. Though never married, the two claimed to be wed by common law and continued the pretense for nearly 20 years.

Alan Hale, the actor playing Nora's husband, was a pioneer film actor in hundreds of films from 1911 to 1950, but he is best known for sharing his name with his son, Alan Hale, Jr., famous for playing Skipper on the *Gilligan's Island* television series. Some of Alan Hale Sr.'s outstanding work was in *Life's Whirlpool* (1917) with Ethel Barrymore, *The Four Horsemen of the Apocalypse* (1921), *Robin Hood* (1922), *The Covered Wagon* (1923), *Susan Lenox* (1931) with Greta Garbo, *The Sin of Madelon Claudet* (1931) with Helen Hayes, *The Lost Patrol* (1934), *Of Human*

Alla Nazimova and Alan Hale in *A Doll's House*
(1922).

*Bondage* (1934), *The Crusades* (1935), *Robin Hood* (1938), and many
more top productions.

*A Doll's House* was made twice since, by Claire Bloom and again by
Jane Fonda, both in 1973. Alla pitted her will to elevate the status of motion
pictures against the male studio heads. She was blind to their criticism and
ultimately proved to be her own downfall.

*Salome* (1923) was a fine motion picture that flashed across the world's
screens and caused critics to bare the heads in wondering awe and mur-
mur a prayer of devout gratitude. Then came the dull, sickening thud
which inevitably occurred when any meteoric masterpiece lands in the
box office. It was a financial disaster. Theater owners thought it suicidal to
book it. The production was noteworthy in every sense of the word: It was
extraordinarily beautiful to look at, rich with exquisitely designed pictorial
values; It was well acted, and the action was continuous with no break in
the sequences or events; It was oddly free of the usual explanatory subtitles marring many films, and Alla earned the gratitude of everyone who

believed in the possibilities of the movies as art. The trade journals of the
time urged exhibitors to book it and proclaim its artistic values. But many
of the critics and those few audience members who paid to see it thought
it degrading, unintelligent. The famous Biblical tale was modernized into
a highly charged, poetic atmosphere.

Thomas Craven, a reviewer for *The New Republic*, described the deba-
cle angrily:

> Nazimova, as the daughter of Herodias, has attempted a part for which she
> has no qualifications. She flits hither and thither with the mincing step of a
> toe-dancer; she has the figure of a boy, and in her absurd costume, a satin
> bathing suit of recent pattern, she impresses one as the old Tetrarch's cup-
> bearer. Try as she will she cannot be seductive—the physical handicap is
> insurmountable; she tosses her head impudently, grimaces repeatedly and
> rolls her eyes with a vitreous stare. The effect is comic. The deadly lure
> of sex, which haunts the Wilde drama like a subtle poison, is dispelled the
> instant one beholds her puerile form. The Dance of the Seven Veils, used by
> the poet to release the hideous consequences of lust, is wholly innocuous.
> Not that one expected, in these censorial days, a *danse du ventre,* but had
> Nazimova appeared in the garb contrived by Beardsley she might at least
> have given a touch of reality to her epicene antics. The other characters can
> be disposed of summarily.

*Salome* was so weird, it has stood the test of time, and copies of it are
still being bought and sold today. It defies description; it is so outland-
ishly stylish and bizarre that it is actually enjoyable. It is a case of a film
being so bad it is good, but it was truly ahead of its time. Audiences of
1923 found it bewildering and unsavory. Many were even sickened by
it. Nazimova's career in films crashed and burned after the release of
*Salome.*

After her production of *Salome* lost her what remained of her fortune,
Alla made a few additional films and returned to the stage during the late
'20s in *Woman of the Earth, Mother India,* and *The Cherry Orchard.* Other
plays included *A Month in the Country, Mourning Becomes Electra,* and
*The Good Earth.*

She flirted with a return to Hollywood, making a sound test for RKO
that neither pleased the studio nor herself. She continued her career, successfully appearing on the stage in *Ghosts* and *The Mother,* along with
sporadic attempts at an autobiography.

Hollywood again invited her to test, this time for the role of Mrs. Dan-
vers in Alfred Hitchcock's *Rebecca,* but she lost the role to Judith Anderson.

An NBC radio presentation of the Everyman's Theater presented Alla in *The Ivory Tower* on July 8, 1939. In August, one week *before* World War II began in Europe, she was broadcast in *This Lonely Heart.*

Louis B. Mayer immediately authorized production of two anti-Nazi movies, *The Mortal Storm* and *Escape.* Edith Vance's suspense novel, *Escape,* was about a renowned actress rescued from a concentration camp by her son. George Cukor was set to direct, and he requested Alla to return to Los Angeles to test for the role of the actress. When Mervyn Le Roy was substituted for Cukor, she was brought back to MGM for a second test, her hair dyed black, and ordered to underplay the scene. This time, she was following the rejected tests of Judith Anderson and appeared to be a front-runner for the role. The film's star, Norma Shearer, lobbied heavily for Alla, and she won the role. She relished the small but pivotal part, especially the scene where she was smuggled out of the concentration camp in a coffin.

In the fall of 1942, along with Blanche Yurka, Flora Robson, and Greta Garbo, she tested for the role of Pilar in *For Whom the Bell Tolls,* directed by Sam Wood, but she failed to obtain the engagement.

She won the role of Madame Ranevskaya in Warner Brothers' *In Our Time,* about a Polish family during the German invasion. The part was relatively small, but she brought to it the fragile quality of an aristocrat living in the past.

David O. Selznick, remembering his father's success with Alla in many films, had a part specially written for her in *Since You Went Away.* Her scenes were filmed in February of 1944, and though they add up to only six minutes of screen time, they reveal an undeniably great actress. She portrayed a drab immigrant mother describing how she and her little son "prayed that God would let us go to the fairyland across the sea," and stunned audiences with a moving recital of the inscription on the Statue of Liberty. The cameo was a fittingly memorable climax to her spectacular film career.

She died in Los Angeles of coronary thrombosis on July 2, 1945. Alla Nazimova was admirable for overcoming the barriers of language and the restrictions of the silent cinema. Her determination to pioneer the presentation of the art of Ibsen within the confines of an industry that stressed commercialism won the praise of critics and the admiration of many fans. In her own way, she loved the movies, and put her time and money into the effort to raise their standards. Her life has become legendary, and as her films resurface one at a time from secluded crypts, her notable performances restore her prestige as an actress to each new generation. *The*

*Red Lantern* has been rediscovered, and hopefully, *A Doll's House* will be found in a surviving print.

## SILENT FILMOGRAPHY OF ALLA NAZIMOVA

War Brides (1916) ★ Revelation (1918) ★ Toys of Fate (1918) ★ Eye for Eye (1918) ★ Out of the Fog (1919) ★ The Red Lantern (1919) ★ The Brat (1919) ★ Stronger Than Death (1920) ★ The Heart of a Child (1920) ★ Madame Peacock (1920) ★ Billions (1920) ★ Camille (1921) ★ A Doll's House (1922) ★ Salome (1923) ★ Madonna of the Streets (1924) ★ The Redeeming Sin (1925) ★ My Son (1925)

# CONSTANCE TALMADGE

Constance Talmadge, one of Hollywood's most popular comediennes, crested at the height of her fame in *Dulcy,* one of her greatest successes. She was a beautiful girl with a great sense of humor who gained the pinnacle of stardom despite inexperience. She achieved film immortality as the Mountain Girl of ancient Babylon in D. W. Griffith's *Intolerance.* She made 84 films from 1914 to 1929, and when sound technology arrested the industry, had the courage to end her film career, turning down offers from the studios that profited from her efforts and walked away from their cameras forever.

Here are some fascinating aspects of her life:

When Grauman's Chinese Theater opened in Los Angeles, she was among the first stars to place foot and hand prints in the cement squares of the forecourt. Her panel is fittingly located directly behind the box office, unique with the imprints of five feet.

Her sister was actress Norma Talmadge, and they both became stars of the movies while in their teens.

She was one of the few women in Hollywood who could drive a chariot.

Her film career was exclusively in silent films. She never made a sound film.

Her first marriage was a double wedding with Dorothy Gish and James Rennie.

She was lovingly nicknamed "Dutch" because, as a child tomboy with blonde hair and brown eyes, friends said she looked like a little Dutch boy.

In 1927, Constance and Norma Talmadge opened the Talmadge Park real estate development in San Diego, California, USA, now known as the Talmadge District, located about a mile southwest of the San Diego State University campus.

Talmadge Street in Hollywood, California, USA, is named for Norma and Constance. Originally it ran along the west side of the Vitagraph studio where the sisters made some of their movies. It is now the site of the ABC Television Center.

Constance was one of the most loved young women working in silent movies. Her older sister, Norma, had become a star at Vitagraph several years before her as a dramatic actress, while Constance's specialty was sharp, witty comedies.

Constance was a vivacious girl, and when she accompanied her sister to the Vitagraph studios, she was often observed playfully imitating their leading ladies. She had no real interest in pursuing a dramatic career, and were it not for the pushing of her mother, teenage Constance would have had none of the discipline required for theatrical success.

In *The Talmadge Sisters* her mother remembered, "I imagined that Constance would come home in a state of perfect adulation. But although she went to admire, she remained to scoff! She returned after her first day, simply bursting with a desire for laughter. Not one of the Vitagraph actors or actresses was exempt from her mimicry."

"Peg," she exclaimed, "they do a love scene like this..." Whereupon she proceeded to give an imitation of Flora Finch, the pinch-faced comedienne of John Bunny comedies, in the throes of the tender passion.

"After the first few days we could not keep Constance away from the studio," recalled her mother. "It must have been instinct, or despair of her doing anything else, that prompted my consent. I must have known intuitively that they would recognize the child's spirit of drollery at the Vitagraph, as we recognized and delighted in it at home. Either they will love her, I thought, or she will make them simply furious. The chances seemed about even."

It was soon after that Thomas Ince, the well-known film director, allowed Constance to appear as an extra in films for 25 dollars a week. D. W. Griffith chanced to see her sister Norma in a film, and offered her a contract to join his Triangle company in Los Angeles, California.

"Of course, Norma cannot go to Los Angeles alone," her mother stated.

"But what shall I do?" wailed Constance, "I don't want to stay here alone either. Why Peg, I couldn't possibly remain by myself, without you and Norma and Natalie. Yet, if I go to California, I'll lose my chance at the Vitagraph just when I was beginning to get somewhere."

"Constance, I promise to see that you do get a chance, if you'll only come with us, dear," Norma said. "I realize it may seem selfish to take you away from Vitagraph, just because I've had the offer, but I'm sure we ought to go. Just think, Constance—Griffith!"

*The Birth of a Nation,* directed by D.W. Griffith, had just taken the world by its astounding power. He was considered the preeminent director of motion pictures.

Constance arose and snapped a dramatic finger. "Write Mr. Griffith on your best party stationery," she said, "that the three Misses Talmadge and their mother are packing tonight!"

Three days later they were en route to Griffith in California, stars in the making. Norma made seven pictures under Griffith's supervision, and Constance took various small parts in films made at the Triangle Company. "Despite the fact that she was doing these small parts and doing them very well, and receiving a very good salary, I always suspected, in the privacy of my own mind, that part of Constance's value to Mr. Griffith lay in the fact that she amused him," Peg Talmadge mused. "I think she made him laugh largely because of her absolute disregard of his importance, in contrast to the awe and respect and head-bowing accorded him by all the others."

"Just sent for you, Constance, because I want to laugh," Griffith would say.

"Well, here I am. Your Majesty may begin at once," was her stock reply. She would make a bow of mock humility, and the very sight of her seemed to set him off immediately. In the back of his mind, Griffith was planning his tremendous production, *Intolerance,* and all the while he had Constance in mind for a certain part, but he said nothing to her until the eleventh hour. The part was that of the Mountain Girl of Babylon. When he finally told her she was to play the part, Constance threw both arms around him and they had a long talk. She promised him, with tears in her laughing eyes, she would do her best and study every angle of the part.

Karl Brown, Griffith's assistant camera man, remembered *Intolerance* was made as four separate motion pictures. As there was no script, each day's shooting was for a particular bit of detail known only to Griffith. He spent much of the film seeing to the details of photography on each setup, often having no idea how the setup fit into the body of the entire film. He recalled in *Adventures with D. W. Griffith* Constance actually played two roles within *Intolerance,* one being a fancy dressed-up part in the French episode, and the other more famous role of a rough and tough, onion-chewing hoyden known as The Mountain Girl of Babylon. "She was so wonderfully well liked that nobody ever thought of calling her Miss Talmadge. She was Connie, and she loved it. Connie had to drive her chariot all over everywhere in a wild ride to the rescue of someone, somewhere, who seemed to be in a lot of trouble, nobody knew just what. Anyway, we got the rides to the rescue all safely on film and maybe later Griffith would come up with someone in dire need of rescuing," Brown reflected.

She took to the role with fervid intensity and was determined and tireless. She became the Mountain Girl as Griffith visualized. "When she described to me what she was to do, including the chariot race, I felt dubious—and a little afraid for her," remembered her mother.

"Don't worry about me and the horses. I'll drive them to a fare-thee-well, you'll see," declared Constance.

For weeks before the scenes were filmed, Constance rehearsed from morning until night, not only learning the management of the horses, but learning to balance herself creditably in a rocking, swerving, swaying chariot. At night she practiced by standing on two rocking chairs side-by-side. And every night of those weeks she came home stiff, black and blue, but undaunted. After the release of *Intolerance* she was immediately acclaimed, and a flood of offers came from various companies.

"No sooner had I breathed freely once more at Constance's escape from death in the *Intolerance* chariot than Jack Pickford came along with a sporty new roadster presented to him by Mary," Constance's mother agonized, "and filled me with a new fear. Jack made boon companions of Constance and Dorothy and their favorite amusement was to have him race up a steep hill at full speed, reach the top, quickly reverse the gears and let the car slide backwards all the way down. Constance assured me that she could recommend this as an 'A-1 thrill' and invited me to join. Needless to say, I found a number of important things to do around the house. But Jack and the girls thought it a marvelous hair-raising sensation and seemed to think that my anxiety was the finishing comedy touch—if their shrieks of mirth at my terrified face meant anything."

Griffith re-edited *Intolerance* repeatedly after its initial release, and even shot new scenes long after it was in distribution. Grace Kingsley found Constance in her dressing room at the Fine Arts Studio, in Los Angeles, in the midst of making up for some new shots.

"Did you really drive those galloping brutes of horses?" asked Miss Kingsley.

"Indeed I did," stated Constance. "Two women sat behind me at the Auditorium the other night. They said, 'Of course she never really drove those horses herself. Somebody doubled for her.' Know what I did? I turned around and told them, 'I wish I could show you my knees, all black and blue even yet from being cracked up against the dashboard of that chariot!'"

So popular was her portrayal of the tomboyish Mountain Girl, Griffith released in 1919 the Babylonian sequence from *Intolerance* as a new, separate film called *The Fall of Babylon*. He refilmed her death scene to allow for a happy ending.

Both Talmadge sisters were quite unconcerned about the eminence they had achieved. The same camaraderie which existed in their family existed in the studios where they worked. Connie, as her friends called her, was interested in the outside life of every member of her companies, and knew the first name of every property man. She loved people and loved good times, and best of all, she had ideals and did not attempt to conceal them.

Her brother-in-law, Joseph M. Schenck, set up the Constance Talmadge Film Company in 1917, solely to produce bubbly, light comedies with her. She was given full control regarding scripts and costars, and her films were enormously popular.

When Constance was asked by *Green Book Magazine* what sort of stories she wanted to do in 1920 she said:

Although no less than sixty manuscripts are submitted to me every week, it is exceedingly difficult to get exactly the kind of comedy I especially want. I want comedies of manners, comedies that are funny because they delight one's sense of what is ridiculously human in the way of little everyday commonplace foibles and frailties—subtle comedies, not comedies of the slap stick variety.

I enjoy making people laugh. Secondly, because this type of work comes easiest and most naturally to me, I am not a highly emotional type. My sister could cry real tears over two sofa cushions stuffed into a long dress and white lace cap, to look like a dead baby, and she would do it so convincingly that 900 persons out front would weep with her. That is real art, but my kind of talent would lead me to bounce that padded baby up and down on my knee with absurd grimaces that would make the same 900 roar with laughter.

You see, in my way, I take my work quite as seriously as my sister does hers—I would be just as in earnest about making the baby seem ridiculous as she would about making it seem real. I am not fitted to be a vamp type. There is nothing alluring, or exotic, or erotic, or neurotic about me. I could not pull the vamp stuff to save my life, but if I am assigned a vamp role in a comedy, and I had such a part in my fourth First National picture, *In Search of a Sinner.*

I play it with all the seriousness and earnestness and sincerity with which a real vamp would play it, except that I, of course, over-emphasize all the characteristics of the vampire. I try to handle a comedy role much the same way that a cartoonist handles his pencils. If he is drawing the picture of the late Theodore Roosevelt, with a few strokes he emphasizes Teddy's eye-glasses and teeth, leaving his ears and nostrils and the lines of his face barely suggestive. One must leave a great deal to the imagination on the screen, because in the span of one short hour we sometimes have to develop a character from girlhood to womanhood through three marriages and two divorces, and perhaps travel half way round the world besides; so, like the cartoonist, I try to emphasize the salient characteristics, which, of course, in my particular work, bring out the humorous side of the person I am portraying.

Constance went on a vacation to Europe with her mother, and on their return, she married her first husband, John Pialoglou, a Greek tobacco importer. He was handsome, and an exceptional ballroom dancer. Constance was flirtatious, a well-known girl about town, liked to stay up late, dance through the night, and play cards with women who harbored hidden liquor stashes during the era of prohibition. Her association with Pialoglou was brief, and after a few months of partying, returned to work in five movies written by Anita Loos and John Emerson: *Dangerous Business, Mama's Affair, Woman's Place, Polly of the Follies,* and *Dulcy.*

Anita Loos and John Emerson commented in the September 4, 1921, *New York Times* about the improved technique they were writing into *Dulcy* and Constance's other films. Emerson commented:

There is a great deal of talk about developments in technique, but one seldom finds any specific statement as to just what these changes are. It is rather difficult to be specific in such matters, but Miss Loos and myself can number off a few of them, at least.

First comes the diminution of the number of sequences, that is, episodes in each picture. Formerly there were literally dozens of sequences, which tended to give the picture a choppy, jumpy effect, with a most syncopated tempo. These sequences are like the acts or scenes of a play, and, just as the play has gradually reduced the number of acts and scenes, so the movies are reducing the number of sequences.

Secondly, there has been a move toward the elimination of what are known as "narrative sub-titles"—those deadly inserts which read, "Little Mary comes home and tells father that mother has gone away forever," thereby ruining all the action which follows.

Pat Talmadge, recalled in *The Talmadge Sisters,* "There too, Anita Loos and John Emerson first crossed out path, and became our very close friends.

Little did we think, then, that the day was not so very distant when we would be in a position to engage these clever collaborators to write and supervise a series of five-reel comedies for our own Constance, and little did they imagine, in those days, that the time was coming when their marriage would be celebrated at the Talmadge country home at Bayside, Long Island."

Anita Loos and John Emerson had many opportunities to study Constance and observe to good account what peculiarities of her personality set people to laughing. When Constance formed her own company, their inimitable comedy vehicles were a large part of Constance's success. "In engaging the Emerson-Loos combination," her mother remembered, "Mr. Schenck recognized the value of having his authors live day by day with their stories, watching their production, and making sure that their works were screened as they were written. Because of the large financial returns John and Anita were to receive for this series, the writer became as important to the motion picture as he had always been to the dramatic stage."

Constance made people laugh because she laughed first at the follies and foibles of modern culture. Mack Sennett, the King of Hollywood's fun factory, has often been credited with developing most of the great comic talent of the silent film. He began in films working with D. W. Griffith as an actor at the same time Anita Loos was writing stories for his one-reel Biograph films. Sennett experienced Griffith's tutelage with Constance, and he understood the comic bent Constance saw in people and their manners. He spoke profoundly of the psychology of film comedy, as he knew it, and as Anita Loos practiced it with her Constance Talmadge films in a 1918 interview with *Motion Picture Classic:*

> Movie fans do not like to see pretty girls smeared up with pastry. Shetland ponies and pretty girls are immune. It is an axiom of screen comedy that a Shetland pony must never be put in an undignified position. People don't like it. You can take any kind of liberties with a donkey. They even like to see the noble lion rough-housed, but not a pony. You might as well show Santa Claus being mistreated.
>
> The immunity of pretty girls doesn't go quite as far as the immunity of the Shetland pony, however. You can put a pretty girl in a comedy shower bath. You can have her fall into mud puddles. They will laugh at that. But the spectacle of a girl dripping with pie is displeasing.
>
> These conventions are more marked in comedy than in other forms of movie drama. In comedy the events are piled on too rapidly to admit of much character drawing. You can't go into the personality of a preacher to show the audience that he is not a proper candidate for sympathy. When you put side-whiskers on him and top him with a stove-pipe hat the movie fans understand the trade-mark. They know that he is due for disasters.

So much of the material out of which comedies are built. Most of the materials are old. All jokes are old, and there are only a few of them. One of the earliest inscriptions found in Egypt was a joke about a mother-in-law told in hieroglyphics.

Skillful comedy direction consists of arrangement of these comedy elements. And the arrangement involves a knowledge—either instinctive or studied—of the psychology of the man sitting out there in the dark in front of the screen. You must know how he thinks and how fast he thinks. The extent to which you get in tune with him is the measure of your screen success.

*Dulcy* is the kind of picture Constance described as appealing to her sense of wit, a sparkling, witty, contemporary comedy of manners that kidded the foibles of the day. It was the kind of comedy of popular culture Anita Loos was so profound in highlighting and which Sennett believed would be palatable to audiences of the era. It was one of her biggest hits, capturing the essence of her personality and presenting her unique wit in a light, silly, escapist vein, the perfect formula for her continued success.

*Dulcy* was released in August of 1923, the same year Constance also starred in *The Dangerous Maid.* Other outstanding films showing at the same time were Charles Ray in *The Courtship of Miles Standish,* Marion Davies in *Little Old New York,* Blanche Sweet in *In The Palace of the King,* George Walsh in *Vanity Fair,* and Richard Dix and Rod La Rocque in Cecil B. DeMille's *The Ten Commandments.* Paramount released a timeless western classic, *The Covered Wagon,* while Selznick released a sequel to *The Prisoner of Zenda* called *Rupert of Hentzau.*

*The New York Times* described *Dulcy* in September, 1923: "A splendid picture has been made of the stage's *Dulcy.* Cynical souls were never doubtful of the ability of the silent drama to do justice to this particular play. The play, they argued, required, as its central figure, merely an adorable nitwit to give it life. Surely, they said, this was one requirement the movies would be able to meet. The actress would have to be one who would lend her talents to a most ungrateful part, as such things are reckoned in the movie world that knows only fat and lean roles. This actress, Constance Talmadge, to reveal the secret and remove the strain, showed a hitherto almost unrevealed sense for delicate light comedy, and that in a medium, the screen, to wit, that has not in the past been known for its ready welcome to delicate light comedy delineators."

The story of *Dulcy* was well known to people in New York, having been based on a popular play by George S. Kaufman and Marc Connelly. The comedy concerned itself with the well-meaning young wife, peculiarly enough known as Dulcy, who almost ruins all her adored husband's

An advertising poster for the world premier of *Dulcy* (1923).

chances for the business successes he craves by a series of good-natured idiocies.

She takes Mr. Forbes, with whom her husband is trying to consummate a big deal, along with his wife and daughter, into their charming home for a weekend, and there submits him to a series of indignities. In the unintentional matters she almost ruins his desire to do business with any one connected with Dulcy or her husband.

Mr. Forbes tells Dulcy about his aversion to sports of all kinds, for example, with a hatred reaching from the present back to his childhood. The well-meaning Dulcy, thinking she could show him the better side of outdoor recreations, plans for him a program of sports-related activities. Forbes feels obligated to adhere to her regime through regard for the courtesy of social amenities, participating even though doing so may kill him. Dulcy provides him with a horse to straddle for a ride with the family. The skittish horse bucks and ultimately throws Forbes. She compels him to go

Constance Talmadge and Jack Mulhall in a scene from *Dulcy* (1923).

in swimming and diving, though he nearly breaks his back. She schedules a round of tennis, and he turns his ankle.

*The New York Times* concluded by noting,

> Constance Talmadge, as has been said, is most adorable. Hers is a most difficult part to play, granted the legitimate movie responses to situations, but she successfully avoids the usual silver screen clinches. She makes her motive for her stupidity, her love for her husband, most plausible, and she is extremely dexterous in her manners of blundering. In the business of her part, too, she has a light effect—with the bumping of her brother off the bench that he shares with her—that may, if developed, take its place alongside the Chaplin shuffle.
>
> Johnny Harron, as Dulcy's brother, and Claude Gillingwater, as her husband, are natural, human and likable. The rest of the cast is adequate throughout and in every way equal to the demands placed upon them.
>
> Some slight fault might be found by carping souls with the captioning of the picture. There is, for example, "The evening falls—but no one is injured."

Constance Talmadge, the star of *Dulcy* (1923).

*Dulcy* was Constance's 72nd film. Although many of her films have been lost, she is joyfully remembered by many who cherish her work in *Intolerance,* the one film which has been seen by more people than all her other films put together. She made eleven more films after *Dulcy,* and when sound films became a reality in the late 1920s and she observed her sister Norma suffering critically in two poorly recorded early talkies, both she and Norma walked away from their careers, rich, married, and content. By the year 1931 both she and her sister were gone from movies and noticeably absent from the popular fan magazines of the day.

Although Norma attempted to continue her career in sound film, Constance did not. *Venus,* her final film in 1929, was made as a silent even as the hammers were pounding soundproof material into the walls of the stages as she worked. The industry was changing from all-silent to all-sound in the brief six months of after the completion of her last film.

In May of 1929 she married a wealthy man and vowed she would never make another film. She walked away from it all and had no reason to look back. Her career was a means to an end, and the end was security. Her mother fostered the belief she might one day return to films. "Success and fame cast a spell that can never been quite shaken off," she pointed out. "A woman, because of her love, may say, and in the fervor of the moment believe, that she is ready to give up her chosen work. But there is sure to come a time when keen longing and strong regret for her lost career dominate over the more placid contentments of love and marriage. Then unhappiness and friction ensue." Constance never gave films another thought, and she never regretted her decision. She gracefully lived 44 more years and died of pneumonia in November of 1973.

Constance Talmadge deserves to be remembered because she excelled in the formative years of the film industry, etching a style that has been rarely duplicated. Despite inexperience, she developed notable skills and made fortunes for many producers. As a young woman in a new industry during World War I, she broke through the barriers that kept women on the lower steps of the corporate ladder and climbed to the top. She was a shining example to millions of girls in America that hard work, determination, and perseverance could open the doors of success.

## SILENT FILMOGRAPHY OF CONSTANCE TALMADGE

In Bridal Attire (1914) ★ Uncle Bill (1914) ★ The Peacemaker (1914) ★ Our Fairy Play (1914) ★ The Mysterious Lodger (1914) ★ The Moonstone of Fez (1914) ★ The Maid from Sweden (1914) ★ In the Latin Quarter (1914) ★ Forcing Dad's Consent (1914) ★ Fixing Their Dads (1914) ★ Father's Timepiece (1914) ★ The Evolution of Percival (1914) ★ The Egyptian Mummy (1914) ★ Buddy's First Call (1914) ★ Buddy's Downfall (1914) ★ The Young Man Who Figgered (1915) ★ Billy the Bear Tamer (1915) ★ The Vanishing Vault (1915) ★ A Study in Tramps (1915) ★ Spades Are Trumps (1915) ★ The Master of His House (1915) ★ The Little Puritan (1915) ★ The Lady of Shalott (1915) ★ A Keyboard Strategy (1915) ★ The Green Cat (1915) ★ Georgia Pearce (1915) ★ Captivating Mary Carstairs (1915) ★ Can You Beat It? (1915) ★ Burglarious Billy (1915) ★ The Boarding House Feud (1915) ★ Billy's Wager (1915) ★ Bertie's Stratagem (1915) ★ Beached and Bleached (1915) ★ The Missing Links (1916) ★ Intolerance (1916) ★ The Microscope Mystery (1916) ★ The Matrimaniac (1916) ★ The She-Devil (1916) ★ A Girl of the Timber Claims (1917) ★ Betsy's Burglar (1917) ★ Scandal (1917) ★ The Honeymoon (1917) ★ The Studio Girl (1918) ★ The Shuttle (1918) ★ Up the Road with Sallie (1918) ★ The Lesson (1918) ★ Good Night, Paul (1918) ★ A Pair of Silk Stockings (1918) ★ Sauce for the Goose (1918) ★ Mrs. Leffingwell's Boots (1918) ★ A Lady's

Name (1918) ★ Who Cares? (1919) ★ Romance and Arabella (1919) ★ Experimental Marriage (1919) ★ The Veiled Adventure (1919) ★ Happiness a la Mode (1919) ★ The Fall of Babylon (1919) ★ A Temperamental Wife (1919) ★ A Virtuous Vamp (1919) ★ Two Weeks (1920) ★ In Search of a Sinner (1920) ★ The Love Expert (1920) ★ The Perfect Woman (1920) ★ Good References (1920) ★ Dangerous Business (1920) ★ Mama's Affair (1921) ★ Lessons in Love (1921) ★ Wedding Bells (1921) ★ Polly of the Follies (1922) ★ The Primitive Lover (1922) ★ East is West (1922) ★ Dulcy (1923) ★ The Dangerous Maid (1923) ★ The Goldfish (1924) ★ Her Night of Romance (1924) ★ Learning to Love (1925) ★ Seven Chances (1925) ★ Her Sister from Paris (1925) ★ The Duchess of Buffalo (1926) ★ Venus of Venice (1927) ★ Breakfast at Sunrise (1927) ★ Venus (1929)

# NORMA TALMADGE

Margaret "Peg" Talmadge gave birth to Norma, her first daughter, on May 26, 1897, in Brooklyn. She and her husband raised Norma with her sisters, Constance and Natalie, in a loving home, often watching them at play and wondering which of the three would become famous as a painter. She bought them crayons and closely observed the girls. "I would watch them attentively, wondering which one would eventually turn out to be the artist," she later wrote in *The Talmadge Sisters.* "It is hard to conceive the importance I attached to these early products of their childish imaginations, not only with painting. I never failed to gather any concrete results of their creative play, study each carefully in my leisure hours, and fondly tuck away those which I thought showed most promise. While I was thus eagerly watching for signs of art, my husband, whose tastes inclined to music, secretly hoped that at least one of our little girls would some day become a famous virtuoso."

To foster this ambition, Norma's father purchased a piano and a mandolin, and insisted on keeping the piano open at all times, hoping the white ivory keys would attract the little girls to his love of music. As Norma grew older, she wavered in her preference for the piano or mandolin, but a chance comment from a visitor pointed her life in a new direction. As Norma sat on the floor strumming the mandolin, the friend, amused at the pose she struck, remarked, "With her dark, snappy eyes and beautiful olive skin, she looks very Latin indeed." Apparently the compliment was not lost on Norma, for she later adopted this pose whenever company was expected. "Why did I not recognize the first, fine traces of the actress in her then?" Margaret later questioned. "We were so bent on having an artistic genius in our family that, later on, we even attributed Natalie's early taste for reading to a subconscious desire to write!"

The girls studied at Public School No. 9 on Vanderbilt Avenue, and after three o'clock there were many amateur attempts in the cellar or back yard as their little neighborhood theater. A number of animal acts were included in the repertoire, for the youngsters were particularly fond of bringing stray dogs and cats into the home to be nursed back to health and then formally adopted. Norma wrote plays, improvised scenery, strung together costumes, and acted the leading parts.

Norma was encouraged to take many a part in the school plays, and when her mother noticed the girl showed a profound expertise, she thought it only natural Norma should go to the Vitagraph Studios in Flatbush with the hundreds of other screen-struck ones. Her pretty face, charming manner, and a little pushing from her mother soon won an engagement for her.

The first week at Vitagraph, Norma did no work. She carefully observed Florence Turner, the reigning star of the lot, working on a film with the other inhabitants of the pioneer lot. She met many of the technicians, asking questions about the proceedings and soaking up the atmosphere of the studio. Years later, in Albert Smith's book, *Two Reels and a Crank,* Norma spoke of those first days at Vitagraph: "Florence Turner was my idol. I never missed a single picture in which she appeared and I would rather have touched the hem of her skirt than to have shaken hands with Saint Peter. Leaning forward in my hard chair, I was as much a part of Florence Turner as was her own reflection on the silver sheet. I laughed when she laughed, suffered when she suffered, wept when she wept. A veritable orgy of emotions for five copper pennies."

Albert Smith recalled, "From the start my confidence in Norma Talmadge was unshakable. There were dissenters on all sides, loud in their praise of her beauty but contending she was difficult to direct. At one time Vitagraph had some sixteen directors who could not see Norma in this, that, or any role."

The second week at Vitagraph passed in much the same manner for Norma. Finally, on the third week she was given a small part in a picture called *The Household Pest,* a film about a horse that was always getting people into hot water. Norma later recalled in *Moving Picture World,* "My bit was to be kissing a young man, whose name I forgot, on a street corner, under a black cloth that was thrown over a camera, until the horse came along and lifted the cloth with her teeth. Only the back of my head was revealed, with my arms around the youth's neck. Then we had to run away. That was a sad humiliation for me—to be in the movies at last and not show my face! At the end of the day I received two dollars and fifty cents for my services, and Constance was given two dollars. But more precious to me than any amount of money was the sweet smile from Miss Turner as she handed us our envelopes.... she had charge of the supers' salaries and doled out their money every evening. Also, she helped her mother with the wardrobe department."

Norma's next role had her appearing in blackface in *A Dixie Mother* with Florence Turner and early matinee idol, Maurice Costello. For the next six years Norma learned the craft of film acting with these veterans of Vitagraph, playing in at least 86 films, an amazingly prolific output. These pioneering films gave her a supreme grasp of the techniques of communication through the medium of silent shadows.

The Vitagraph players often visited picture theaters to gauge the reaction of audiences to their latest release, and Norma was usually the center of attraction. She developed a big following and received hundreds of letters each week from fans around the world. Vitagraph was convinced that she had the making of a star. In the years before World War I Vitagraph films were among the best-sellers, and from Europe came demands for more of Norma's pictures. The Vitagraph, before the war, was one of the best-sellers abroad. European sales paid all the studio expenses and the American market added rich profits into the company. Low salaries were paid all around, and Margaret began to entertain offers from other studios.

Norma's mother noted her daughter's success in films began to accelerate after she was featured in a three-reel adaptation of *A Tale of Two Cities.* "Things began to take a turn," she remembered. "After her success in *A Tale of Two Cities* Norma was given several comedy parts and one or two emotional roles. Her versatility was often discussed by producers and directors."

Rex Ingram, pioneering director of *The Four Horsemen of the Apocalypse* and many outstanding films, remembered in *The Griffith Actresses* seeing Norma in the film *A Tale of Two Cities:*

In 1913, when I was studying drawing and sculpture at the Yale School of Fine Arts, a motion picture play, founded upon Charles Dickens' famous story, *A Tale of Two Cities,* came to New Haven. It followed in the wake of many cut and dried one-reel subjects, and while this picture was necessarily full of imperfections, common to all pioneer films, it marked a tremendous step ahead in the making of them. I left the theater greatly impressed; absolutely convinced that it would be through the medium of the film play to the production of which the laws that govern the fine arts had been applied, that a universal understanding and appreciation of art finally would be reached. I brought several friends of mine, most of them either students of the art school, or members of the Yale Dramatic Association, the following day to see this picture, which had been made by the Vitagraph Company of America, and each and every one of them was as much impressed as I. All of us thereupon decided to enter the motion picture field.

James Morrison, an actor at the American Academy of Dramatic Arts, specialized in pantomime and wangled a job at Vitagraph. In an interview with Kevin Brownlow for *The Parade's Gone By* he remembered appearing in the same film with Norma: "The first thing I did was *A Tale of Two Cities*—and this was one of Norma Talmadge's first appearances, too. I played the peasant brother, and Lillian Walker played my sister. In one scene I had to leap a balustrade and attack the Marquis, while a big ball was going on. I went back as far as I could to get momentum, about twenty-five feet against the wall—then I ran forward, and as I leaped the balcony I let out a loud yell. Afterward, Julia Swayne Gordon told me, 'When I heard that cry, it really struck truth to me. I was in the toilet at the time, but I had to come out to see who on earth had done it.' So my training had not been in vain!"

Mrs. Talmadge knew her daughter was destined to be a part of something bigger than even her dreams could imagine. "And when Commodore Blackton decided to startle the film world with a big feature picture, *The Battle Cry of Peace,* the forerunner of what we call super-productions today, he chose Norma for the big part," she told. "This picture really lived up to that hackneyed phrase 'it took the public by storm,' and Norma literally woke up famous." Albert Smith remembered hearing Blackton bemoaning his lot before making the film. It seemed he had an incredible story ready to be filmed, then discovered all the suitable Vitagraph actresses were busy in other pictures. Smith suggested Norma for the leading female role in *The Battle Cry of Peace.*

"Norma! I'm doing *The Battle Cry of Peace,*" Blackton exclaimed, "and she wouldn't possibly be right for that."

"Why not?" challenged Smith.

"Look, Al, there's a scene in that picture which requires the girl to turn her lovely bare back to the audience and act out her deep emotional feelings in that position—with her back!"

"Look, I'll use her but only at your risk," surrendered Blackton.

"Right." Smith later claimed the film was one of Norma's best, and the high spot of her portrayal was the sinuous bareback scene.

Marshall Neilan, director of the Mary Pickford films, *Stella Maris,* *Amarilly of Clothesline Alley,* and *Daddy Long Legs,* analyzed Norma's

Norma Talmadge earned film stardom with her
role in *The Battle Cry of Peace* (1915).

appeal for the *Photoplay Research Society:* "An analysis of this attractive
star's success places her in the forefront of those who hold their admirers
through *temperament.* Often it is attributed to actresses but seldom pos-
sessed to such an extent as Norma Talmadge possesses it. It is her extreme
sensitiveness to every possible emotion, her poignant response to a hundred different moods, which, expressed in vivid play of features and gestures, mark her as a truly superior personality."

Herbert Brenon, who later directed Norma in *The Passion Flower*
(1921), said in *Motion Picture Magazine,*

> *Temperament* is more sensed than actually seen. I know that to many, the
> words "artistic temperament" bring to mind ranting and tearing of hair. Of
> course, some temperaments have expressed themselves in that way. Other
> natures have found an outlet in complete isolation from their fellow beings.
> Tears bring relief to some temperaments. Others turn to silence. And some
> to a forced, unnatural gaiety. During my years as a director, it has been my
> pleasure, my pleasure, to work with some of the most temperamental stars

One-sheet poster from the 1915 film, *The Battle Cry of Peace*.

on the screen.... I find that the more temperamental an actor is, the easier it is for him to grasp all the subtleties of a role and imbue it with life, instead of merely playing a part.... Pola Negri is very temperamental, but she has her temper under tight control. She, like such other high-strung actresses as Norma Talmadge and Anna Q. Nilsson, resorts to tears if anything goes wrong. These three women I rate among the best on the screen today. It is a joy to direct them, they are so sensitive to impressions. But if any one of them is asked to portray a character in a way that she thinks is alien to the part, she will not be able to go on.

Norma went on to make her breakthrough impression with a landmark film by J. Stuart Blackton. *The Battle Cry of Peace* could have been taken straight out of the newspaper headlines of September 11, 2001, when a seemingly defenseless America was attacked at the Pentagon and the New York World Trade Center by invading forces. Ironically, the film premiered in September, 1915 at the Vitagraph Theater on Broadway.

J. Stuart Blackton's screen version of Hudson Maxim's *Defenseless America* presented a picture of the ruthless crushing of New York by an invading force. The screen filled with glimpses of foreign emissaries at work in America and was designed to cast suspicion on all those who opposed the hoped-for Army and Navy appropriations for the looming World War I. With its spectacle of the chief of the pacifists rapturously releasing doves at the peace meeting at the very moment a hostile fleet is approaching our shores, the film was intended to rout with ridicule the peace-at-any-price followers.

World War I motivated some filmmakers to call for productions that showcased the excitement of war and the theme of preparedness. In 1915 many people were still debating whether America should play a part in the war, and millions of people came to the box office to see this film.

In *The New York Times,* September, 1915, a reviewer wrote: "It is entirely interesting and has the accent of authority lent by the presence on its screen of such men as the Secretary of War, Admiral Dewey, Major Gen. Wood and others. Furthermore, it has been heartily endorsed by such bodies as the Navy League, the National Security League, the Army League, the American Red Cross and the American Legion." Most conspicuously, it was warmly endorsed by then-Colonel Theodore Roosevelt.

Kenneth Macgowan, a movie critic in Philadelphia in 1915, remembered in *Behind the Screen* there were Censor Boards demanding objectionable scenes be cut from the release prints. "I encountered many of the absurdities of censorship," he said. "Often the cuts in films were so obvious that audiences knew something had been removed, and many must have imagined far worse episodes than those that had actually been cut. If the censor cut a certain vital subtitle, the management stopped the film and lowered a lettered sign into a spotlight in front of the screen. When the censor cut a whole scene from *The Battle Cry of Peace,* the theater raised the screen and had the episode played in pantomime by actors in a stage set."

In the story, enemy agents under the leadership of Emanon conspire with pacifists to keep the American defense appropriations down at a time when forces of the enemy are preparing to invade. The invasion comes, and New York, Washington, and other American cities are devastated. A handful of survivors retreat to the nearest cover, a little farmhouse a quarter of a mile away; still, they remain under the watchful eye of their enemy, who observes them from the air and reports their movements in detail by wireless communication to their forces on the ground. They are hunted down like animals.

A small force is detailed to take the prisoners back to New York. On either side of Broadway, as far as the eye can see, stretch lines of the enemy troops, standing rigid and immovable as stone figures. Down between them limp a straggling band of American troops, weary and broken in body and spirit, hopelessness written on their haggard countenances. In

Americans suffer defeat when invading soldiers devastate Washington, D.C. The Capitol dome, blown apart by bombs, looms in the background in *The Battle Cry of Peace* (1915).

the widest part of the street a great pile of rifles grows constantly as each man is forced to deposit his weapon on the stack.

The Capitol at Washington is shown in shocking images of ruin, the white dome rent and blackened. The film warned the public to be prepared and encouraged men to enlist. Audiences were urged to remember the beat of distant drums, the echo of the bugle cry calling to the spirit of American ancestors who served at Gettysburg and Valley Forge. The mother in the story, who had been brutally murdered earlier, was then shown alive and well, passing her husband's sword to her sons with words admonishing them to "Wear it in memory of the life he gave for his country. Draw it only in your country's defense!"

Norma appeared in nine other films in 1915 in addition to *The Battle Cry of Peace.* This was also the year Sarah Bernhardt appeared in *Jeanne Doré,* produced immediately after the amputation of her leg, when most of the world thought she would never act again. Mae Marsh was winning applause in *The Birth of a Nation* and Pauline Frederick debuted in films in *The Eternal City, Zaza, Bella Donna,* and *Sold.* Theda Bara helped Fox forge ahead as one of the leading film companies with their release of *A Fool There Was,* Pearl White thrilled audiences the world over with *The Exploits of Elaine,* and Dorothy Gish charmed crowds with *Out of Bondage.*

*Variety,* August 13, 1915, wrote of the powerful story:

The punch of the picture comes after the bombardment of New York, when the two Harrison boys return to their home to find the house has been wrecked by one of the shells and both their mother and their sister have been slain.

The acting cast with which Charles Richman, who is the star of the production, has been surrounded is one of tremendous Strength, and the work of Mrs. Mary Maurice, Miss Louise Beaudet and Norma Talmadge is particularly worthy of individual mention. From a pictorial standpoint the panorama scenes, some of which have been taken from hydroplanes flying over New York, which are little short of wonderful. The picturing of the bombardment of the city has been worked out in a manner which will win universal admiration, and the fleets and forts in action add much to the stirring value.... it is a film that will come in for nationwide discussion. In publicity way [*sic*] it should be worth columns of space. Its value to Sunday editors throughout the country should be immense for it contains material for a series of special stories that could run for weeks. Take each and every town and hamlet in the entire country and bring the question of the national defense home to them by taking their own buildings and tearing them asunder, in imagination, with the shells of the big guns of the enemy.

The production was not without its problems. James Morrison remembered in *The Parade's Gone By:* "In *The Battle Cry of Peace* I remember one marvelous effect. There were some huge columns flanking a great stairway built into the Vitagraph tank. They were supposed to come crashing down into the water. Well, everybody held their breath. Down came the columns—but the damn things floated, because they'd been made of wood. It broke their hearts."

*The Battle Cry of Peace* has survived only in a three-minute fragment. The George Eastman House has this footage preserved, according to film historian Kevin Brownlow in a letter to the author.

D. W. Griffith watched Norma in the film and decided he wanted her for part of his new Triangle film company. They engaged a number of big Broadway stars who had hitherto despised the screen, including Billie Burke, Douglas Fairbanks, De Wolfe Hopper, and Sir Herbert Beerbohm Tree. It was a wonderful opportunity and the salary seemed astounding to her. It included a promise to give her sister Constance a few roles, so the whole family shook the dust of Brooklyn from their feet and moved to California. Mr. Talmadge quit his job in the advertising business and led the family to support his daughter and her new career.

It proved to be a profitable trip in many ways. Norma had several good roles but her work in *Panthea,* following soon after Madam Petrova's appearance in the stage version, made a tremendous success. This one part alone was enough to stamp her as a star of great ability.

Norma was shepherded into film work by her mother, and though her work was the central and most valued fact of her life for many years, she grew bored with stardom and was known to be indifferent to each new film in the beginning days of production. Once involved, she worked hard, became interested, and roused herself to give credible performances.

When asked about her plans for future films, Norma said she wanted to play strong, dramatic, emotional roles which have in them something more than just the opportunity to act, which, besides being true character portrayals, would at the same time, be helpful.

"I have turned down a number of good stories," she said in *Photoplay* in 1926, "because I am not satisfied to have people see in my pictures entertainment only. I want them to always feel an underlying psychology in what I do, and I like a story with a purpose, a story that gets somewhere. I believe the moral can be brought out more subtly and be so cleverly interwoven in the story that it becomes the very soul of the character and the play."

At the height of her career she received in the neighborhood of 3,000 letters a week. At least half of those came from girls between the age of 14 and 25. For the actress on the speaking stage there were curtain calls to tell her when her work was at its best, but to Norma reliance came on these letters. "In the studio there is no applause. The most we ever get is when the director says 'Good—hold it!,' and the army of girl adorers throughout the country are my guide."

Norma commented in *Photoplay* on her belief in the power of film: "The motion picture camera has the power of witchcraft, almost. It is a curious and miraculous thing to find that the very soul of a woman is occasionally revealed on the screen. The least bit of insincerity or artificiality is apparent. The innermost thoughts of the actress somehow seem to show in her eyes, and she cannot hide them. You cannot explain it, and it defies analysis. Personality means far more on the screen than it does on the stage—in fact, it means everything."

Her marriage to Joseph M. Schenck in 1916 permanently changed her career and her personal life. Schenck saw in Norma's beauty and talent an opportunity to make a fortune, and he immediately took charge of her career, establishing in 1917 a producing company called the Norma Talmadge Film Company. His supervision took her career to a new level, beginning with *Panthea,* the story of a woman who sacrificed herself to help her husband produce an opera.

"Mr. Schenck makes definite decisions and effects them rapidly," Peg noted with admiration. "Shortly after he had decided to organize Norma's own company, the deed was done. The contract was drawn up with the

Select Company, the first story bought, and the first cast selected, with Allan Dwan as director. Early in 1917, came the great moment, when *Panthea,* Norma's own, her very own, first picture was finished and ready for release. *Panthea* had been played on the legitimate stage by the beautiful and exotic Olga Petrova. Norma hung over this first Norma Talmadge production like a child over a favorite doll, or a mother over a first baby, except that, unlike fond mothers, she had the critical eye. It was wonderful for all of us!"

The picture had a stunning opening in two theaters simultaneously in Manhattan, the Rialto and the New York. Schenck surrounded her with elaborate, first-rate sets, costumes, and the direction of Allan Dwan. The auspicious debut of Norma as a producer ordained the hope that her future productions would be of equal caliber. Her ranking in the front lines of box office champions was cemented.

Mae Marsh was one of Norma's greatest admirers. She claimed in *Screen Acting,* "No screen actress makes a shrewder use of *emphasis* than Norma Talmadge. She seems invariably to hold much in reserve with the result that when she does let go in a big emotional scene, the effect is brought home to the audience with telling force. There are other actresses who play with reserve. But it is important that with Miss Talmadge her repression seems ever illuminated by the fires of potential emotion. The student of the screen will do well to study these matters of emphasis and repression. They are all important. Our manner of life itself is an accepted repression, outlined by laws for the streets and conventions for the drawing room. From the screen viewpoint repression is a vital thing, if for no other reason than the fact that it gives the audience a breathing spell. After a breathing spell it is the better disposed to appreciate emphasis."

Under the careful management of her husband, Norma climbed to the top rank of film stars in 1917. Although critics often noted the extravagant production values of the many films she made over the next three years, the plots were frequently silly. Fans poured out in droves. Schenck wanted his wife to be featured in material with a high-level tone to it, and he bought plays, novels, and historical documents bolstering her image as the Queen of the Motion Picture. The ongoing succession of films included a dual role in *The Forbidden City.* Sidney Franklin directed the old-fashioned melodrama of the Madame Butterfly story. Her work was artistic and eloquent, and soon led her to a banner year in 1922 with *Smilin' Through* and *Love's Redemption.* Both films were so successful they were remade a few years later in sound.

Her last silent films were *Kiki, Camille, The Dove,* and *The Woman Disputed,* all made as the industry was in the chaos of converting to sound. A striking portrait of Norma looking fearfully at an ominous microphone the size of an artillery shell dangling from a wire above her head was widely circulated on the cover of *Photoplay* magazine.

When talking pictures arrived, she wisely stayed off the screen during 1929, and rallied to the challenge by studying with voice coaches to eliminate her Brooklyn accent. *New York Nights,* her first talkie, was well received, but her second talkie, *DuBarry, Woman of Passion,* was a famous example of the difficulty directors encountered in 1929 with the early technology and the challenge of reconciling the technique of the silent film with the new requirements of sound. *DuBarry* was not a very good film, and the interminable absurdities of its story heralded Norma's downfall. One wry comment about her sound-debut diction, the source of which is buried in antiquity, has been handed down through the years as a legendary Hollywood quote: "She speaks the Belasco dialogue with a Vitagraph accent." With three pictures contracted to be filmed, Norma realized the folly of proceeding further. She cancelled the contract with a firm announcement that she was retiring from films. She was still young, beautiful, and very rich. Divorced from Joseph Schenck and without a career, she soon became addicted to cocaine.

"Quit while you are ahead, and thank God for the trust funds Mama set up," was the urgent advice her sister Constance wired to her after the bad reviews *DuBarry* earned.

Many years later, she attempted a comeback, unsuccessfully testing for the role of Pilar in *For Whom The Bell Tolls.* She died in 1957, still addicted to cocaine and married to a doctor who made her last years as comfortable as possible.

Norma was one of Hollywood's biggest stars for nearly 20 years. In spite of her fame and marriage to Joseph Schenck, the president of United Artists, she is forgotten by audiences of today. Billy Wilder remembered her when writing his classic script for *Sunset Boulevard.* The character of Norma Desmond was named using parts of names from the famous Norma of the Talmadge family and the infamous William Desmond Taylor, whose murder has intrigued mystery enthusiasts for decades.

Norma broke through the ranks of ingénues without previous experience and rose from minor parts to the pinnacle of film stardom. She persevered, with the iron determination of her mother, Margaret "Peg" Talmadge, to indelibly connect with world audiences. She pleased her generation and served as a role model for many young women in an era when women first emerged from the confines of the home to vote, work, and succeed in industry.

## SILENT FILMOGRAPHY OF NORMA TALMADGE

The Household Pest (1910) ★ A Dixie Mother (1910) ★ The Love of a Chrysanthemum (1910) ★ Uncle Tom's Cabin (1910) ★ In Neighboring Kingdoms (1910) ★ A Broken Spell (1910) ★ A Tale of Two Cities (1911) ★ The Sky Pilot (1911) ★ The General's Daughter (1911) ★ The Thumb Print (1911) ★ The Child Crusoes (1911) ★ Forgotten, or An Answered Prayer (1911) ★ Her Hero (1911) ★ His Last Cent (1911) ★ Paola and Francesca (1911) ★ The Four Poster Pest (1911) ★ Captain Barnacle's Messmates (1912) ★ The First Violin (1912) ★ Mrs. Carter's Necklace (1912) ★ Mrs. 'Enry' Awkins (1912) ★ Counsel for the Defense (1912) ★ Fortunes of a Composer (1912) ★ The Extension Table (1912) ★ The Troublesome Step-Daughters (1912) ★ Wanted: A Grandmother (1912) ★ The Lovesick Maidens of Cuddleton (1912) ★ A Fortune in a Teacup (1912) ★ Captain Barnacle's Waif (1912) ★ His Official Appointment (1912) ★ Captain Barnacle, Reformer (1912) ★ O'Hara, Squatter and Philosopher (1912) ★ Mr. Butler Buttles (1912) ★ Casey at the Bat (1913) ★ Just Show People (1913) ★ O'Hara's Goldchild (1913) ★ The Silver Cigarette Case (1913) ★ An Old Man's Love Story (1913) ★ The Other Woman (1913) ★ Father's Hatband (1913) ★ His Silver Bachelorhood (1913) ★ An Elopement at Home (1913) ★ The Blue Rose (1913) ★ The Honorable Algernon (1913) ★ Wanted: A Stronghand (1913) ★ Under the Daisies (1913) ★ Stenographer Troubles (1913) ★ The Solitaires (1913) ★ Omens and Oracles (1913) ★ O'Hara as a Guardian Angel (1913) ★ The Midget's Revenge (1913) ★ The Lady and Her Maid (1913) ★ Fanny's Conspiracy (1913) ★ Extremities (1913) ★ 'Arriet's Baby (1913) ★ The Vavasour Ball (1914) ★ The Sacrifice of Kathleen (1914) ★ A Helpful Sisterhood (1914) ★ Cupid Versus Money (1914) ★ Miser Murray's Wedding Present (1914) ★ A Wayward Daughter (1914) ★ Fogg's Millions (1914) ★ Memories in Men's Souls (1914) ★ The Loan Shark King (1914) ★ The Curing of Myra May (1914) ★ A Question of Clothes (1914) ★ Under False Colors (1914) ★ Sunshine and Shadows (1914) ★ The Salvation of Kathleen (1914) ★ The Right of Way (1914) ★ Politics and the Press (1914) ★ The Peacemaker (1914) ★ Old Reliable (1914) ★ Officer John Donovan (1914) ★ The Mill of Life (1914) ★ John Rance, Gentleman (1914) ★ His Little Page (1914) ★ The Hidden Letters (1914) ★ The Hero (1914) ★ Goodbye Summer (1914) ★ A Daughter of Israel (1915) ★ The Barrier of Faith (1915) ★ Janet of the Chorus

(1915) ★ Elsa's Brother (1915) ★ The Criminal (1915) ★ The Battle Cry of Peace (1915) ★ The Crown Prince's Double (1915) ★ A Pillar of Flame (1915) ★ A Daughter's Strange Inheritance (1915) ★ Captivating Mary Carstairs (1915) ★ The Missing Links (1916) ★ Martha's Vindication (1916) ★ The Children in the House (1916) ★ Going Straight (1916) ★ The Devil's Needle (1916) ★ The Social Secretary (1916) ★ Fifty-Fifty (1916) ★ Panthea (1917) ★ The Law of Compensation (1917) ★ Poppy (1917) ★ The Moth (1917) ★ The Secret of the Storm Country (1917) ★ The Ghosts of Yesterday (1918) ★ By Right of Purchase (1918) ★ De Luxe Annie (1918) ★ The Safety Curtain (1918) ★ Her Only Way (1918) ★ The Forbidden City (1918) ★ The Heart of Wetona (1919) ★ The New Moon (1919) ★ The Probation Wife (1919) ★ Dust of Desire (1919) ★ The Way of a Woman (1919) ★ The Isle of Conquest (1919) ★ A Daughter of Two Worlds (1920) ★ She Loves and Lies (1920) ★ The Woman Gives (1920) ★ Yes or No (1920) ★ The Branded Woman (1920) ★ Passion Flower (1921) ★ The Sign on the Door (1921) ★ The Wonderful Thing (1921) ★ Love's Redemption (1921) ★ Smilin' Through (1922) ★ The Eternal Flame (1922) ★ The Voice from the Minaret (1923) ★ Within the Law (1923) ★ Ashes of Vengeance (1923) ★ The Song of Love (1923) ★ Secrets (1924) ★ The Only Woman (1924) ★ The Lady (1925) ★ Graustark (1925) ★ Kiki (1926) ★ Camille (1926) ★ The Dove (1927) ★ The Woman Disputed (1928) ★ Show People (1928) ★ New York Nights (1929) ★ DuBarry, Woman of Passion (1930) (Sound film)

# LAURETTE TAYLOR

> Beautiful women seldom want to act. They are afraid of emotion and they do not try to extract anything from a character that they are portraying, because in expressing emotion they may encourage crow's feet and laughing wrinkles. They avoid anything that will disturb their placidity of countenance, for placidity of countenance insures a smooth skin.
>
> Laurette Taylor, as quoted in *Actors on Acting*
> by Toby Cole and Helen Krich

Forty-ish Laurette Taylor was never called a great beauty; after many years as a leading stage actress, she courageously debuted without her voice in silent motion pictures as an 18-year-old heroine, a career challenge few women would dare attempt. With the aid of innovative lighting, King Vidor's motion picture version of Laurette's most famous play was a smash hit. She placed her masterpiece in the time capsule of film, made two other pictures, and left the screen forever. Many stage actresses followed her lead, at least to the extent of immortalizing their talent or acclaimed performances in films, when they, too, were long past the ingénue stage. Ruth Gordon, Uta Hagen, Ina Claire, Shirley Booth, Lynn Fontanne, and Katherine Cornell were some who imprinted their art, albeit briefly, on film, trailing the venturesome Laurette Taylor.

Laurette was born on April 1, 1884, as Loretta Cooney. Her mother, Elizabeth, and father, James, moved from Newark to New York, and took her to see her first stage shows from the 25-cent gallery seats of the Harlem Opera House once a week.

Irrepressible Loretta was dismissed from high school during her first year. Her father took over her career, put a stop to her singing and dancing lessons, and, against Loretta's desires, enrolled her in a nearby business school for stenographers. She was regularly disciplined with whippings for any infraction. Her attraction to the stage was voracious, and she was determined to start a career using her talent. She printed and sent cards around to the theatrical agencies and won an audition at Keith's Vaudeville on 14th Street before a gathering of agents and managers. Her audition consisted of an ambitious program, much longer than was the custom. The judges were so taken aback by the sheer elaboration of her detailed audition, they allowed her to unroll the entire performance without interruption. She failed to get a job.

Charles Taylor, a playwright and producer, noticed her and soon a dizzying friendship blossomed between Loretta and the prolific author of melodramas. He married her, and wrote a play about their relationship called *Child Wife,* which debuted at the Cordray Theater, Portland, Oregon on September 14, 1901, the day President McKinley died. The play went on a 40-week tour, failed to make money, and closed.

Laurette, as she was now called, announced the January 1, 1902 birth of her son, Dwight Oliver Taylor, in *Theatrical News,* published by Charlie's friend, Charles Blaney.

She toured in more plays by her husband for the next several years, and appeared in other roles including *East Lynne* and *Camille.* Another play by Charlie, *Yosemite,* opened in Buffalo, December 8, 1908. It created a storm of criticism over the leafy costume Laurette wore as a child of the forest. The play failed, and a week later, Laurette left to sign with the Shuberts for three years. She appeared in six plays for the Shuberts, and seldom saw Charlie Taylor. In 1910 they divorced, and Laurette took part in a comedy by J. Hartley Manners, *The Girl in Waiting.* It was a big hit at the opening in Philadelphia, and Laurette saw her name in lights for the first time. The Shuberts offered Laurette a five-year contract. She soon fell in love with Hartley and they married. His love for her was profound, and he penned a new play specially to fit her personality. *Peg O' My Heart* was first read to Laurette in Hartley's beautiful voice and impeccable diction. It was the play that was to make the fame and fortune of both.

The year 1912 saw Laurette Taylor win stage stardom with stunning success in *The Bird of Paradise,* featuring Guy Bates Post and Lewis S. Stone. Near the end of the same year she opened in *Peg O' My Heart,* the charming comedy written by her husband. The play ran for 603 performances, the longest running play of her career. *Peg* was a winner from the debut, breaking records for runs in Los Angeles with 101 performances to standing room only.

Laurette's dog, Michael, exhibited a captivating allure for audiences. His burning devotion to his mistress caused him to unwittingly portray an unforgettable performance. From the Los Angeles opening in 1912 through the New York and London recreations, Michael played in every performance of *Peg O' My Heart.* He reprised his role again in the 1921 revival. He ultimately held an unbeaten record for a stage dog of 1,250 performances, earning an immortal position in the annals of the theater.

In November, 1913, the play broke the record for continuous performances, beating the previous record held by Maude Adams in *The Little Minister.* During the First World War she took the play to London, and gave more than a thousand performances.

Laurette and Hartley returned to America and she appeared mostly in his plays, including *The Harp of Life, Out There,* and *The National Anthem.* She liked to sing, and Hartley wrote a song into each play for her. "My voice isn't so good," she said, "but I work hard on my songs. It's good training, and I like it."

*Happiness,* another play by J. Hartley Manners, was another huge hit for Laurette. She followed it with several attempts at Shakespeare and another Hartley play, *One Night in Rome.* After running for five and a half months, *One Night in Rome* went to London on April 29, 1920, opening at the Garrick Theater for 104 performances.

Frances Marion, long before she began her unrivaled work as a scenarist of motion pictures, struggled as an artist. One day she was invited to sketch a portrait of Laurette in her dressing room. As Laurette was posing for her, gowned in a creamy white outfit and looking like the pearl in an oyster, her eyes noticed the drab walls and worn, stained carpet surrounding the dilapidated sofa and chairs. She mentioned the shabby condition of the room to the star, who smiled and indicated the floor would be completely hidden by huge baskets of flowers from fans and friends on the night after the play opened and she would be surrounded with visitors bearing dozens of cards wishing her success, a long run, and unending profit. "As her voice trailed off on a happy note, I wondered if she would receive such praise and adulation when she opened in this *Peg O' My Heart* nonsense," Frances fancied in *Off With Their Heads.* "To me, a talent like hers was wasted on this sentimental little play which I referred to, only in my diary, as *Cinderella in the Doghouse.*"

"I'm trying to maintain an expression of childish wonderment," Laurette explained. "After all, Peg is a girl of eighteen, tiptoeing into life's adventure. An experienced actress doesn't find it very difficult to play a girl still in her teens. Do you think I'm achieving this?" she asked Frances.

"Absolutely," Frances declared, though thinking Miss Taylor had tiptoed quite a distance from her teens. She painstakingly and deliberately failed to etch into her drawing the character lines Laurette was trying to tiptoe around. As her pencils traced the beautiful eyes and radiant smile of the star, the artists noticed the detail in her enormous eyes when in repose, a glint reflecting some nameless fear. Frances remembered musing to herself if the barely hidden emotion was the eternally human fear of growing old, a particular grief among actresses.

While discussing the rising influence of the movies with the posed star, Frances recorded Laurette's pointedly emphatic, off-hand statement, "I shall never be lured into it, though they have trapped Madame Bernhardt, Lillie Langtry, and Minnie Maddern Fiske."

*Peg O' My Heart* earned the Manners family more than a million dollars by the year 1919. Ten different companies toured the play across France, Italy, Hungary, Holland, South Africa, Australia, New Zealand, and the Far East. In 1921 Laurette went back into another production of it for three months in New York, then took the play to Chicago. It was inevitable that the play would attract the lust of Hollywood. The play was such a hit, movie producers were eager to transfer the story to the screen. *The New York Times* began watching developments involving the great stage actress Laurette Taylor and the looming interest in wooing her to the movies. On March 31, 1918, the newspaper reported,

Something more than a year ago, Roi Cooper Megrue, acting as a Goldwyn emissary, called Laurette Taylor on the telephone and asked her what sum she would ask to become a movie star. "One million dollars," replied Miss Taylor, promptly, and dismissed the incident as closed. A few days later Mr. Megrue again rang the Taylor number, and informed her that the Goldwynites were willing to talk business. Miss Taylor, however, decided that she did not want to enter pictures after all, and accordingly the matter was dropped.

Now, however, the movie people have returned to the attack and according to all accounts, they have found Miss Taylor in a more receptive mood. Whether the Goldwyn people are among the concerns which are bidding for Miss Taylor's services is not known; the petitioners are more than one in number and probably include nearly all of the prominent movie companies. The important point, however, is that Miss Taylor seems inclined to fall. Although nothing definite has as yet been decided, she admitted, a few nights ago, that the prospect of earning a huge sum of money easily was not entirely unalluring. In the event of her capitulation the picture will be made in New York almost immediately, and will be seen here this Spring. A condition made by George C. Tyler, Miss Taylor's manager, is that the picture must not be released as a part of a so-called "program," but that it must be put into a New York playhouse for a run. As to the picture in which Miss Taylor will appear, it will be *Peg O' My Heart* or nothing.

Nearly every screen actress in the world had been eager to act *Peg O' My Heart* in pictures ever since the play was first produced. Included in that number was Mary Pickford, who, according to report, made an offer considerably in excess of the highest amount ever paid for the picture rights to a play or a story. The value of *Peg O' My Heart* to the movie producers and wishful stars lies less in the simple story of the play than in the prestige value attached to the title. The massive publicity wrung from the numerous traveling exhibitions of the play for several years also packaged with the story a built-in audience, name recognition, and proven appeal. Almost any actress in the famous role would be assured of a resounding success, however Laurette doggedly clung to the movie rights for her own use, should she ever commit to appearing in a film.

The heads of more than one prominent company were particularly desirous of securing Laurette's services and the commercial potential her great following would bring with an appearance in movie theaters in *Peg O' My Heart.* Rather than become just another movie actress, however, Laurette steadfastly declared that she would stay out of the films forever. Her own idea was to make one picture and one only—*Peg O' My Heart*—and then eschew the celluloid forever.

It took years for the play to reach the moving picture screen. King Vidor remembered in his autobiography, *A Tree Is A Tree,* "I soon landed a job at the old Metro studio on Romaine Street—the assignment: to direct Laurette Taylor in *Peg O' My Heart.* Although I had never seen Miss Taylor, her name carried with it a certain magic to my young ears."

Vidor was dismayed, when given a copy of the play, to find that all the action took place on a single set. He couldn't envision how the stage talk could be translated into a silent motion picture. To make matters worse, a screen test of Laurette Taylor, filmed in New York by Billy Bitzer, the head cameraman for D. W. Griffith, was appalling. To his astonishment, the test made Miss Taylor look 70 years old. Noting that Peg's first line in the play was a remark about her father saying she was old enough to start thinking about going to college, it was obvious the character of Peg was certainly no more than 18 years old. The character did not age any during the course of the story, and Vidor was tempted to abort the whole project. Unfortunately for him, the star and her husband were due to arrive in California within days to begin consultations on the production. He had no choice but to wait and meet the actress in person before finalizing his judgment. He hoped the actress would be better in person than she had appeared on the crude screen test.

"I was met at the hotel by a charming, vivacious woman with sparkling eyes who simply oozed personality from her entire being," the surprised Vidor revealed. Soon after their arrival, the star and her husband read the play to Vidor, emphasizing the moments of high spirits and hilarity that proved effective with live audiences. Vidor began to see that much of the dialogue could find a substitute in pantomime, and much of the talk about action outside of the single setting could be shown rather than verbally described. As the play was read to him he realized the possibilities of a cinematic treatment, and became anxious to film a new test of the 40-ish Laurette. Remembering the beauty of certain still photos of another actress of similar age, images accomplished with the use of a flattering portrait lens, he devised a plan to film a test of motion picture film on a camera fitted with a similar lens. The results were astonishing.

Another age-reducing gadget, a spotlight beamed from slightly higher than the camera and aimed through a rifle sight, focusing a circle of light no larger than the actress's face, burned out some of the lines around her eyes and firmed a sharp jaw and chin shadow. When the tests were projected, Laurette looked sixteen instead of forty. "Another trick I employed with great effectiveness in all medium and long shots where we could not use the still-camera lens was to play some joke or prank just before each 'take' to get Laurette in a laughing mood," Vidor revealed. "Then without warning we could start the camera. When she would hear the grinding of the camera, she would start acting the already rehearsed scene, but the playful and youthful expression would remain until the scene had ended."

In the story, Peg is a variation of the eternal Cinderella theme. She goes to the English manor of the Chichesters as rather an ugly duckling, but she blossoms forth in a way that wins over her snobbish relatives and captures the heart of the English lord who lives close by.

Filming began with a scene to be taken on a very hot location near Sherwood Lake. A house had been erected days before to appear as Peg's cottage on the location, and wild geese and goats were lodged the previous night within the makeshift structure. King Vidor planned for the set to double as Laurette's dressing room in the wilds. It was a little Irish hut overlooking the lake. Nancy Dowd and David Shepard, interviewing the director for *King Vidor,* quoted Vidor remembering, "We got out to the location together that morning. Hartley was wearing his white shoes and Laurette brought her maid and her dog along. We had to climb a very steep, dusty trail to the top of the hill where the house was. She damn near quit the film while climbing the hill and slipping and sliding in the dust. The usual Hollywood cast never thought anything about the hardships on location." Bright tin reflectors surrounded the exterior where the camera was set up. Hot, searing sunlight blasted from them onto Laurette as she posed for the camera. One of the actors, deviating from the prescribed wording of the script, said some flippant line instead of what he had been rehearsed to say, and Laurette, thrown by the transgression, got very angry. Vidor agonized when the actress announced her angry frustration with the blinding reflectors. She also was stymied by the peculiar demands of shooting the story out of sequence and the requirement forcing her to turn on hot and cold emotions at the moment when the director yelled, "Action!" Within minutes, her emotional upset aggravated by the stifling heat caused her to finally pass out. The horrified crew carried her unconscious into the house and laid her down on the floor. When she came to, she was dumbstruck by the outrageous sight of all the goats and geese leaping around the room. Laurette saw the unplanned pandemonium and jumped up, screaming, "It's impossible. I'll never be able to do it." She rushed out the door and down the hill with her maid, Michael the dog trailing faithfully behind.

Vidor went to work and tried to smooth out all of the ruffled feelings, and the following day the cast and crew returned to the location and resumed work on the same scene aborted the previous day. Vidor implored the supporting actors to stay to the letter of the rehearsed script and refrain from whimsical ad-libbing, knowing the star would only play the script as she had done so many nights on the stage. The production ran smoothly from then on.

The filmed play turned out beautifully. *The New York Times* reviewed it on January 22, 1923:

The same spontaneous, irrepressible Peg who enlivened J. Hartley Manners' play on the stage for so many years has not been brought to life on the screen in the motion picture version of the play, which is at the Capitol this week. She is, of course, embodied in Laurette Taylor herself. No other could be the real Peg.

It's a Peg without her voice that you see now, and something is lost, too, in the absence of her physical presence, but it's a true Peg, nevertheless, for Miss Taylor has taken naturally to the studio, and by her pantomime, her vitality and variety of manner she has made Peg an actively present person despite the fact that she is silent and only a shadow. The others in the cast do well, too, and the settings and general direction of the film are good, but it is Miss Taylor who makes the photoplay stand up and go as the play did.

It doesn't go as well as the play, of course. No one would pretend that he would rather see the picture than the stage production. Through necessity,

Laurette Taylor made her motion picture debut in *Peg O' My Heart* (1923).

or by choice, the producers have made the screen version merely a reflection of its original. Though it begins further back in Peg's life and goes further on to a rather useless scene of Peg's presentation at court, it is in the main concerned with Irish Peg's adventures in the home of the snobbish English Chichesters, and the principal sets might well be those used on the stage, with the same action, and its accompanying conversations, carrying forward the comedy and the story of the play. This means that the picture is full of spoken subtitles, taken from the stage dialogue, and upon these the photoplay largely depends for its humor and its human interest.

Vidor's finished work was not a distinctly cinematographic piece. The screen adaptation was more of a transliteration than a translation of the play. He wisely availed himself of every opportunity to open the story to other settings when possible, going to the extent of showing story elements that were merely described in the spoken play. These enhancements served to magnify the impact of the story while staying as faithful to the spirit of the original as possible. No audience viewing the film would sense any

Laurette Taylor in *Peg O' My Heart* (1923).

element missing from the story, if they had seen one of the many versions of the live theater presentations. All the ingredients so popular in the original were readily apparent in the screen adaptation. At the worst, audiences would hopefully welcome the skillfully made substitutes, which, if just as good, were adequate as a substitute could be when considering the need to express in images what had been previously expressed in words.

Laurette's pantomime was an extra treat for those who were seeing her for the first time. Her performance, due largely to the direction of King Vidor, was polished and in keeping with the techniques common among experienced film performers. He was able to make Laurette appear to be the living embodiment of the character. The production was of such a high caliber, it stood on its own merit as a motion picture production. Persons unfamiliar with the star or the story found it engrossing and enjoyable.

The others in the cast, some of whom were hired for their appearance as a specific type, ably supported the star and gave a realistic texture to the authentic reproduction of the Irish villages.

*Photoplay,* February, 1923, noted,

> The screen Peg goes back into the girl's past to show her a restless wanderer with her beloved father—an Irish gypsy in truth. And it extends on to show Peg being received by the king. Possibly this addendum isn't necessary, but, on the whole, Director King Vidor and his scenarist, Mary O'Hara, have done a very satisfying job with the popular play, never deviating in any essential particular from J. Hartley Manners' original footlight thesis.
>
> Miss Taylor's screen work is unusual. Her performance is very well sustained and there are but one or two perceptible let-downs in spontaneity.
>
> *Peg O' My Heart* rather encourages us in regard to Mr. Vidor. It is workmanlike and sincere. Somehow, we can't understand why Vidor has been in eclipse recently. Surely no one had a more human touch in his direction. But the ways of motion picture business are many and varied.

*Film Daily,* December 17, 1922, said,

> A very valuable piece of stage property has at last reached the screen and the much enjoined J. Hartley Manners play, made famous by Laurette Taylor several years ago, has been recorded in pictures with Miss Taylor as *Peg*. The picture is a very delightful entertainment and an unusually amusing and wholesome one. There has been so much controversy regarding the rights of the play and its production that the result has been anticipated with a little more than the usual interest.
>
> Both Miss Taylor, and King Vidor, who directed, have fulfilled the hopes of those who have been waiting to see *Peg O' My Heart* in pictures. The star, to begin with photographs surprisingly well and proves that she knows the art of pantomime. Her facial expressions are delightful and she can say a lot with her eyes. They are going to love that frolicking left eye wink and the pensive expression when she finds herself in love with Jerry. Miss Taylor is a real trouper and her charming characterization of Peg, her first film role, will certainly gain many admirers for her.
>
> King Vidor has handled the production very well and the material has been used to good advantage and with good judgment. The exterior shots are very pretty and production values in general are first rate. There is one change that nearly everyone will probably suggest and that is taking off the second ending that has been tacked on, showing Peg, now Lady Adair, being presented to the King and Queen. The shot of Peg, happy with her English sweetheart who has come for her, is the logical and prettiest ending.
>
> The director has brought out the humor of the story in splendid style and it is always wholesome. Added to his efforts are some fine titles that fit

the pictures very well. A good supporting cast includes Mahlon Hamilton as Jerry, Peg's lover, Russell Simpson as her father, Ethel Grey Terry, Vera Lewis and D.R.O. Hatswell as the English cousins. Vera Lewis is not the most suitable type but Hatswell, who resembles Von Stroheim, is fine as the son. Michael, Peg's dog, has his usual place in the story.

The film version goes back a little introducing Peg at home in Ireland and the death of her mother. Then comes the parting from her father when she goes to live with her mother's rich sister, Mrs. Chichester. Peg's discomfort in her surroundings and the abuse of her relatives who are only tolerating her because it means money to them, finally sends her back to their father in Ireland. Jerry, really Sir Gerland Adair, a neighbor of the Chichesters follows Peg whose "divil of a tongue" had kept her from admitting her love before she left England.

*Variety,* January 25, 1923 said,

Peg on the screen isn't the full, rich, racy character she was on the stage, but still stands head and shoulders over almost any pantomimic comedienne the screen has. Miss Taylor does a unique piece of work here. New to the camera, she has mastered that pitiless instrument by sheer naturalness and abandon. She looks 20 and acts 16 with an exquisite grace that is memorable.

There can be no question of the box office value of *Peg.* It is almost in the *Ben-Hur* class as a draw, for it played from one end of the country to the other with half a dozen actresses in the same part for more than 10 years, and was in the *Way Down East* class as a repeater. It is one of the dozen or so titles that will appeal to the whole public, for it is as standard as *David Copperfield.*

Metro and Mr. Vidor have done handsomely by the production. It has some exquisite settings, authentic scenic background taken abroad, and interiors done in the best form of the best modern practice. The playing is in the same mood of restraint.

On completion of the photography, Laurette was so pleased with her appearance and performance that she obtained her own print of the film for showing in her home. Ethel Barrymore wrote in her autobiography, *Memories,* "Another of the happy memories is of going to Sunday night dinners with that magical Laurette Taylor and her husband, Hartley Manners, in their big house on Riverside Drive. She had made a silent picture of *Peg O' My Heart* and always after dinner they would show it to us. Some years afterward she said to me, 'Ethel, did you ever see my picture *Peg O' My Heart?'* I said, 'All one winter.' I hadn't meant to be funny, but Laurette loved it and kept repeating it."

As far as eschewing the celluloid forever, Laurette was quite entranced with her performance in the film, and proceeded to star in two more motion pictures, *One Night in Rome* (1924) and *Happiness* (1924).

Gardiner Carroll wrote in *Photoplay* about his discussion with Laurette in 1924,

> When asked which she like better and thought the higher art—the screen or stage—Laurette laughed and gave the Irish answer... Both! I believe a thorough actress should be effective on screen or stage. If the screen is incomplete, the stage is not yet perfect, but the art of acting might be made complete by the actress at her best in spoken and silent drama too.
>
> While I have had far more experience on the stage, I cannot agree that the stage requires greater physical effort. The waits and the rests necessitated in screen work convince me that patience is indeed a virtue.
>
> The films appeal to me because they are permanent. What would the world give today to see Duse in her youth or Bernhardt at the height of her power on the screen? The picture I made of *Peg* will be treasured as long as I live, and by my children's children long after I'm gone, I hope.
>
> That's vanity, but I'm human, and I believe that the same feeling may inspire the preference of many actresses for the screen.
>
> On the stage, we can see our audience, it's true, but never ourselves. On the screen, we can see ourselves and be part of our own audiences as well.
>
> An important advantage that the screen possesses is the ability of the camera to reveal one's soul. The lens strikes below the surface and reveals nuances of emotion that cannot be shown on the stage.
>
> Those who scoff that motion pictures lack depth should beware the camera or they'll find their souls exposed when they may least desire it!
>
> The variety of the screen appeals strongly to me, and the thrill of seeing rushes is something like that of a first night—but I am sustaining the screen when I'm a stage actress! Doesn't it sound like heresy?"

She returned to the stage for many years and, as her youth faded, she retreated into semiretirement. She returned occasionally, scoring hits with *Alice Sit By The Fire* (1932), *Outward Bound* (1938), and, notably, *The Glass Menagerie* (1945). No sound film was ever made with her of either *Peg O' My Heart* or *The Glass Menagerie;* however, she did make a sound recording on 78 rpm discs of *The Glass Menagerie,* and *Peg O' My Heart* was recorded in a 1934 radio broadcast of the play.

Laurette Taylor showed a courage attempted by few other actresses: daring to debut in motion pictures at middle age; audaciously portraying a character in her teens. She also influenced many other actors who previously disdained work in films to transfer their trademark productions to the screen, a packaging and promotional idea still in use today. Her work

Laurette Taylor appeared in the 1945 Broadway stage-play of Tennessee Williams' *The Glass Menagerie.*

in *Peg O' My Heart* was a determined attempt at self-preservation, casting her best work in the semipermanence of film. She succeeded admirably and won both public and critical approval.

## SILENT FILMOGRAPHY OF LAURETTE TAYLOR

Peg O' My Heart (1923) ★ Happiness (1924) ★ One Night in Rome (1924)

# PEARL WHITE

The dynamic Pearl White, immortalized in cinema history in the serial *The Perils of Pauline,* created an image that freed women from Victorian passivity.

Pearl White was born in Green Ridge, Missouri, and lived on a small farm with her four brothers and sisters. She was the youngest child of the family. Her parents moved to the town of Springfield, Missouri, where she had a normal childhood, growing up with a developing interest in the theater. She obtained a role with the Diemer Theater Company while in her second year of high school. In 1907, at the age of 18, she went on the road with the Trousedale Stock Company. For several years she played a variety of small roles until she was spotted by the Powers Film Company in New York. While in Oklahoma City, she married another actor with the company, Victor Sutherland, on October 12, 1907. They later divorced in 1914.

She claimed to have also performed in Cuba for a time under the name of Miss Mazee, performing American songs in a dance hall. Her travels as a singer took her through South America, performing in casinos and dance halls.

In 1910 she was having trouble with her throat, and her voice began to fail from the rigors of nightly theatrical performances. She made her debut in films that year, starring in a long series of one-reel dramas and comedies for the Powers Film Company in the Bronx, New York.

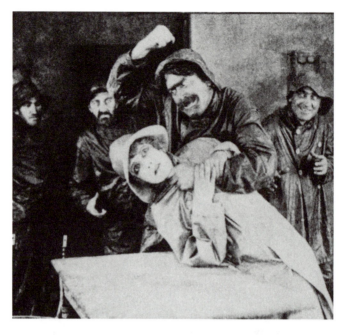

Pearl White in *The Perils of Pauline* (1914).

Her big break came in 1913 with a three-reel film titled *Through Air and Fire,* the beginning episode of the famous serial, *The Perils of Pauline.* In this film, Pearl plunged into daring, physical adventure, including a suspenseful flight in a runaway balloon. Her depiction of an emancipated woman caught in hair-raising calamity struck a nerve with audiences all over the world. The studio planned *The Perils of Pauline* as a 20-episode series of daredevil stories in which her evil guardian attempted to kill her to gain her inheritance. The series became an international favorite, catapulting her to the highest level of popularity. The series was translated into many different languages and cemented her name and image as an icon of the silent cinema. For a time, her fame eclipsed that of Mary Pickford.

Pearl found a niche with frightening serials thrusting her into danger each week and ending with a cliff-hanging climax plotted to leave audiences on the edge of their seats. To experience how she escaped from each deadly peril, audiences had to return each week for the next episode. *The Exploits of Elaine* series followed in 1914, then *The New Exploits of Elaine* and *The Romance of Elaine,* both in (1915). Other serials continued her worldwide popularity in spellbinding horrors: *The Iron Claw* (1916), *Pearl of the Army* (1916), *The Fatal Ring* (1917), and *The House of Hate* (1918). These serials featured Pearl performing a variety of acro-

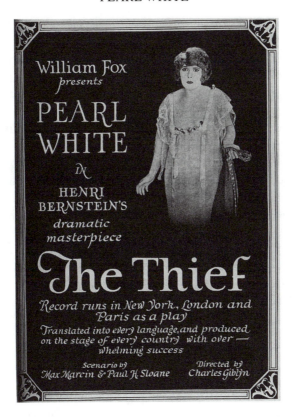

Magazine advertisement for Pearl White in *The Thief* (1920).

batic stunts, including dangling from aerial wires, escaping from sunken submarines, and nearly dying in sabotaged airplanes.

Pearl married Major Wallace McCutcheon, a World War I veteran, in 1918. Together they starred in *The Black Secret* (1919). McCutcheon suffered nerve gas affects from the war, disappeared in 1920, and resurfaced in a Washington, D.C. sanitarium. He committed suicide in January 1928.

Unfortunately, most of these serial episodes have been lost to the ravages of time and decomposition. Their vogue waned in the 1920s, and Pearl transitioned to the new genre of feature films.

Pearl White was destined to be remembered as a serial star, but her feature films are fascinating because of the courage it took for her to defy the restrictions of typecasting and break free. One of these, released by William Fox in November of 1920, is *The Thief*.

*The Thief* was the third of Pearl White's feature productions, and it was a screen version of Henri Bernstein's great play, recalled by theatergoers as a notable stage success in New York, London, and Paris, after which it gathered many honors on the road. The film was adapted by Max Marcin, a well-known Broadway playwright, and Paul H. Sloane, one of the Fox scenario forces who had contributed several successful original screen plays. In the cast supporting Miss White was Charles Waldron as leading man, adding another to the steadily growing list of stage figures who had answered the call of the screen.

Under the direction of Charles Giblyn, who also staged another of her vehicles, *The Tiger's Cub,* this story gave the famous star her first opportunity to wear the fashionable gowns which gained for her in her serial career a reputation as one of the best-dressed stars of the silent drama. The costumes figured strongly into the story.

Pearl White was one of several actors and actresses making attention-getting career changes in 1920. This was the year Charlie Chaplin made his first, independent feature-length film, *The Kid,* released in 1921. Pioneer star Florence Lawrence made her final bid for fame with *The Enfoldment,* baseball legend Babe Ruth left the sand to go Hollywood in *Headin' Home,* and Harry Houdini left vaudeville to venture into films with *Terror Island.*

As *The Thief* hit screens in November of 1920, *Moving Picture World,* December 11, 1920, prompted Robert C. McElravy to call it, "Tense, exciting dramatic material that has been extracted for the screen."

In another review from the same publication, he wrote,

> Pearl White is cast in the role of the wife, a part to which she brings her usual animation and trained abilities. She rises to one after another of the many big situations in this gripping play, which has sufficient substance to equip several ordinary features.
>
> *The Thief* is compactly built, most of the scenes occurring in and around a country house. Not a great many characters are involved, and the guilt is not passed about from one to another in the usual haphazard way. Only two characters are suspected of having taken he stolen money, so that this production differs from many others of somewhat similar settings. It is a study of motives, running broader and deeper than the average thief story. It should interest all spectators, as in addition to its tense drama, it also has a strong intellectual interest.
>
> E. Featherstone makes a good juvenile in the part of Fred Lenwright, possessing clear-cut, sensitive features. The rest of the cast play creditably. The settings are adequate throughout, but it is the unfolding of the drama itself which chiefly grips the spectator.

The release of the film was extremely successful for showmen who reported from all directions that Pearl White was an even better draw when she appeared in full-length films instead of serials. The showing of *The Thief* at the Terminal Theater in Newark, New Jersey broke all house records. Similar reports were gathered from other cities such as San Francisco, Chicago, Kansas City, Cleveland, and Michigan, to name only a few.

The story is about Mary Vantine, who, with her husband Andrew, is visiting for the summer at the home of Richard and Isabelle Lenwright. Mary and Isabelle were friends at college and swore eternal friendship, even though one might succeed in the world and the other might remain poor. Isabelle has won social position, but Mary soon realizes that her cheap attire has marked her as dowdy at the country place. She determines to get some new gowns, and everyone, including her husband, is astonished when she suddenly blossoms out in beautiful, new clothes.

Mary soon finds herself persistently wooed by Fred Lenwright, the impressionable young son of her friends, and also by an unscrupulous millionaire, Ralph Blake. Fred writes her endearing love notes, which he leaves carelessly about, and Blake takes it upon himself to pay her bill at the modiste's when she is pressed for funds.

She soon finds herself in an extremely compromising position. Some stolen money and the presence of detectives in the house increase her discomfort. At length her husband begins to suspect, and the stolen money is traced to Fred and the love affairs to Mary. Fred is about to be sent away to South America, when Mary makes a dramatic confession, assuming guilt for the stolen funds, but denying her complicity in the love affairs. She and her husband then decide to go away and begin life anew.

In February, 1921, Adele Whitely Fletcher, a writer for *Motion Picture Magazine,* steeled herself for what resulted as an amusing, personal encounter with Pearl White at the Fox Studios. In previous interviews, Fletcher remembered being shocked by the revelations she witnessed as she encountered actresses renowned for a specific type later revealed in a different guise: a famous vamp who was discovered demurely rocking a cradle, and an innocent ingénue revealed luridly curled on a divan while philosophizing through shallow tea talk and scented cigarette smoke. With heightened sensitivity, she approached her appointment to meet Pearl White, her impressions guarded with mental shock absorbers firmly in place. "Seeing Pearl White," she later wrote, "if only for a comparatively short time in her dressing room, causes you to reconsider her. On the screen, until recently, she has defied death in *The Perils of Pauline* and other thrillers, apparently immune to fear. And while she has always been attractively clothed in these serials, and has looked quite as intelligent as it would seem humanly possible for anyone to look while they perform some feat, you would not expect her to be just as she is."

Portrait of Pearl White, ca. 1915, famous for her work in the
cliff-hanging serial, *The Perils of Pauline.*

The star was not yet at the studios when the writer arrived. An emissary from the Press Department at Fox Studios told her Miss White was
expected any moment, having telephoned that she would be a few minutes
late. A few minutes later, a dignitary announced that she had arrived, and
Fletcher was hurried to the studio. After halting at a huge, fireproof door,
the escort announced, "Miss White is right inside. I've been standing here
so she couldn't get away." The writer girded herself anew, thinking the
young star was either temperamental or irresponsible, two attributes to
be expected of one so famous and not uncommon in the motion picture
profession.

"We passed through the doorway and in the passage stood a girl, not
very large and cloaked in dark blue with a fuzzy, wool checked collar and
a big blue and white straw hat," recounted Fletcher. Pearl White looked
up from beneath the broad hat brim and offered, "If you'll come up to my

room and there are two chairs not occupied by clothes, being either packed or unpacked, we can talk there."

The two ladies entered the hall and were surprised to be accosted by none other than William Fox, president of the company. He smiled warmly in greeting Miss White, who simply looked at him blankly. As the writer marveled at her failure to recognize the film studio head, she recalled feeling additionally shocked as Miss White suddenly blurted, "Oh, I remember you, you're Mr. Fox. Of course." Mr. Fox laughed, Pearl laughed, and the mortified writer continued her way following the star through a log cabin and a conservatory until reaching the end of the studio and Pearl's room. They were led by her maid, and something in rapid French was exchanged between the two of them. The writer ensconced herself on a chintz-covered lounge and recovered from the further shock of hearing Miss White converse in eloquent French, something unexpected from someone seemingly preoccupied with jumping chasms and climbing perilous precipices.

Pearl attached a small, electric heater and sat, posing her feet inches from its warmth, inviting the writer to do the same. She removed her hat and threw it on another chair. "I'm the only person in New York wearing a straw hat," she announced, running her fingers through her blonde hair, "and now that I'm leaving for the South on exteriors it will probably save me buying a velvet one. When I get back it will be very cold and straw hats will be the vogue."

Miss White explained she was about to begin the work on her fourth feature for Fox, and after exchanging a few rapid and frank remarks about her travels, she was interrupted several times as she attended to various details of the film. "From what I could gather she is quite as capable of taking care of the lights and technical details as the experts engaged for this purpose," the interviewer approvingly mused.

"I've always worried about such things," Pearl sighed. "ever since I did serials for Pathé, but it's foolish now when every company under the sun pays somebody for worrying especially about that certain thing. But, as a matter of fact, I'll probably go on worrying about them just the same. It's a habit I have—a bad habit." The actress went on to discuss her career, describing her admirers as customers in the manner fitting a woman tending to a business. For Pearl, working in films was a business, and it was her attention to details that made the difference between failure and success.

Sarah Bernhardt, like millions of other women, had a great enthusiasm for the adventures of Pearl White. When director Edward Jose took the cast and crew of his serial, *Pearl of the Army,* down to Savannah, Georgia, Pearl had the rare privilege of meeting the great French actress, who was playing an engagement at the Savannah theater. On hearing that Miss

White was in town, Sarah could not resist the opportunity of making her acquaintance. She sent word by a courier to the actress, inviting her to visit her in her dressing room at the theater after the evening's performance.

Miss White accepted the invitation, and through an interpreter, had an extended interview with Sarah. The great star revealed to Pearl that her fame was as widespread in France as it was in the United States. Sarah had viewed *The Exploits of Elaine,* retitled for European consumption under the name *The Mysteries of New York.* Identifying with the incredible, cliff-hanging, weekly escapades of torture and intrigue suffered by Pearl White, Sarah saw herself as Pearl outfoxed Indians, withstood submarine bombs, dangled from aerial wires, and blew unfettered through the clouds in hot air balloons. Both actresses were kindred spirits in their wild lust for adventure. "If they had made films when I was young, what a career I would have had," Sarah later remarked in a *Moving Picture World* article.

Pearl's final work was in one more serial, believed by most contemporary reviewers to be the best of her body of work, a 15-chapter serial called *Plunder.*

In 1923, after having earned and saved millions of dollars, she retired to France. She came out of retirement to make one additional film, *Terror* (1924).

In Paris she resurfaced again to star in several popular stage reviews at the Montmartre Music Hall. She was later seen in London in a revue with George Carney, then drifted happily into a very wealthy retirement until her death in Neuilly, France, on August 4, 1938.

## SILENT FILMOGRAPHY OF PEARL WHITE

The Girl from Arizona (1910) ★ The Missing Bridegroom (1910) ★ Tommy Gets His Sister Married (1910) ★ The Horse Shoer's Girl (1910) ★ The Burlesque Queen (1910) ★ The Matinee Idol (1910) ★ The Hoodoo (1910) ★ The Music Teacher (1910) ★ A Summer Flirtation (1910) ★ A Woman's Wit (1910) ★ The New Magdalene (1910) ★ The Woman Hater (1910) ★ When the World Sleeps (1910) ★ The Maid of Niagara (1910) ★ Her Photograph (1910) ★ Helping Him Out (1911) ★ The Angel of the Slums (1911) ★ The Stepsisters (1911) ★ His Birthday (1911) ★ Memories of the Past (1911) ★ Through the Window (1911) ★ A Prisoner of the Mohicans (1911) ★ For Massa's Sake (1911) ★ Love Molds Labor (1911) ★ Terms of the Will (1911) ★ Love's Renunciation (1911) ★ The Reporter (1911) ★ The Lost Necklace (1911) ★ Her Little Slipper (1911) ★ The Power of Love (1911) ★ Home Sweet Home (1911) ★ For the

Honor of the Name (1912) ★ The Arrowmaker's Daughter (1912) ★
The Hand of Destiny (1912) ★ Pals (1912) ★ The Girl in the Next
Room (1912) ★ The Man from the North Pole (1912) ★ McQuirk, the
Sleuth (1912) ★ Her Dressmaker's Bills (1912) ★ The Only Woman
in Town (1912) ★ Bella's Beaus (1912) ★ A Pair of Fools (1912) ★
The Blonde Lady (1912) ★ Oh, Such a Night! (1912) ★ The Gypsy
Flirt (1912) ★ Her Old Love (1912) ★ The Chorus Girl (1912) ★ The
Quarrel (1912) ★ Locked Out (1912) ★ A Tangled Marriage (1912)
★ The Mind Cure (1912) ★ His Wife's Stratagem (1912) ★ Her Visi-
tor (1912) ★ Mayblossom (1912) ★ The Mad Lover (1912) ★ The
Life of Buffalo Bill (1912) ★ Her Kid Sister (1913) ★ A Night at the
Club (1913) ★ Heroic Harold (1913) ★ The Fake Gas-Man (1913)
★ A Dip Into Society (1913) ★ Pearl's Admirers (1913) ★ The False
Alarm (1913) ★ Accident Insurance (1913) ★ With Her Rival's Help
(1913) ★ Box and Cox (1913) ★ Her Lady Friend (1913) ★ Strictly
Business (1913) ★ An Awful Scare (1913) ★ That Other Girl (1913)
★ Schultz's Lottery Ticket (1913) ★ An Innocent Bridegroom (1913)
★ Ma and the Boys (1913) ★ Knights and Ladies (1913) ★ Who is
the Goat? (1913) ★ Lovers Three (1913) ★ His Twin Brothers (1913)
★ The Drummer's Note Book (1913) ★ Pearl as a Clairvoyant (1913)
★ Forgetful Flossie (1913) ★ The Veiled Lady (1913) ★ Our Parents-
In-Law (1913) ★ Two Lunatics (1913) ★ His Romantic Wife (1913)
★ A Joke on the Sheriff (1913) ★ Where Charity Begins (1913) ★
When Love is Young (1913) ★ Pearl as a Detective (1913) ★ Oh!
Whiskers! (1913) ★ His Awful Daughter (1913) ★ Our Willie (1913)
★ Homlock Shermes (1913) ★ Toodleums (1913) ★ A Supper for
Three (1913) ★ Mary's Romance (1913) ★ The New Typist (1913) ★
False Love and True (1913) ★ Her Joke on Belmont (1913) ★ A Call
from Home (1913) ★ The Smuggled Laces (1913) ★ Who is in the
Box? (1913) ★ The Paper Doll (1913) ★ An Hour of Terror (1913)
★ Muchly Engaged (1913) ★ The Girl Reporter (1913) ★ Pearl's
Dilemma (1913) ★ The Hall-Room Girls (1913) ★ The Broken Spell
(1913) ★ College Chums (1913) ★ What Papa Got (1913) ★ A Child's
Influence (1913) ★ True Chivalry (1913) ★ Starving for Love (1913)
★ Oh! You Scotch Lassie (1913) ★ Pearl and the Tramp (1913) ★
The Greater Influence (1913) ★ Caught in the Act (1913) ★ That
Crying Baby (1913) ★ His Aunt Emma (1913) ★ Much Ado About
Nothing (1913) ★ Lost in the Night (1913) ★ Some Luck (1913) ★
Pleasing Her Husband (1913) ★ A News Item (1913) ★ A Night in
Town (1913) ★ Misplaced Love (1913) ★ Pearl and the Poet (1913)
★ His Last Gamble (1913) ★ Dress Reform (1913) ★ The Woman

and the Law (1913) ★ Hearts Entangled (1913) ★ Willie's Great Scheme (1913) ★ Robert's Lesson (1913) ★ The Rich Uncle (1913) ★ A Hidden Love (1913) ★ When Duty Calls (1913) ★ Oh! You Pearl (1913) ★ Her Secretaries (1913) ★ The Cabaret Singer (1913) ★ Hubby's New Coat (1913) ★ The Convict's Daughter (1913) ★ A Woman's Revenge (1913) ★ Pearl's Hero (1913) ★ First Love (1913) ★ The Soubrette (1913) ★ The Heart of an Artist (1913) ★ The Lure of the Stage (1913) ★ The Kitchen Mechanic (1913) ★ Will Power (1913) ★ Through Air and Fire (1913) ★ Girls Will be Boys (1913) ★ The Lifted Veil (1914) ★ Shadowed (1914) ★ The Ring (1914) ★ It May Come to This (1914) ★ The Shadow of a Crime (1914) ★ Oh! You Puppy (1914) ★ A Grateful Outcast (1914) ★ What Didn't Happen to Mary (1914) ★ For a Woman (1914) ★ Getting Reuben Back (1914) ★ A Sure Cure (1914) ★ McSweeney's Masterpiece (1914) ★ Lizzie and the Iceman (1914) ★ The Perils of Pauline (1914) ★ The Lady Doctor (1914) ★ Get Out and Get Under (1914) ★ A Telephone Engagement (1914) ★ The Dancing Craze (1914) ★ Her New Hat (1914) ★ The Girl in Pants (1914) ★ What Pearl's Pearls Did (1914) ★ Willie's Disguise (1914) ★ Was He a Hero? (1914) ★ The Hand of Providence (1914) ★ East Lynne in Bugville (1914) ★ Some Collectors (1914) ★ Pearl's Mistake (1914) ★ Oh! You Mummy (1914) ★ A Father's Devotion (1914) ★ The Exploits of Elaine (1914) ★ The Mashers (1914) ★ Going Some (1914) ★ Easy Money (1914) ★ The New Exploits of Elaine (1915) ★ The Romance of Elaine (1915) ★ A Lady in Distress (1915) ★ Hazel Kirke (1916) ★ The Iron Claw (1916) ★ Out of the Grave (1916) ★ Pearl of the Army (1916) ★ Mayblossom (1917) ★ The Fatal Ring (1917) ★ The House of Hate (1918) ★ The King's Game (1918) ★ The Lightning Raider (1919) ★ The Black Secret (1919) ★ The White Moll (1920) ★ The Tiger's Cub (1920) ★ The Thief (1920) ★ The Mountain Woman (1921) ★ Know Your Men (1921) ★ Beyond Price (1921) ★ A Virgin Paradise (1921) ★ Any Wife (1922) ★ The Broadway Peacock (1922) ★ Without Fear (1922) ★ Plunder (1923) ★ Terror (1924)

# APPENDIX: PRODUCTION CREDITS, CASTS, AND SYNOPSIS OF FEATURED FILMS

### *Romeo and Juliet*

Quality Picture Corporation

Distributor: Metro Pictures Corporation

Released October 19, 1916

8 reels

Director: John W. Nobel

Producer: Maxwell Karger

Cinematography: R.J. Bergquist

Scenario: John Arthur, Rudolph de Cordova and John W. Noble

Musical Accompaniment: Irene Berg and Samuel Berg

Source: *Romeo and Juliet* by William Shakespeare

Cast:

Francis X. Bushman (Romeo)

Beverly Bayne (Juliet)

Horace Vinton (Escalus)

John Davidson (Paris)

Eric Hudson (Montague)

Edmund Elton (Capulet)

Leonard Grover (Old Man)

Fritz Leiber (Mercutio)

Olaf Skavlan (Benvolio)

W. Lawson Butt (Tybalt)

Robert Cummings (Friar Laurence)

Alexandre J. Herbert (Friar John)

Edwin Boring (Balthasar)

William Morris (Abraham)

Joseph Dailey (Peter)

Adella Barker (Nurse to Juliet)

Helen Dunbar (Lady Capulet)

Genevieve Reynolds (Lady Montague)

Ethel Mantell (Rosaline)

Story: Two youths, Romeo and Juliet, from rival families, fall in love in medieval Italy. After secretly marrying, circumstances prevent their union from blossoming. Thinking Juliet has died, Romeo drinks poison and dies next to her in a tomb. Juliet awakens, discovers her lover dead, and stabs herself to death. The warring families vow to settle their differences.

### *Salome*

Fox Film Corporation

Distributor: Fox Film Corporation

Released August 18, 1918

8 reels

Director: J. Gordon Edwards

Producer: William Fox

Cinematography: George Schneiderman

Scenario: Adrian Johnson

Source: *The Jewish Antiquities* by Flavius Josephus

Cast:

Theda Bara (Salome)

G. Raymond Nye (King Herod)

Albert Roscoe (John the Baptist)

Herbert Heyes (Sejanus)

Bertram Grassby (Prince David)

Genevieve Blinn (Queen Miriam)

Vera Doria (Naomi)

Alfred Fremont (Galba)

Story: Miriam, the sister of Prince David, marries Herod, the king of Judea, after he usurps the throne rightfully belonging to the Prince. To placate the Judeans, Salome, the beautiful but treacherous cousin of Herod, convinces him to make David the high priest. She secretly arranges his assassination and conspires to have Miriam killed, and is publicly denounced by John the Baptist. During his imprisonment, John rebuffs the advances of Salome. She vows to have him destroyed. Salome performs a sensuous dance at Herod's birthday feast and demands the head of John the Baptist as a reward. She kisses his lifeless lips, an abomination that outrages God. A fierce storm arises and Herod orders the execution of Salome.

## Camille (La Dame aux Camélias)

Le Film d'Art Society

Distributor: French-American Film Company

U.S. Released February 24, 1912

2 reels

Director: Andre Calmettes and Henri Pouctal

Cinematography: Clement Maurice

Scenario: Henry Pouctal

Source: *La Dame aux Camélias* by Alexandre Dumas Fils

Cast:

Sarah Bernhardt (Marguerite Gautier)

Lou-Tellegen (Armand Duval)

Paul Capellani (Sadoul)

Charmeroy

Suzanne Seylor

Henri Desfontaines

Pitou

Story: While recuperating from an illness at her home in the country, Marguerite Gautier receives a visit from the father of her lover, Armand Duval, demanding she end their relationship. She tearfully writes him a letter stating she is returning to a former lover and leaves. Armand arrives for a visit, discovers the letter, and is devastated. Later, at a party, Armand is winning at the gambling table when Marguerite arrives. She is shocked to encounter Armand, and when he humiliates her by throwing a deck of cards at her face, she crumbles on a sofa. Armand still loves her, and they reconcile after Marguerite explains why she wrote the letter. In her salon, Marguerite succumbs to the ravages of consumption and dies in the arms of Armand.

## *America*

D. W. Griffith, Inc.

Distributor: United Artists

Released February 21, 1924

13 reels

Director: D. W. Griffith

Producer: D. W. Griffith

Cinematography: G. W. Bitzer, Marcel Le Picard, Henrik Sartov, Hal Sintzenich

Musical Arrangement: Joseph Carl Breil

Cast:

Neil Hamilton (Nathan Holden)

Erville Alderson (Justice Montague)

Carol Dempster (Miss Nancy Montague)

Charles Emmett Mack (Charles Philip Edward Montague)

Lee Beggs (Samuel Adams)

John Dunton (John Hancock)

Arthur Donaldson (King George III)

Charles Bennett (William Pitt)

Frank McGlynn, Jr. (Patrick Henry)

Frank Walsh (Thomas Jefferson)

Lionel Barrymore (Captain Walter Butler)

Arthur Dewey (George Washington)

Sydney Deane (Sir Ashley Montague)

W. W. Jones (General Gate)

Harry O'Neill (Paul Revere)

Henry Van Bousen (John Parker)

Hugh Baird (Major Pitcarm)

James Miland (Jonas Parker)

Louis Wolheim (Captain Hare)

Riley Hatch (Chief of Mohawks)

Emil Hoch (Lord North)

Lucille La Verne (A Refugee Mother)

Downing Clarke (Lord Chamberlain)

P. R. Scammon (Richard Henry Lee)

Ed Roseman (Captain Montour)

Harry Smith (Hikatoo, Chief of Senecas)

Story: The romance of Boston patriot, Nathan Holden, and the daughter of a Virginia Tory is plunged into the middle of the Revolutionary War. A highlight is the spellbinding ride of Paul Revere.

## A Slave of Vanity

Robertson-Cole Studios, Inc.

Distributor: Robertson-Cole Distributing Corporation

Released November 28, 1920

6 reels

Director: Henry Otto

Source: *Iris* by Arthur Wing Pinero

Cast:

Pauline Frederick (Iris Bellamy)

Nigel Barrie (Laurence Trenwith)

Willard Louis (Frederick Maldonado)

Maude Louis (Fanny Sullivan)

Daisy Robinson (Aurea Vyse)

Arthur Hoyt (Croker Harrington)

Ruth Handforth (Miss Pinsent)

Howard Gaye (Arthur Kane)

Story: Iris Bellamy becomes the widow of a wealthy man. His will prescribes that if she remarries, his fortune will be donated to charity. Iris is in love with an impoverished artist and a rich, Italian millionaire. When the artist decides to go to America to seek his fortune, Iris agonizes over going with him and sacrificing her inheritance. She almost gives herself later to the millionaire when the artist returns and the furious millionaire throws her out into the streets. Iris awakens, discovering the drama was only a dream, and then gives herself to the artist she loves.

## From the Manger to the Cross

Kalem Company

Distributor: States Rights

U.S. Released January, 1913

5 reels

Director: Sidney Olcott

Producer: Frank J. Marion

Cinematography: George K. Hollister

Scenario: Gene Gauntier

Cast:

> Robert Henderson-Bland (Jesus, the man)
>
> Percy Dyer (Jesus, as a youth)
>
> Gene Gauntier (Mary)
>
> Alice Hollister (Mary Magdalene)
>
> Samuel Morgan (Pilate)
>
> James D. Ainsley (John the Baptist)
>
> Robert G. Vignola (Judas)
>
> George Kellog (Herod)

Story: The life of Christ depicted in scenes closely following Biblical literature, including the Annunciation, the flight of Joseph and Mary into Egypt, the youth of Jesus, the baptism by John the Baptist, the calling of the disciples, the miracles, Christ's last days, the Last Supper, and the Crucifixion.


### Street Angel

Fox Film Corporation

Distributor: Fox Film Corporation

Released April 9, 1928

10 reels

Director: Frank Borzage

Producer: William Fox

Cinematography: Ernest Palmer

Scenario: Marion Orth

Source: *Cristilinda* by Monckton Hoffe

Cast:

> Janet Gaynor (Angela)
>
> Charles Farrell (Gino)
>
> Gino Conti (policeman)
>
> Guido Trento (Neri)
>
> Henry Armetta (Mascetto)
>
> Louis Liggett (Beppo)
>
> Milton Dickinson (Bimbo)
>
> Helena Herman (Andrea)
>
> Natalie Kingston (Lisette)
>
> David Kashner (The Strong Man)

Jennie Bruno (Landlady)

Story: Angela, a poor girl desperate for medicine for her sick mother, steals supplies and is caught by the police. After a prison term, she finds refuge with a circus and meets Gino, an artist, who poses her for a portrait of the Madonna. The authorities track Angela to the circus and imprison her again. After release, Angela sees her portrait in a church and reunites with Gino.

## Flying Pat

New Art Film Company

Distributor: Famous Players–Lasky Corporation

Released December 5, 1920

5 reels

Director: F. Richard Jones

Cinematography: Fred Chaston

Scenario: Virginia Philley Withey

Cast:

Dorothy Gish (Patricia Van Nuys)

James Rennie (Robert Van Nuys)

Morgan Wallace (William Endicott)

Harold Vizard (Butler)

William Black (Detective)

Porter Strong (Reporter)

Tom Blake (Policeman)

Kate Bruce (Old Lady)

Mrs. Waters (Cook)

Miss Waters (Housemaid)

Story: Patricia Van Nuys decides to get a job and selects the occupation of aviatrix, with a plan to become the first woman to cross the Atlantic by plane. A friend of her husband offers to teach her to fly. While practicing, the plane nosedives into a crash, and the pilot and Pat emerge safely. She leaves town on a train, only to return disguised as a Swedish maid. After a series of comic incidents, Pat's identity is revealed and the couple reunite.

## The Little 'Fraid Lady

Robertson-Cole Company

Distributor: Robertson-Cole Distributing Corporation

Released December 14, 1920

6 reels

Director: John G. Adolfi

Cinematography: George Benoit

Scenario: Joseph W. Farnham

Source: *The Girl Who Lived in the Woods* by Robert A. Odell

Cast:

Mae Marsh (Cecelia Carne)

Tully Marshall (Giron)

Kathleen Kirkham (Mrs. Helen Barrett)

Charles Meredith (Saxton Graves)

Herbert Prior (Judge Peter Carteret)

Gretchen Hartman (Sirotta)

George Bertholon, Jr. (Bobby Barrett)

Jacques III (a dog)

Story: Neighbors call Cecelia Carne the little 'fraid lady because she hides from society in the solitude of her little house in the forest where she paints. One day she accidentally wanders onto the estate of Judge Peter Carteret and meets Saxton Graves, who recognizes her talent and hires Cecelia. They fall in love. She soon learns the judge is to try a case in which her father Giron, a bootlegger, is implicated. Complications and blackmail follow, Cecelia testifies against her father, and Giron shoots himself on the witness stand, opening the door to happiness for his daughter and Saxton.

### Fascination

Tiffany Productions

Distributor: Metro Pictures

Released April 10, 1922

8 reels

Director: Robert Z. Leonard

Producer: Robert Z. Leonard

Cinematography: Oliver T. Marsh

Scenario: Edmund Goulding

Cast:

Mae Murray (Dolores de Lisa)

Creighton Hale (Carlos de Lisa, her brother)

Charles Lane (Eduardo de Lisa, her father)

Emily Fitzroy (Marquesa de Lisa, her aunt)

Robert Frazer (Carrita)

Vincent Coleman (Ralph Kellogg)

Courtenay Foote (The Count de Morera)

Helen Ware (Parola, a dancer)

Frank Puglia (Nema)

Story: Dolores de Lisa, an impulsive American girl, while visiting her aunt in Spain, disguises herself in a native costume and attends a bullfight. At a party that evening she meets the bullfighter, Carrita, and entrances him with her exotic dance of the bulls, while her aunt receives word of the arrival of her family from America. In a thwarted blackmail attempt, Dolores is wounded, and begs her American fiancé, Ralph, to help her accept the more simple life of an American wife.

## A Doll's House

Nazimova Productions

Distributor: United Artists

Released February 12, 1922

7 reels

Director: Charles Bryant

Producer: Charles Bryant

Cinematography: Charles Van Enger

Scenario: Peter M. Winters

Source: *A Doll's House* by Henrik Ibsen

Cast:

Alan Hale (Torvald Helmer)

Alla Nazimova (Nora)

Nigel De Brulier (Dr. Rank)

Elinor Oliver (Anna, a nurse)

Wedgewood Nowell (Nils Krogstad)

Cara Lee (Ellen, a maid)

Florence Fisher (Mrs. Linden)

Philippe De Lacy (Ivar)

Barbara Maier (Emmy)

Story: Nora Helmer approaches a money lender, Krogstad, and forges her father's name to a note, hoping to procure enough money to enable her husband, Tovald, to retire and recover his health. Six years later, when Krogstad applies for a position in the bank where Tovald is a manager, he is denied employment. He threatens Nora with exposure unless she influences his hire. Despite her efforts, Tovald denounces Krogstad as a criminal, and the man exposes Nora's forgery from years earlier. Tovald is infuriated, and instead of shielding his wife, explodes over the threat to his reputation. When Krogstad relents and withdraws his accusation, Nora sinks into depression, and with her illusions of her marriage shattered, sees the truth of her doll-like existence. She asserts her right to live her own life and walks out on her husband and children.

### Dulcy

Constance Talmadge Film Company

Distributor: Associated First National Pictures

Released August 27, 1923

7 reels

Director: Sidney A. Franklin

Cinematography: Norbert Brodin

Scenario: Anita Loos and John Emerson

Source: *Dulcy* by George S. Kaufman and Marc Connelly

Cast:

Constance Talmadge (Dulcy)

Claude Gillingwater (Mr. Forbes)

Jack Mulhall (Gordon Smith)

May Wilson (Mrs. Forbes)

Johnny Harron (Billy Parker)

Anne Cornwall (Angela Forbes)

André Beranger (Vincent Leach)

Gilbert Douglas (Schuyler Van Dyke)

Frederick Esmelton (Blair Patterson)

Milla Davenport (Matty)

Story: A scatterbrained bride attempts to improve her absent husband's finances by inviting two of his business prospects to dinner. She does get him an improved deal, but the confusing arrangements cause comic complications to ensue.

### The Battle Cry of Peace

Vitagraph Company of America

Distributor: V-L-S-E, Inc.

Released September 9, 1915

9 reels

Director: J. Stuart Blackton

Producer: J. Stuart Blackton

Cinematography: Leonard Smith and Arthur T. Quinn

Scenario: J. Stuart Blackton

Musical Accompaniment: S. L. Rothapfel

Source: *Defenseless America* by Hudson Maxim

Cast:

> Charles Richman (John Harrison)
>
> L. Rogers Lytton (Mr. Emanon)
>
> James Morrison (Charley Harrison)
>
> Mary Maurice (Mrs. Harrison)
>
> Louise Beaudet (Mrs. Vandergriff)
>
> Harold Hubert (Mr. Vandergriff)
>
> Jack Crawford (Poet Scout)
>
> Charles Kent (The Master)
>
> Julia Swayne Gordon (Magdalen)
>
> Evart Overton (Vandergriff's son)
>
> Belle Bruce (Alice Harrison)
>
> Norma Talmadge (Virginia Vandergriff)
>
> Lucille Hamill (Dorothy Vandergriff)
>
> George Stevens (The butler)
>
> Thais Lawton (Columbia)
>
> Lionel Braham (The War Monster)
>
> Joseph Kilgour (George Washington)
>
> Paul Scardon (General Grant)
>
> William J. Ferguson (Abraham Lincoln)
>
> Hudson Maxim (Himself)

Story: Hudson Maxim, a patriotic writer, delivers a patriotic lecture witnessed by John Harrison. Harrison becomes an advocate of military preparedness. Mr. Emanon, a family friend, is a peace movement leader and secret enemy agent. American's worst fears are realized when the enemy opens fire on New York City, killing citizens and humiliating survivors. The invaders ravage women and dismantle the resistance. A plea for preparedness is made in an allegorical finale.

## Peg O' My Heart

Metro Picture Corporation

Distributor: Metro Picture

Released December 18, 1922

8 reels

Director: King Vidor

Producer: J. Hartley Manners

Cinematography: George Barnes

Scenario: Mary O'Hara

Source: *Peg O' My Heart* by J. Hartley Manners

Cast:

   Laurette Taylor (Margaret O'Connell—Peg)

   Mahlon Hamilton (Sir Gerald Adair)

   Russell Simpson (Jim O'Connell)

   Ethel Grey Terry (Ethel Chichester)

   Nigel Barrie (Christian Brent)

   Lionel Belmore (Hawks)

   Vera Lewis (Mrs. Chichester)

   Sidna Beth Ivins (Mrs. Jim O'Connell)

   D. R. O. Hatswell (Alaric Chichester)

   Aileen O' Malley (Margaret O'Connell, as a child)

   Fred Huntly (butler)

   Michael (a dog)

Story: Peg, the daughter of a poor, Irish farmer, is sent to England to live with the Chichesters. She is alienated by their snobbishness and makes friends with Jerry, a neighbor living on an adjacent estate. Peg learns the Chichesters' only interest is in the money paid to them by her uncle. Jerry is revealed to be Sir Gerald Adair, and the disillusioned Peg returns to Ireland, only to be pursued by the lovesick Jerry who persuades Peg to marry him.


## *The Thief*

Fox Film Corporation

Distributor: Fox Film Corporation

Released November, 1920

6 reels

Director: Charles Giblyn

Producer: William Fox

Cinematography: Joe Ruttenberg

Scenario: Max Marcin and Paul H. Sloane

Source: *Le Voleur* by Henri Bernstein

Cast:

Pearl White (Mary Vantyne)

Charles Waldron (Andrew Vantyne)

Wallace McCutcheon (Ralph Blake)

George Howard (Richard Lenwright)

Dorothy Cumming (Isabelle Lenwright)

Eddie Featherstone (Fred Lenwright)

Sidney Herbert (Long)

Anthony Merlo (Valet to Long)

Story: Mary Vantyne and her husband are guests at the home of her old friend, Isabelle Lenwright. The wealth of her friends is starkly contrasted by the impoverished state of her mate. When Mary overhears a comment about her dowdy appearance, she resolves to purchase an entirely new wardrobe. When she appears decked out in new clothes, she both astonishes her family and attracts the attention of two new suitors. The bills for dressmaking arrive, and Blake presents her with a receipt for the wardrobe marked paid in full. Lenwright discovers the theft of $3,000 and hires a detective to discover the true culprit. Fred is fingered for the crime, and when Andrew is about to wreak revenge on both men, Mary confesses that she stole the money to pay for her new clothes. She learns her lesson and all is forgiven.

# BIBLIOGRAPHY

"A Doll's House." *Motion Picture World,* 25 February 1922.

Agney, Frances. *Motion Picture Acting.* New York: Reliance Newspaper Syndicate Publishers, 1913.

*American Film Institute Catalog of Feature Films.* Berkeley, Calif.: University of California Press, 1997.

Ardmore, Jane Kesner Morris. *The Self-Enchanted: Mae Murray, Image of an Era.* New York: McGraw-Hill, 1959.

Arvidson, Linda. *When the Movies Were Young.* New York: Dover Publications, 1969.

Bangley, Jimmy. "The Rise to Stardom of Mae Murray." *Classic Images,* August 1996.

Bardou, Odette. "Un Visage … Un Grand Talent." *Avant Scene,* 15 January 1981, 85.

Barry, Iris. *D. W. Griffith American Film Master.* New York: Doubleday, 1965.

Barrymore, Ethel. *Memories.* New York: Harper and Brothers, 1955.

Beach, Barbara. "The Worms Will Get You!" *Motion Picture Classic,* December 1925.

Berg, A. Scott. *Goldwyn.* New York: Grosset & Dunlap Publishers, 1953.

Bernhardt, Sarah. *Memories of My Life.* New York: Benjamin Blom, 1908.

"Bernhardt Meets Pearl White." *Moving Picture World,* 31 July 1915.

"Big City Theatres From Coast to Coast are Playing Pearl White in The Thief." *Moving Picture World,* 25 December 1920.

"Big Reception for Human Wreckage." *Moving Picture World,* 28 July 1923.

Blackton, Commodore J. Stuart. "The Battle Cry of Peace." *Motion Picture Classic,* January 1916.

Blaisdell, George. "At the Sign of the Flaming Arcs." *Moving Picture World,* 3 January 1914.

———. "Romeo and Juliet." *Moving Picture World,* 4 November 1916.

Blum, Daniel. *A Pictorial History of the Silent Screen.* New York: Alfred A. Knopf, 1989.

Bodeen, De Witt. "Pauline Frederick." *Films in Review,* February 1965, 69–90.

Borzage, Frank. "Directing a Talking Picture." In *Hollywood Directors, 1914–1940* edited by Richard Koszarski. New York: Oxford University Press, 1976.

Brenon, Herbert. "Must They Have Temperament?" *Motion Picture Magazine,* February 1926.

Brown, Karl. *Adventures with D. W. Griffith.* New York: Farrar, Straus and Giroux, 1973.

Brownlow, Kevin. *The Parade's Gone By.* New York: Ballentine Books, 1968.

Brownlow, Kevin, and John Kobal. *Hollywood: The Pioneers.* New York: Alfred A. Knopf, 1980.

Bush, W. Stephen. "From the Manger to the Cross." *Moving Picture World,* 26 October 1912.

Carr, Harry. "Griffith: Maker of Pictures." *Motion Picture Magazine,* August 1922.

Carroll, Gardiner. "Why Jane Cowl Avoids the Screen, Norma Talmadge Avoids the Stage, Laurette Taylor Appears on Both." *Photoplay,* July 1924, 72–73.

Casselton, Harold. *Remembering Dorothy Gish.* Minneapolis, Minn.: The Society for Cinephiles, 1986.

Chapman, John. "Magnificent Yankee a Beautiful Piece of Sentimental Biography." *New York Daily News,* 23 January 1946.

Cheatham, Maude. "Vamp by Accident." *Motion Picture Classic,* June 1922.

Claire, Ina. "Moving Picture Practice Makes Better Legitimate Acting." *Paramount Pictures Magazine,* June 1915.

Courtney, Marguerite. *Laurette.* New York: Rinehart, 1955.

Craven, Thomas. "Salome and the Cinema." *The New Republic,* 1923.

Croy, Homer. *Star Maker: The Story of D. W. Griffith.* New York: Duell, Sloan and Pearce, 1959.

Cugat, F. "Mae Murray's Victory." *Movie Weekly,* 19 August 1922.

De Lacy, Edythe. "The Nurse Takes the Child." *Film Fun,* November 1922.

De Mille, Cecil B. *The Autobiography of Cecil B. de Mille.* Upper Saddle River, N.J.: Prentice-Hall, 1959.

Don, Val Jo. "I'm Tired of Smother Roles." *Photoplay,* December 1928.

Dowd, Nancy, and David Shepard. *King Vidor.* Metuchen, N.J.: The Directors Guild of America; London: The Scarecrow Press, 1988.

Elwood, Muriel. *Pauline Frederick on and off the Stage.* Chicago: A. Kroch, 1940.

Farrar, Geraldine. *Such Sweet Compulsion.* Richmond, Va.: The William Byrd Press, 1938.

Fletcher, Adelle Whitely. "Reconsidering Pearl." *Motion Picture Magazine,* February 1921.

Foster, Charles. "Sidney Olcott and the Making of *From the Manger to the Cross.*" In *Stardust and Shadows: Canadians in Early Hollywood.* Toronto, Canada: Dundurn Press, 2000.

Franklin, Joe, and William K. Everson. *Classics of the Silent Screen.* New York: Citadel Press, 1971.

Frederick, Pauline. "The Story of My Life." *Motion Picture Magazine,* December 1918.

Frohman, Daniel. *Daniel Frohman Presents.* New York: Claude Kendall and Willoughby Sharp, 1935.

Gassaway, Gordon. "Anna with the Lid Off." *Picture Play,* November 1923.

Gauntier, Gene. "Blazing the Trail." *Woman's Home Companion* 55, no. 11 November 1928, 15–16, 132, 134.

Geduld, Harry M. *Focus on D.W. Griffith.* Upper Saddle River, N.J.: Prentice-Hall, 1971.

Gish, Dorothy. "And So I Am a Comedienne." *Ladies Home Journal,* July 1925.

Gish, Lillian. *Dorothy and Lillian Gish.* New York: Charles Scribner's Sons, 1973.

———. *The Movies, Mr. Griffith, and Me.* Upper Saddle River, N.J.: Prentice-Hall, 1969.

Golden, Eve. "Pauline Frederick, Empress of Stormy Emotion." *Classic Images,* October 2001.

Goldwyn, Samuel. *Behind the Screen.* New York: George H. Doran Company, 1923.

Griffith, David Wark. "Pictures vs. One Night Stands." In *Hollywood Directors, 1914–1940,* edited by Richard Koszarski. New York: Oxford University Press, 1976.

Griffith, Richard. "Is It the Machinery?" In *The Movie Stars.* New York: Doubleday, 1970.

Hall, Gladys. "Carol Dempster." *Motion Picture Magazine,* July 1922.

Hall, Mordaunt. "Sombre Naples—Street Angel." *New York Times,* 10 April 1928.

Harrison, Louis Reeve. "Flying Pat." *Moving Picture World,* 25 December 1920.

Hart, Jerome. "Famous Juliets." *Motion Picture Classic,* March 1923.

Henderson, Robert M. *D. W. Griffith His Life and Work.* New York: Oxford University Press, 1972.

Ingram, Rex. *Opportunities in the Motion Picture Industry.* Los Angeles: Photoplay Research Society, 1922.

Johnson, Julian. "The Shadow Stage—Intolerance." *Photoplay,* December 1916.

———. "The Shadow Stage—Romeo and Juliet." *Photoplay,* January 1917.

Kingsley, Grace. "The Wild Woman of Babylon." *Photoplay,* May 1917.

Knight, Arthur. *The New York Times Directory of the Film.* New York: Arno Press, 1971.

Lahue, Kalton C. *Ladies in Distress.* New York: A.S. Barnes, 1971.

Lambert, Gavin. *Nazimova.* New York: Alfred A. Knopf, 1997.

"Laurette Taylor a Delight in Adaptation of Her Stage Success." *Film Daily,* 17 December 1922.

MacGowan, J. P. "From Jerusalem to the Sea of Galilee." *Motion Picture Stories,* August 1912.

Mack, Grace. "The Sunshine Girl—Mae Murry." *Picture Play,* September 1918.

Mantle, Burns. "The Love Flower." *Photoplay,* November 1920.

Marion, Frances. *Off with Their Heads!* New York: Macmillan, 1972.

Marsh, Mae. *Screen Acting.* New York: Frederick A. Stokes Company, 1921.

Martin, Mary. *My Heart Belongs.* New York: Quill, 1984.

Maturi, Richard, and Mary Buckingham Maturi. *Beverly Bayne, Queen of the Movies.* Jefferson, N.C.: McFarland & Company, 2001.

———. *Francis X. Bushman: A Biography and Filmography.* Jefferson, N.C.: McFarland & Company, 1998.

McElravy, Robert C. "The Thief." *Moving Picture World,* 11 December 1920.

Mcgowan, Kenneth. *Behind the Screen.* New York: Delacourte Press, 1965.

Miles, John P. "D. W. Griffith's Twenty-Year Record." In *D. W. Griffith Papers, 1897–1954.* Frederick, Md.: University Publications of America, 1982.

Mitchell, George. "Sidney Olcott: He Was the First American Director to Go on Location Abroad." *Films in Review,* April 1954.

Moreno, Antonio. "Estelle Taylor." *Photoplay,* July 1924.

Neilan, Marshall. "Opportunities in the Motion Picture Industry." In *Hollywood Directors, 1914–1940,* edited by Richard Koszarski. New York: Oxford University Press, 1976.

"Norma Talmadge Looking for Plays Which Will Offer Strong, Dramatic Emotional Roles, while Constance Wants to Play in Subtle Comedies." *Moving Picture World,* 25 December 1920.

O'Brien, Eugene. "Norma Talmadge." *Photoplay,* July 1924.

Olcott, Sidney. "The Present and the Future of Film." In *Hollywood Directors, 1914–1940,* edited by Richard Koszarski. New York: Oxford University Press, 1976.

O'Leary, Liam. *The Silent Cinema.* New York: E. P. Dutton and Co., 1965.

Paine, Albert Bigelow. *Life and Lillian Gish.* New York: Macmillan, 1932.

"Peg O' My Heart." *Photoplay,* February 1923.

"Peg O' My Heart." *Variety,* 25 January 1923.

Perry, Montanye. "From the Manger to the Cross." *Motion Picture Story Magazine,* November 1912.

Pratt, George C. *Spellbound in Darkness.* New York:  New York Graphic Society, 1966.

Ramsaye, Terry. *A Million and One Nights.* New York: Simon and Schuster, 1926.

Robbins, E. M. "The Two Strange Women." *Photoplay,* August 1919.

"Robertson-Cole Offers Mae Marsh in a Sumptuously Produced Play From Novel." *Moving Picture World,* 18 December 1920.

"Romeo and Juliet." *Variety,* 27 October 1916.

"Romeo and Juliet." *Wid's Daily,* 26 October 1916.

"Salome Ready for Exhibitors." *Moving Picture World,* 11 January 1919.

Sennett, Mack. "The Psychology of Film Comedy." *Motion Picture Classic,* November 1918.

Sergent, Epes W. "The Little 'Fraid Lady." *Moving Picture World,* 18 December 1920.

———. "The Photoplaywright." *Moving Picture World,* 24 August 1912.

Slide, Anthony. "From the Manger to the Cross." *Magills Survey of the Cinema.* Englewood Cliffs, N.J.: Salem Press, 1980.

———. *The Griffith Actresses.* New York: A. S. Barnes and Company, 1973.

———. "Mae Marsh in an Interview with Robert B. Cushman." *The Silent Picture.* New York: Arno Press, 1977.

Smith, Albert E. *Two Reels and a Crank.* New York: Doubleday, 1952.

Smith, Frederick James. "Intolerance in Review." *The New York Dramatic Mirror,* 16 September 1916.

———. "Those Nazimova Eyes!" *Picture Play,* September 1918.

———. "Unwept, Unhonored and Unfilmed." *Photoplay,* July 1924.

Society for Cinephiles. *Remembering Dorothy Gish.* Minneapolis, Minn.: Society for Cinephiles, 1986.

Spehr, Paul C. *The Movies Begin.* Newark, N.J.: The Newark Museum, 1977.

Spensley, Dorothy. "My Life So Far." *Photoplay,* December 1928.

St. Johns, Adela Rogers. "A Flyer in Pasts." *Photoplay,* November 1923.

———. "Mae Murray—A Study in Contradictions." *Photoplay,* July 1924, 38.

———. "What Happened to Pauline Frederick?" *Photoplay,* June 1926, 38.

Stern, Seymour. *Griffith: The Birth of a Nation.* New York: Film Culture, 1965.

"Street Angel." *The Film Daily,* 15 April 1928.

"Street Angel." *Harrison's Reports,* 21 April 1928.

"Street Angel." *Variety,* 11 April 1928.

Swanson, Gloria. *Swanson on Swanson: An Autobiography.* New York: Random House, 1980.

Synon, Katherine. "Beautiful Beverly Bayne." *Photoplay,* May 1914.

Talmadge, Constance. "The Quality You Need Most." *Green Book Magazine,* April 1914.

Talmadge, Margaret L. *The Talmadge Sisters.* New York: J. B. Lippincott Company, 1924.

Vidor, King. *A Tree Is a Tree.* New York: Harcourt, Brace and Company, 1952.

Wagenknecht, Edward. *The Movies in the Age of Innocence.* Oklahoma City, Okla.: The University of Oklahoma Press, 1962.

Weitzel, Edward. "Elinor Glyn Throned on Her Tiger Skin Sets a New Pace for Speedy Interviews." *Moving Picture World,* 11 December 1920.

Welsh, Robert E. "David W. Griffith Speaks." *The New York Dramatic Mirror,* 14 January 1914.

Zukor, Adolph. *The Public Is Never Wrong.* New York: G. P. Putnam's Sons, 1953.

# INDEX

**About the Author**

DAVID W. MENEFEE is a contributing writer for *The Dallas Times Herald* and *The Dallas Morning News.* He is the author of *Sarah Bernhardt: In the Theater, Film and Sound Recordings*, the first-ever comprehensive study of the actress's recorded work.